Constitutional Predicament

Constitutional Predicament

Canada after the Referendum of 1992

EDITED BY

CURTIS COOK

McGill-Queen's University Press
Montreal & Kingston • London • Buffalo

© McGill-Queen's University Press 1994
ISBN 0-7735-1192-X (cloth)
ISBN 0-7735-1202-0 (paper)

Legal deposit third quarter 1994
Bibliothèque nationale du Québec

Printed in Canada on acid-free paper

Publication of this book has been supported by a
grant from the William H. Donner Foundation.

Canadian Cataloguing in Publication Data

Main entry under title:
Constitutional predicament: Canada after the referendum
  of 1992
Includes index.
ISBN 0-7735-1192-X (bound) –
ISBN 0-7735-1202-0 (pbk.)
1. Consensus Report on the Constitution (1992).
2. Canada – Constitutional law – Amendments.
3. Canada – Politics and government – 1984–1993.
I. Cook, Curtis, 1937–   .
JL65.1994 c67 1994   342.71'03   c94-900167-8

Typeset in Baskerville 10/12 by
Caractéra production graphique inc., Quebec City.

To my father

Contents

Preface

The papers in this collection were delivered at a Colloquium on the Canadian Constitutional Crisis and the 26 October Referendum. The colloquium was held on 13–14 November 1992 in Colorado Springs and was sponsored by the North American Studies Program at the Colorado College. The college's creation of the program in 1989 was based on the conviction that the multiplication of economic, social, and political ties among Canada, the United States, and Mexico needed to be accompanied by greater scholarly understanding and contact. Reflecting this goal, the North American Studies Program sponsors an ongoing series of scholarly discussions and meetings, funds faculty and student research and travel, supports courses taught in all three countries, and directs a North American Studies minor at the Colorado College. Since its inception, the program has received funding from the William H. Donner Foundation, the William and Flora Hewlett Foundation, and the Canadian government. Thanks to the generous support of these institutions, prominent Canadians and Mexicans have lectured and taught at the college over the last three years. They include Antonine Maillet, Anne Wheeler, Mordecai Richler, Carlos Fuentes, Elena Poniatowska, Jesus Reyes Heroles, Soledad Loaeza, Jorge Castaneda, and Lorenzo Meyer as well as the distinguished group of participants in this colloquium.

Juan D. Lindau
Assistant Professor of Political Science
Director, North American Studies Program

Constitutional Predicament

Introduction:
Canada's Predicament

CURTIS COOK

"Has Canada proliferated its solitudes into three or more?" asked Alan Cairns, drawing on the famous Hugh MacLennan novel. "Remember," replied James Tully, "that MacLennan took the 'two solitudes' phrase from a Rilke poem about love." The essays that follow explore the "Canada round" according to the nationalisms involved, the nationalistic and particularistic pulls, the principles of constitutionalism and constitution making, the quality and appropriateness of popular participation in constitution making, what the Charlottetown events might tell us about future efforts to revisit the matter, and the referendum as an illustration of worldwide trends. The Canada round of popular discussion and leadership negotiation, running from defeat in 1990 of the Meech Lake Accord through the Charlottetown Accord and the referendum of 26 October 1992, was Canada's fifth effort in "mega-constitutional politics."[1]

The Constitution Act, 1867 (the British North America Act, a law of the British parliament), along with amendments to it and written and unwritten tradition, served Canada as a constitution until 1982. The rounds of constitutional politics beginning in the mid-1960s transformed this law into an indigenous Canadian constitution. The

The Canadians I worked with in this project were generous with their time, patient, intellectually demanding, and stimulating as associates. My colleagues at Colorado College were endlessly supportive. To all of these people, I give my thanks. On behalf of all the authors, I wish to thank the William H. Donner Foundation, which made publication of this book possible.

transformation was in fact accomplished by Canada and the United Kingdom in 1982, adding to the former Constitution Act a bill of rights (the Canadian Charter of Rights and Freedoms) and amending procedures, to create a Canadian constitution for Canada. This transformation, the third round of constitutional politics, is referred to as "patriation" of the constitution. The Government of Quebec did not join in patriation and thus left an anomaly, which the fourth round of constitutional politics, running from patriation to 1990, attempted to resolve. The fourth round ended unsuccessfully with defeat of the Meech Lake Accord.

Cairns tells us in the next chapter that the "first major contemporary attempt to find a constitutional reconciliation between Quebec nationalism, Aboriginal nationalism, incipient ROC [Rest of Canada] nationalism, and the inherited pan-Canadian nationalism occurred in the post-Meech process that led to Charlottetown." Just as the 1987 Meech Lake constitutional reform proposals were instructed by the flawed patriation of the constitution in 1982, the Charlottetown agreement showed the influence of what Canadians had learned in the Meech Lake effort. Patriation had been without Quebec's consent, and Meech attempted to gain that consent with constitutional protection for Quebec's way of life. Meech failed in part because it gave protections to Quebec but ignored Aboriginals. Charlottetown was designed to build on the earlier efforts and add protection for the Aboriginal way of life. But a majority of Canadians still found cause to object to the proposed constitutional reforms. This learning process may well continue, but of all the essays that follow, Alain Noël's is the only one to conclude that we should expect an early reengagement of the constitutional question.

The authors concur on several fundamentals. They agree, for example, that Canadian voters rejected the Charlottetown proposals because they disapproved of both the content of the proposals and the procedure by which the proposals had been drawn up. Three qualifications follow from this conclusion. First, Quebec remains the chief problem for the Canadian constitution. Barry Cooper has argued that Canada and Quebec would each be better served by deconfederation. Nor does he retreat from this view in chapter 3 here. But his preference for deconfederation arises from the fact that he believes that Quebec and Canada together cannot have a proper constitutional order. Quebec is central to the Canadian constitutional problem, and whatever the many dimensions of the problem are, a condition of progress may be for Quebec to set forth its own preferences, whether for sovereignty or for Canada. Quebec has, in effect, rejected three constitutional options (sovereignty, the 1982 Constitution Act, and

Charlottetown). In this line of argument, the next move is Quebec's. But compare the view in Noël's and Tully's chapters that all Canadians must increase their recognition and rationalization of diversity.

Second and closely related, Quebec was not the sole constitutional issue or voting issue this time. Rather, the scope of the accord and doubts about the feasibility, sincerity, and desirability of the proposals for Aboriginal self-government added materially to questions about provisions for Quebec. Third, all of the essays agree that Canada is multinational and that the three major nationalisms (Aboriginal, Canadian, Québécois) have valid claims on the political system. The validity of the nationalisms was less the issue than the resolution offered in the referendum. The essays also agree that the decentralizing forces at work in Canada are not limited to these valid nationalistic claims.

On the other hand, we do not find these essays uniform in explaining how the Charlottetown Accord came to read as it does. F.L. Morton's chapter attributes some of the reforms to a strategy for dealing with patriation's "constitutional losers." Cairns explores the "revolutionary" constitutional advances which the accord represented for Aboriginal people. Tully offers a way of understanding why these constitutional advances would be just, and gives a thorough explanation of the Canada clause. (Americans may wish to understand the Canada clause as a statement of principle analogous to the U.S. Declaration of Independence, but with a more direct connection to constitutional affairs.) While it is understandable that the Charlottetown reforms would be more accommodating to Aboriginal demands than earlier reform efforts had been, the exact provisions are less explicable. They were widely criticized as incoherent or unrealistic. Certainly, much would have been left to later drafters, politicians, and courts in meshing the third order of (Aboriginal) government with the two existing orders (national and provincial) and with the Charter of Rights and Freedoms. Nor do we have a good explanation of why the negotiators at Charlottetown so misjudged public opinion.

The essays also do not agree on the prognosis for constitution making. Alain Noël expects constitutional reform to remain on the agenda. Tully provides a way of plotting a solution, without saying when reform might return to the agenda. The same can be said of Cooper's essay. Decidedly less optimistic are Janet Ajzenstat, who places her hopes on apathy (about constitutional reform), and Peter Emberley, who relies on common sense and common decency rather than on formal measures, even though it is his view that the world is increasingly disorderly and therefore less receptive to these commonalities.

CHARLOTTETOWN ACCORD: RENEWING CANADA

The Charlottetown Accord (*Consensus Report on the Constitution, Charlottetown, August 28, 1992, Final Text*, appended hereto), completed by the first ministers at Charlottetown, is self-consciously about more than mere constitutional amendment. It refers (in the preface) to "renewal of the Canadian federation," citing the numerous steps already taken to involve Canadians in a consultative process intended to culminate in renewal through constitutional change. Set out in six chapters, the 20-page Charlottetown Accord is not itself a constitutional amendment; but it would have become, after referendum, the consensus of the people of Canada concerning changes to their constitution.

The *Consensus Report*'s chapter 1, "Unity and Diversity," sets forth the Canada clause, about "fundamental Canadian values" such as parliamentary and federal government and the rule of law, and the objectives of Canada's economic and social union. Chapter 2, "Institutions," is chiefly about the newly designed Senate, in which provinces would be represented equally by elected or appointed senators. Chapter 3, "Roles and Responsibilities," allocates governing between the national and provincial governments. Chapter 4, "First Peoples," advances the third order of government under which Aboriginal people would govern themselves according to their own way of life. Chapter 5 revises the amending procedure for the constitution, and chapter 6 lists the matters which the first ministers chose not to include in this constitutional deliberation.

THE VOTE: ROOM FOR INTERPRETATION

Voting data which readers might want as they read this volume are given in the following tables. However, some seemingly important questions about the demographics of the vote cannot be answered with certainty. For example, one cannot be exact about the vote among Aboriginal people. Although it is possible that they voted against the Charlottetown proposals in the aggregate – a judgment that can be supported by examining the vote in polling places on reservations – it should be noted that the count at such polls may have included some non-Aboriginal people. And, of course, some status Indians voted at polling places off reserves. Voting by province is exact, but other demographic divisions, such as the comparison of voting by men and women, can only be estimated. Opinion polling offers some basis for judgments, but it is subject not only to

Table 1
Provincial Vote, Referendum of 26 October 1992

Province	Total Votes	Number/% Yes	Number/% No
Alberta	1,219,887	484,472 – 39.8%	732,457 – 60.2%
British Columbia	1,673,947	528,773 – 31.7%	1,139,127 – 68.3%
Manitoba	523,193	199,905 – 38.4%	320,918 – 61.6%
Newfoundland	212,393	133,583 – 62.3%	77,742 – 36.8%
New Brunswick	381,996	234,469 – 61.8%	144,885 – 38.2%
Northwest Territories	24,172	14,723 – 61.3%	9,280 – 38.7%
Nova Scotia	450,722	218,967 – 48.8%	229,690 – 51.2%
Ontario	4,834,742	2,409,713 – 50.1%	2,395,465 – 49.9%
Prince Edward Island	65,974	48,541 – 73.9%	17,128 – 26.1%
Saskatchewan	456,610	203,525 – 44.7%	251,441 – 55.3%
Yukon Territory	12,342	5,360 – 43.7%	6,916 – 56.3%
Total for Canada outside Quebec	9,855,978	4,482,031 – 45.7%	5,325,049 – 54.3%
Quebec	4,033,021	1,709,075 – 43.3%	2,236,114 – 56.7%
Total for Canada including Quebec	13,888,999	6,191,106 – 45.0%	7,561,163 – 55.0%

Sources: Elections Canada and Le directeur général des élections du Québec. Percentages based on votes.

Table 2
Aboriginal Vote, Referendum of 26 October 1992

Total Votes	Number/% Yes	Number/% No
111,015	41,503 – 37.4%	68,906 – 62.1%

Source: Assembly of First Nations; supplied with cautionary explanation that the error may be as much as 17%. This count is from reservation polling stations; it may include non-Aboriginal voters. These figures do not take account of Aboriginal voters voting off-reservation. Totals do not add because of rejected votes.

customary tolerances but to the variables of turnout and change of heart. Exit polling was not done in this referendum. The Noël essay in this volume nonetheless has good analysis and persuasive insights about the 26 October results, as does Cairns's essay.

CAIRNS: MULTINATIONALISM AND THE CONSTITUTION

Alan Cairns argues that several nationalisms were at work in the referendum. The various nationalisms in Canada include pan-

Canadian nationalism, Quebec nationalism, and "Rest of Canada" (ROC) nationalism. All Canadians feel some attachment to the Canadian nation, pan-Canadaism. But Quebec claims to be one of two founding nations of Canada, leaving Canada outside Quebec – ROC – as the other founding nation. Thus, Quebec's self-absorption (especially the possibility that it might resolve into separatism) generates in the rest of Canada a nationalism about ROC. Compared with Quebec nationalism, ROC nationalism is complicated by having no government to focus it, since the federal government represents all of Canada. Added to these three is the Aboriginal nationalism represented by the Assembly of First Nations and other Aboriginal groups. As real and deserving as these nationalisms may be, their demands on the common political system have introduced new and so far irreconcilable pulls.

The pattern of interaction between Quebec and ROC differs from that between Aboriginals and Canada. Quebec and ROC bring as much introspection as bilateral negotiation to the process of constitutional reform. This condition is more understandable perhaps for ROC, since its nationalism is contingent – it exists as a response to Quebec's own nationalism. Indeed, the current constitutional crisis would not exist save for Quebec. Other essays in this collection concur in this assessment of Quebec's centrality to the crisis, and to the primacy of Quebec's making up its mind whether to be in Canada or not. These two entities, Quebec and ROC, have nevertheless conducted themselves as partners seeking some modus vivendi.

Cairns goes on to argue that English Canada's and Quebec's understanding of each other as founding nations explains some of the differences in how they treat each other compared to how they treat Aboriginal nations. If the intention in 1982 was to have a constitution for Canada, then the reforms of Meech Lake were to validate and accommodate the constitutional requirements not just of Canada but also of Quebec. The role of Aboriginals in defeating the Meech Lake Accord dramatized and validated Aboriginal demands and the distinct governing practices which Aboriginal culture and traditions would supply. This experience made Canada ready to face a potential third (Aboriginal) order of government. But if Quebec and English Canada could live together only by providing Quebec with some assurances captured in the "distinct society" phrase, these two were still fundamentally in the republican-flavoured liberal tradition which the European explorers and settlers brought with them. Aboriginal traditions are not just distinct, they are different.

The Cairns essay wrestles with the theory of representation implied both in the negotiations at Charlottetown and in the third order of government provisions of the referendum proposal. Were the people negotiating on behalf of the Aboriginal peoples at Charlottetown actually representative? Were they more representative than the first ministers of the respective provinces in which Aboriginal people live? How should non-Aboriginal Canada treat the defection of some Aboriginal women's groups, and perhaps even a majority of Aboriginal voters, from the consensus reached at Charlottetown? Even more daunting, how in fact would liberal Canadian governments coexist with non-liberal and for that matter perhaps non-territorial Aboriginal governments in their midst? How in Parliament would we assess the representativeness of a non-Aboriginal member elected to represent a riding that had numerous Aboriginal constituents, compared to an Aboriginal member elected from a non-territorial riding made up entirely of Aboriginal people? This was uncharted territory.

In the political-constitutional dynamics of Canada's constitutional reform efforts, Quebec attained priority in the Meech Lake round, but Aboriginals gained significantly greater attention in the Charlottetown round. How are we to explain these changing priorities? One can speculate, Cairns says. Aboriginal negotiators may have been more effective at Charlottetown. Quebec had refused all along to participate in the ongoing negotiations on the grounds that it was one of two founding nations, not one of ten provinces. Quebec's non-participation might have left unbalanced opportunity for Aboriginal negotiators throughout the post-Meech period. The public, still concentrating on the Quebec dimension of the issue in the interval between Meech and Charlottetown, may have ignored the more radical concessions to Aboriginal preferences which were brewing and were then made at Charlottetown. Liberal guilt and other factors may have motivated the rest of Canada to make concessions that amounted to letting Aboriginal peoples catch up. Perhaps the referendum was a political graduation for Aboriginals.

At a deeper level of political psychology, both ROC and Quebec see themselves as part of the same Canada, although they differ about the meaning of Canada. Hence, whatever was done by way of constitutional reform, ROC and Quebec were doing it to themselves. The existing principle of equality of provinces would inhibit giving to Quebec authority that other provinces would not have. Because Aboriginals were truly different in the eyes of European Canada and because historically they had been treated differently, negotiators were not constrained by this perspective. For example, the third order of government was not constrained by the equality of provinces principle and perhaps not even by federalism, and it was possible that the Charter would not apply to Aboriginal government (through the section 1(2)(3) non-derogation provisions of the Canada clause) in cases where it would be at odds with Aboriginal culture.

In sum, Aboriginals gained more in the Charlottetown negotiations than Québécois did, for reasons relating both to the event and to deep-seated constitutional principle and practice. Canadian federalism, moreover, may not be able to adapt to Canadian multinationalism.

COOPER: QUEBEC AND THE CONSTITUTIONAL CRISIS

Seeing Quebec as the centre of Canada's constitutional problem, Barry Cooper moves first to explain how Quebec became such a problem; he then explains why the constitutional reform processes have misfired. Quebec has been a constitutional problem for Canada only recently, and the constitutional reform measures that misfired are those of the last ten years. Historians explain that while the British government initially decided in 1760–63 to anglicize Quebec, it then reversed the decision. Quebec would be easier to govern with its civil law, Roman Catholic traditions, and leadership left intact. (Tully, in his essay below, attaches greater significance to these British decisions.) In particular, this strategy would avoid French-Canadian unrest at a time when the Thirteen Colonies to the south were becoming fractious.[2] In due course, the Catholic church in Quebec proceeded to exercise custodianship of Quebec society, providing many services, such as welfare and education, which political authority might otherwise have provided. As Cooper explains, this division of responsibility fitted well into a republican perspective, which distinguishes between state and society. Political figures could manage Quebec's political agenda at home and in Ottawa, while sectarian figures could manage the distinct society. Constitutional protection for the distinct society was not called for because government had little role in maintaining the distinctiveness.

One of the social changes in Quebec during its Quiet Revolution in the 1960s was secularization of its society. Correspondingly, some of what had been provided to society by the Catholic churches became a responsibility of government. The provision of these collective goods in a manner unique to Quebec – the protection of Quebec's culture, that is – was politicized and the distinct society became a guaranty to be embedded in constitutional arrangements. Thus, the distinct society became a matter of constitutional politics.

Canadians were much readier to see Quebec as a distinct society, which it had been for over three centuries, than to see the Government of Quebec gain special powers. Yet gain special powers the Quebec government would, because the distinct society clause (section 1(2)(1)(c) of the Charlottetown Accord) assigned the Quebec government to protect the distinct society (section 1(2)(2)), while the other provincial governments had no comparable responsibility. In this way the resistance in the rest of Canada to most of the constitutional reform proposals of the past ten years as they relate to Quebec is understandable, not as objection to the distinct society but as objection to the constitutionalization of it.

As a further step back into the groundwork of this argument, Cooper seeks to say what the Canadian constitution is, the better to understand what it might become. Borrowing from Alan Cairns, Cooper says the Canadian constitution has three parts: parliamentary government, federalism, and the Charter. Arguing from the perspective of political philosophy that legitimacy for a constitution rests on its justice, Cooper asserts that a just constitution is one that results in the best regime. The best regime would embody the first principle of democracy: equality, at least equality of people as citizens. Cooper understands a democratic constitution in this sense to be free of partisan advantage. Otherwise, the constitution could not embody the principle of equality. But the constitutional reform processes in Canada, beginning with patriation of the constitution, have been the occasion for rich partisan contest. The result could not be a just or legitimate constitution.

Whatever else may motivate the partisan contest in constitutional reform, the Charter bears central responsibility. The Charter protects not only individual rights but group rights. Protection of group rights hands government a positive role. Whereas government, in the main, need only avoid infringing individual rights, it must act in pursuit of group rights. Group rights imply inequality – the members of a mentioned group have advantage over unmentioned groups or the unorganized; and the advantaged group can be expected to call on government to carry out its responsibilities to provide for the welfare of the group. This condition bodes ill for constitutional reform. In the reform process, groups must seek to protect their advantages or to gain them, and either quest raises partisan politics to the level of constitutional politics.

Cooper identifies a further pathology associated with group rights. When government is transformed into a provider of rights, the people involved need not assert their own rights. Thus, citizens give over to the state what had been their own responsibilities, and their dependence on the state gets amplified. This argument is especially applicable in the case of Quebec, because it identifies the distinct society as a group right; indeed, it would be the "most egregious" instance of group rights in the Canadian constitution. To give any provincial government such responsibilities, Cooper implies, would be inconsistent with inclusion of that government in a larger constitutional framework.

Has Canada any recourse? Cooper believes that the interests of Canada and of Quebec are better served by a sovereign Quebec. He concludes that as Canadians revisit the fundamentals of constitutionalism, they must come to rely on the twin principles of equality of citizens and equality of provinces. Then they can look beyond a principle of mere survival to a constitutional goal of the good life.

NOËL: REFERENDUM AS DEMOCRATIC DELIBERATION

The referendum of 26 October could be seen from south of latitude 49°, if too casually, as a crisis of legitimacy. Canadian leadership had, with near uniformity, asked approval from the citizens for a course of action. After ten years of continual wrangling, the path to constitutional stability had been mapped out, leaders said. With a mandate from voters, officials would proceed down that road, giving constitutional substance to the mandate. Then, in large numbers, Canadians rejected what their leadership had urged. Was this not a rejection not only of the referred constitutional proposals but also of the leadership that had recommended them? Did this not open the door to different and possibly radical leadership? This reading of the referendum results, Noël reports, was at first offered by some Canadian commentators.

But in Noël's view, the referendum was neither a crisis of legitimacy nor a triumph of confusion, ignorance, or intolerance. Instead, Canadians voted No because they compared the constitutional package to the norms of justice which they expected of a constitution, and found the package wanting. This was, in that sense, a case of democratic deliberation. According to Noël, the tests of democratic deliberation are these:

• Public opinion actually changes, as a result of discussing options in a situation in which the outcome of the deliberation and subsequent vote are uncertain. Noël gives evidence that opinion in

Canada changed between the announcement of the Charlottetown package on 28 August and the vote on 26 October.
- The criteria adopted for the voting decision are conceptions of justice, rather than simply readings of personal or group interest. Again, Noël offers evidence that Canadians applied a criterion of justice defined as some form of equality.
- Finally, in democratic deliberation, the people narrow the applicable definitions of justice and the options for action to a few, making choice possible.

Admittedly, the traditional explanation of Canadian politics will not do for the referendum of 26 October. Preparation of the Charlottetown package may seem to have fitted the model of elite accommodation, in which important decisions are made by leadership with little consultation with the public, but the campaign and vote did not. In fact, the explanatory power of elite accommodation had been declining since 1982, with all of its elements coming into doubt. The political style associated with the Charter of Rights and Freedoms differed from executive federalism in its pluralism and participatory ways. Failure of the Meech Lake reforms spelled the end of consociationalism as elites, some of whom had even been associated with preparation of the reforms, moved in opposing directions about the political system itself; and the "absent mandate" from Canadians as the open-ended condition for government decision ended with the fall 1988 election, conducted as a referendum of sorts on ratification of the U.S.–Canada Free Trade Agreement. Thus, while the voters did not signal a crisis of legitimacy in the fall of 1992, they did illustrate the new Canadian politics that had been evolving for at least ten years.

The new Canadian politics, Noël explains, may be new but are not wholly at odds with the old. The new politics are characterized not by the rational, individualistic, and rights-oriented behaviour explained best by theories such as public choice, but rather are characterized by community, public interest, and democratic deliberation. Canadian politics had not abandoned its republican component in the 1980s, but instead had nourished and vitalized it.

Noël's essay goes on to analyse the campaign for and against the referred package according to this democratic deliberation model. Voters commonly support the status quo in referenda, he says, unless given a rationale not to do so. But as F.L. Morton asks in his comments on the essay, which side was the status quo? Since the Charlottetown package would change the constitution, Yes would at first appear to be a vote for change and No a vote for the status quo. Noël answers the question this way, but with a twist: Yes was at the same time a vote for change and a conservative vote. Seeing the Charlottetown package as the minimum necessary to preserve the Canadian federation, Yes was a vote for the changes necessary to preserve the status quo. No, in this sense, might have been insistence on even greater constitutional reform. So a substantial burden of persuasion still fell on the No side.

The proponents of the package began with positive appeals about the virtue of compromise to accommodate the major constituencies in Canada and about the ability of Canadian unity to overreach and comprehend Canadian diversity. But the proponents then slipped into a crude something-for-everybody variation on this argument and finally campaigned on the adversities that would follow rejection of the package. The opponents held to a consistent line, pointing out the inconsistencies and inequalities of the Charlottetown Accord; and it was the equality issues that exposed the underpinnings of justice on which Canadians would finally base their decision. The vote should be understood, then, not as anti-Quebec or anti-Aboriginal or even anti-Mulroney, but rather as the widespread conclusion that inequalities in the package concerning Aboriginal government and the Government of Quebec had not been reconciled with the enduring principles of equality of provinces, equality of founding peoples, and equality of persons.

Is constitutional reform to be put aside now, frozen for a later and unspecified thaw? Is the vote to be read as favouring the boredom of ordinary legislation over the drama of constitutional politics (as Ajzenstat, in her essay, hopes)? Noël doubts that these conclusions are either reasonable or possible. While the referendum removed a deadline (the promise by Quebec's government to offer citizens a referendum on Quebec's future), it did not remove the underlying instability. The dynamics of Canadian politics will prevent retirement of constitutional reform. Aboriginal claims remain unresolved and Quebec is divided down the middle on the question of federalism versus sovereignty or sovereignty association. The issues that Charlottetown attempted to resolve are as alive as ever. So Canadians will not be spared their never-ending story.

Constitutional reform may continue to follow the path of democratic deliberation. Meech Lake was a lesson and so was Charlottetown. Quebec, admittedly the key, is learning more about itself and what it wants from constitutional reform while the rest of Canada may decide that "there are many ways of being a Canadian," as Noël

puts it. Equally, Quebec and the rest of Canada may decide it best
to go their separate ways.

AJZENSTAT: PROPRIETY IN CONSTITUTION MAKING

In fact, should constitution making follow a democratic deliberation
process, in Canada or anywhere else? Scarcely, says Janet Ajzenstat.
While amendments to a constitution may be treated according to
ordinary political processes, preparation of a constitution is extraordinary and liberal democratic theory treats it that way, she argues.
What Canada was doing in the Charlottetown package was no less
than a "refounding," a point endorsed by Robert Jackson in his
comments on Ajzenstat's essay. Lamentably, preservation of the difference between legislation and constitution making has been lost in
Canada, probably forever. The result is a dilemma for Canada.

The Canada Act of 1981 (which resulted in the British parliament's
passage of the Constitution Act, 1982) was not entirely an elite affair.
While formal influence was limited to the prime minister, first ministers, and Parliament, the debate was widespread. Still, the process
of patriation had been too closed, in the eyes of many. Two popular
participatory processes emerged as possible successors, in Ajzenstat's
view. One participatory successor is interest group pluralism, an
arrangement in which all groups and interests press their demands
to eventual resolution. The other is reform by constituent assembly.
The virtue of a constituent assembly is to uncover or build consensus.
Consensus, which is not simply the majority opinion but rather the
general consent in the polity, implies a comprehensive deliberative
process.

Groups were thoroughly involved in the 1981 Canada Act, Ajzenstat explains, and some of them were notably successful in their
efforts. Feminists won section 28 of the Charter, for example, and
other groups obtained their sections. The result was that the constitution could be seen as consisting of "listed" and "unlisted" groups.
This condition evidently did not bring unity, however, for constitution
making has remained prominently and divisively on the Canadian
agenda. In fact, Ajzenstat notes, unity in Canada has never been
about individual rights, since Canada is not individualistic in outlook.
Rather, the listing in the constitution created a sort of have/have-not
status. Thus, in the Meech Lake process (and presumably Charlottetown), the constitutional haves – those whose chief collective concerns
gained constitutional protection – opposed re-tailoring the constitu-

tion to make it fit the requirements of the constitutional have-nots. Domination of constitution making by groups turned the process into a sort of zero-sum game. For example, full recognition of women's rights could not coexist with full recognition of Aboriginal rights to self-government. (Morton explores this theme well in his essay, too.)

But might we not look past the group to the persons who make up the group, avoiding the probable discrepancy between what the leadership of the group wants and what the members of the group want? Moreover, might we not wish to accommodate the unorganized in a constitution-making process? These correctives could be made in a constituent assembly, allegedly. In a broadly based consultative and voting process, the people might individually register their views and be educated to a clearer and enlightened understanding of their own interests and the interests of the community. This understanding could then be written into a constitution. The Beaudoin-Dobbie process was an effort to carry out this method of constitution making.

The argument for a constituent assembly is that however popularized constitution making has become, it has not become sufficiently so. Yet further popularization of constitution making offers no good prospect, argues Ajzenstat. Popularization in combination with post-materialist new politics turns the process from a conventional contest among groups to a struggle among ideologies. Every constitution embodies an ideology, but the one in place has the virtue of being in place. The goal of a constituent assembly, to strip away interests as the basis for decision, leaves ideology, on which there may be neither consensus nor conditions for compromise.

The search for consensus as a basis for constitution making has an even darker side, in Ajzenstat's view. If a nation searches for general agreement but does not find it, the next step may be imposition of a doctrine. But a People's Democracy of Canada is scarcely a prospect, and the outcome of any such tendency as this simply ends with more divisiveness. For most of their history, Canadians accepted their form of liberalism and the disproportionate influence it gave to elites, satisfied that whatever bias was in the constitution would not intolerably taint the political process. But in the past thirty years, Canadians have come to a richer appreciation of the ideological implications of a constitution and of the opportunity presented by constitution making to entrench some advantage. The result has not been success in constitution making, nor will it be. Canadians can hope that contestants, seeing the futility of constitutional politics, will return to ordinary politics for satisfaction of their demands.

Aside from this choice, Ajzenstat concludes, Canadians may hope for a period of apathy, at least about the constitution.

MORTON: THE SUPREME COURT AS CAUSE OF THE CRISIS

Relying on the Supreme Court's treatment of Charter-related litigation on behalf of group rights, F.L. Morton's essay finds support for the hypothesis that the Supreme Court is a cause of Canada's constitutional crisis. Judicialized politics are new for Canada, he shows, but they were taken up enthusiastically once the Charter of Rights and Freedoms was in place. Finding the court receptive, groups were equally enthusiastic about advancing their demands as Charter-based lawsuits. And since Quebec's demand for constitutional protection of its distinct society can be categorized as a demand by a group, Quebec was fitting squarely with the trend of judicialized politics.

Morton also raises the observation made by others in this volume that some groups succeeded in gaining protection in the Charter while others did not. For example, the Charter is explicit about legal equality of men and women (articles 15 and 28), protection of the treaty rights of Aboriginal peoples (article 25), and "preservation and enhancement" of multiculturalism (article 27). But while the Charter has lengthy provisions to ensure equal French and English language rights, it does not take up protection of Quebec's distinct society. The Quebec government may have generous latitude when measured against the latitude reserved to constituent governments in many federal systems. But Quebec's latitude is the same as that of any other province in Canada. In the sense that any group not singled out in the Charter is less protected than the groups that are mentioned, Quebec was a Charter loser. Morton explains how Quebec came to see itself as a Charter loser.

One might note that the protection that would satisfy Quebec goes beyond mere protection of the French language to include whatever else might come under the open-ended label of "distinct society." The French legal tradition would be protected, and Morton offers further examples. Yet an American observer might still be puzzled at first by Quebec's position. Canadian provinces have more authority than states in the United States. A provincial legislature is empowered (article 33), for example, to legislate contrary to the individual freedoms and legal rights that are explicitly protected in the Charter. This greater latitude in all provinces may be seen as sufficient power for Quebec to assure that its government could act to guarantee the distinct society. But according to Morton's analysis, Quebec had from the period of patriation opposed the Charter and other constitutional reforms emplaced in the Constitution Act, 1982, to no avail. That Quebec's constitutional authority is the same as that of other provincial governments is not a persuasive argument to Québécois, who can see that other groups enjoy the advantages of constitutional mention which they do not.

The Meech Lake round of constitutional reform was intended to satisfy Quebec's requirements. The Aboriginal people, with other Charter groups and Senate reformers, were seen as significant in defeating the Meech Lake constitutional proposals. In this line of reasoning, opposition to Meech by Aboriginal people was because they did not want their constitutional position diluted. The obvious conclusion about strategy for constitutional reform was to avoid constitutional losers. The solution adopted at Charlottetown, in this rationale, was to make everyone a constitutional winner. That is Morton's reading of the Canada clause of the Charlottetown Accord – it tried to make all groups into constitutional winners. The Canada clause paved a road for every group to travel to the Supreme Court, where an activist court gives good hope of blessing the group's pleas. Morton thus sees the activist court as a stronger explanation of the expansive work at Charlottetown than the Charter itself.

TULLY: NEGOTIATING A CONSTITUTION FOR A DIVERSE SOCIETY

Do Canadians have the common basis for a constitution? James Tully searches deeply for the answer to this question and comes up with some surprising answers and a qualified optimism. The doctrinal underpinnings of the constitutional order in the United States are said to be organic – the nation and its doctrine came about simultaneously. Most nations can be seen to exist separately from their doctrines. They existed as nations before they held to any particular doctrine, and in some cases they have attached themselves to different doctrines at different times in their histories. Not so the United States, whose highly individualistic form of liberalism is the only doctrine it has ever known. If the doctrine seems lacking in the coherence one expects of a doctrine, this objection can be put aside by relaxing the idea of doctrine and calling the structure of ideas a creed, as Samuel P. Huntington does.[3] In any case, a common array of ideas found in the Declaration of Independence and the Constitution of 1787 is available to solve the common affairs of the polity.

Admittedly, this view of the American creed is harsh in some of its applications. The United States does have its own first nations and some non-European cultures which might claim that the creed fits them poorly. If the United States were to indulge in constitution making in the latter twentieth century, such discrepancies might undermine the process. But the contrast to Canada remains instructive. The nations that make up the Canadian constitutional association have not claimed any doctrine organic to Canada, and this is a complication when the project is constitution making.

Canada seems to be an especially successful realization of the republican tradition. It has implemented communitarianism in its public policy, and Canadians seem less destructive of each other than Americans do. Canada has made do with greater constitutional uncertainty than the United States has, letting laws and charters from abroad serve for a long time as fundamental law. Such loose constitutionalism would never do in the rights-oriented United States, where citizens want to know that they have generous private space and what its boundaries are. Canadian confidence in the community – in each other – is a different attitude, and it might lead one to expect an easier course of constitution making than would be the case in a more individualistic polity.

For Tully, the Canadian "spirit of diversity" means that Canada harbors several visions of itself. Aboriginal people have a certain vision, which is derived from their history and doctrine. That vision contrasts with the Quebec vision and with the vision of English Canada, women, the West, and so forth. These visions cannot simply coexist, because they are not discrete and do not admit to their partiality. National and provincial governing institutions comprehend the holders of the several visions, and the holders of the differing visions interact with each other in political and economic life. They interact now, but they have a record of interactions as well that has been laid down over more than three centuries of common history. Nor are the visions soluble, because they imply contrasting constitutional allocations of power. To dissolve the visions into a common vision would be to reallocate power, a political act that could not be consensual. Canadians may be grateful that the holders of the contrasting visions of Canada are constituencies that overlap. That francophones are also Canadians and Ontarians and women, or that anglophones are also Canadians and Quebeckers and immigrants, should bind people together and confront them with their common fate. Balkanization of Canada would not be the danger. But at the same time, constitution making requires some reconciliation of these visions, and this is the more important question that Tully addresses.

Despite the differing visions, Canadians do have a shared sense of procedural justice residing in the background, or what Tully calls "middle ground." This shared sense of justice can be articulated as three "conventions of justification" with deep roots both in Aboriginal and in Western philosophy. These conventions are:

- *Continuity.* When peoples come together, whether voluntarily or by conquest, they all must mutually recognize one another and grant continuation of one another's way of life. A new constitutional association should not erase its predecessor associations or constituencies.
- *Negotiation.* A constitutional association should result from application of fair multilateral negotiation. A constitutional order, however fair and just, should not be imposed on peoples who had no part in the preparation of it. The test of good constitutional association is not one of efficiency or abstract justice alone.
- *Consent.* Corresponding to the rule of negotiation, a just constitutional order must have the consent of all the peoples who will be part of the order, and change in the constitutional order must have the consent of all the peoples who are affected by the change.

Failure to observe these conventions of justification explains why the five constitutional rounds since 1964 have been unsuccessful in the sense that the question remains unsettled. Tully analyses the recent reform efforts to show how this is so, and then moves back in Canadian history to show that the peoples and nations of Canada have relied on these conventions in jurisprudence and in constitutional arrangements throughout. Significant for his analysis is his showing that Canada has a "parallel constitutional history" of dealings with Aboriginal people relying on these same conventions.

Will application of the conventions of justification move Canada past the many impasses that have surfaced in the 1980s and 1990s episodes of constitutional reform? Some of the impasses, Tully concedes, would be resistant to this treatment. The rights of native women in Aboriginal law as compared with Charter law do not resolve easily, for example. But constitutional reform through application of the three conventions holds promise, says Tully, because it shifts constitutional criteria away from the partial and irreconcilable visions to "Canada as a diversity."

EMBERLEY: WHAT IN THE WORLD IS GOING ON?

One of the responses to Fukuyama's famous end-of-history essay complained that no liberal should be pleased with belief in an end to history, since the belief violates the fundamental liberal stance that history advances indefinitely as a result of the free, individual confrontation of the human condition.[4] Similarly, Peter Emberley asks how a liberal can seek closure of Canada's constitutional debate. His answer begins with the observation that the debate about constitutional reform made an assumption that is no longer valid – that there is a common ground. Canada and all other contemporary nations may lack such common ground, Emberley warns.

That the West has no common ground for constitution making tells us that it has reached a watershed, no less that it did in the fourth century before the Christian era and again in the thirteenth century. What happened in those two earlier intervals, and what is happening again now, is the "decline of the primary political unit." Today, the nation-state is in decline, a decline which Emberley carefully calls a decline in status and an inanition. He thus fortifies his argument against the response, offered in the comments by David Hendrickson, that the power of the nation-state remains great and that some disorder in the world today is by nations seeking their own political system – their own state. One surmises that the power of the nation-state may mask its decline. Emberley analyses both the theoretical and practical decline, establishing that what is happening in Canada is exemplary rather than being unique.

Following Arendt, Emberley says that the nation-state was ever an unstable combination. The nation implies conformity and exclusivity while the state implies freedom of persons and equality in law. The state's authority is from consent, rationally given by each citizen. The state need not stand for justice but simply for procedures that are expected to bring just solutions. A government's task is to promote a homogeneous population in the sense that the population of citizens agree on the procedures. The nation, in contrast, gets its authority from the history shared by its members. It has a version of justice and is not satisfied simply with a procedure. One's obligation to it is not from rationally given consent but from received and perhaps unexamined culture. The universalism of the state would exist uneasily with the particularism of the nation, and the tension between them grew. For example, the tension necessarily would grow as the state was called on, for good economic reasons, to extend its control beyond its borders.

Today, the result of this tension, with its first order implication about the decline of the nation-state, is no less than a "disruption of modern consciousness." The context for political action during the modern state system was the nation-state and the method was power. The context is now uncertain as the number and kind of political units has multiplied. The method is even more elusive but is best understood as technology of a sort. Technology, a way of "seeing human nature as something to be controlled and managed," is the new dominant global and mass process. Technology brings values and capabilities with it. The notable value is efficiency, which is the elimination of tension. Efficiency is greatest when friction is least, when all parts of a process work together perfectly. Fundamental among the capabilities that technology brings is communication. The "global village" is upon us.

This analysis gives us at least three reasons why the contemporary nation-state provides no ground for constitution making. First, with the estrangement of nation and state, the number of nations has proliferated. States may remain intact (or not), but the nation as a reference point has no containment and breaks out into groupings of real or imagined history or other segregating features, which must pass an increasingly fine screen. Second, communication enables the manufacture or remanufacture of sub-state and sub-national groupings which have no basis other than the communication links themselves. Take away the point of identification which the nation-state represented, then fragment the nation, and we cannot predict what people will rally to, except that the number of rallying points can be numerous. Third, in contrast, people can be linked together without the mediating structures of the nation-state and its corollaries. We stand unprotected before the barrage of signals unleashed by contemporary communications. Aboriginals of Canada may find common cause with Aboriginals of Brazil, as much in common as with fellow citizens.

In sum, the familiar structures of nation-state surround us but without the differentiated value structure that legitimated them. Therefore the nation state cannot mobilize its citizens to solve common problems, especially problems of such magnitude as constitution making. What was attempted at Charlottetown may not have been doomed, but it would have been doomed to resist the tide of history. Worse, what actually came out of Charlottetown simply ignored the theoretical incompatibilities of the compromises. The accord accommodated the centralizing and decentralizing pulls by embodying both. It empowered Ottawa (for example, on trade matters), subnational groups (for example, the Aboriginals) and subnational governments (for example, those permitted to opt out of national programs), leaving for later the sorting out when these authorities collided. Trying to be all things to all people, the accord was not a compromise but an amalgam. Emberley concludes that in the new world of disorder, Canada must depend on other than the now inapplicable processes of constitution making.

WHAT IS NEXT?

According to a Decima opinion poll of late 1992, the referendum and the constitution were not first on the minds of Canadians. Eighty-two percent of the sample were "somewhat" or "very dissatisfied" with the federal government, but this judgment seems to have been driven chiefly by distress about the economy. On the other hand, people reported that their opinion of politicians, already low, had gone down as a result of the referendum.[5]

James Madison wrote, in "Federalist Paper 37," that "among the difficulties encountered by the convention, a very important one must have lain in combining the requisite stability and energy in government, with the inviolable attention due to liberty and to the republican form." "Energy in government," he went on, "is essential to that security against external and internal danger, and to that prompt and salutary execution of the laws which enter into the very definition of good government. Stability in government is essential to ... that repose and confidence in the minds of the people, which are among the chief blessings of civil society."[6] Good government is energetic and stable – it secures society and gives citizens confidence, without attacking their liberty; that is, government must be effective without being oppressive. Canada's leadership, acting through government, has not been effective in promoting this most fundamental of assignments, renewed constitutional expression of a Canadian social contract. Canadian leaders are the losers from this ineffectiveness, as shown in the polling result cited above; and perhaps Canadians are also the losers.

But the game is not over. Canadian leadership still has the assignment to present Canadians with a proper constitution. Promises were made in the Meech Lake Accord and in the Charlottetown Accord, even though in the end the promises were not transformed into a binding contract. In particular, Québécois and Aboriginal peoples were promised that they would govern themselves according to their cultures and traditions, within the framework of Canadian constitutionalism. One expects these promises to form the starting point of new efforts to articulate the constitutional order. Specific reforms may, however, be disaggregated and dealt with incrementally (for example, Aboriginal issues) or resolved through practice outside megaconstitutional politics, as part of the unwritten constitution (for example, Quebec's distinct society). In this sense, the referendum was a setback for Canadians, though it need not be a loss.

This starting point is easier to see than the course following it, however. In the early aftermath of the referendum, other matters in Canadian politics have crowded the constitutional question off the agenda. Yet one doubts that the constitutional question will be allowed to rest. Those whose constitutional position would have been improved – those to whom the promises were made – will want the promises executed. Some other political players may gain partisan advantage from energizing the constitutional question. So even if a majority of Canadians might prefer a respite from it, we can expect the constitution to re-enter the agenda.

The negotiators at Charlottetown knew they were proposing more than ordinary amendments to the constitution. What they may not have appreciated were the tensions this effort would expose, tensions which might even be characteristic of the latter twentieth century and which might have significantly altered the parameters of constitution making. Most of the essays here doubt that constitution making can create its own preconditions. They point to the failing preconditions: the political containment of nations which would give a sufficient context for constitutionalism; commitment to both individualism and community sufficient to counter the growing "ideology of difference"; and a place for constitution making outside the realm of ordinary politics. On the other hand, if the principles of justice on which a constitution for Canada can be negotiated are available, as Tully claims, and if democratic deliberation were to re-establish the preconditions, as Noël thinks possible, then Canada's constitutional renewal might still occur.

While this outside observer is apprehensive that repeated failure in national attempts to renew its constitution will bring Canada to crisis, the essayists in this volume conclude that Canada has a predicament or impasse, but not a crisis.

1 The Charlottetown Accord: Multinational Canada v. Federalism

ALAN C. CAIRNS

THE BATTLEGROUND OF RECENT CONSTITUTIONAL HISTORY

Traumatic events, such as the recent constitutional referendum, heighten self-consciousness without generating agreement on what has transpired. Indeed, the reverse is more likely true, since the particularistic self-consciousness activated by the referendum process informs the subsequent competition to affix self-interested meaning to this latest Canadian constitutional episode. As rival interpretive claims battle for attention, the pre-referendum constitutional past also gets subtly redefined. Interpretations of the Charlottetown Accord and referendum are indirectly reinterpretations of Meech Lake, of the 1982 Constitution Act and the Trudeau legacy, of past relations between Aboriginal peoples and the Canadian state, and of historical patterns of relationship between Quebec and the "Rest of Canada" (ROC). For the constitutional competitors, the intense constitutional conflict of recent decades makes the past a political resource that is too valuable to be left to one's opponents, or to the academics.

The unavoidable political uses of the past do not preclude the raising of larger and different questions of meaning and interpretation by academics. Indeed, the latter have an obligation to step back, to adopt a longer-run perspective, and to raise issues that the more directly involved may overlook or prefer to leave unexamined. A constitutional process dealing with issues of nationhood, survival, identity, and community at a time of crisis shakes the inertia and ongoingness characteristic of society in normal times. When the dust has settled on such existential episodes, they should receive intense academic scrutiny for the light they may throw on what normality conceals. This paper's contribution to that constitutional introspection analyses the accord and the referendum from the perspective of the inchoate emergence of Canada as a multinational state,[1] and the latter's entanglement with an inherited federalism.

THE EMERGENCE OF MULTINATIONAL CANADA

The process leading up to the accord, its contents, and the verdict of the electorate reveal a multinational society struggling for constitutional expression in a federal constitutional order that defines Canadians in the traditional terms of province and country. Canadian identities, however, are no longer adequately accommodated by the coexisting provincial and countrywide identities natural to a federal people. They are supplemented and challenged by various internal national identities – Québécois, Aboriginal, and, haltingly, ROC.

Québécois not only see themselves as a distinct people but also recognize two "others" – ROC, or English Canada, and, somewhat ambivalently, the Aboriginal nation(s). The latter, in turn, seek recognition as a third founding nation.[2] They are also intensely cognizant of Quebec/ROC differences, fully appreciating that Quebec-Aboriginal relations could be bitter and acrimonious should Quebec leave Canada. The ROC is unhappily aware that its former hegemony over all of Canada is challenged by both Québécois and Aboriginal nationalisms. These reciprocal national recognitions and the struggles they precipitate are played out in the context of a still surviving, if retreating, pan-Canadian nationalism to which varying allegiance is given by the adherents of the other nationalisms. Described as above, Canada's multinational nature, in terms of each national community's recognizing and engaging in conflict with the others, is a commonplace, the appreciation of which challenges federalism's traditional stranglehold over high constitutional politics.

These nationalisms do not confront one another as such. Québécois, Canadian, and ROC nationalisms confront one another in a federal system that reduces Quebec to the status of a province and muffles the voice of ROC, which lacks the jurisdictional clothing to shape its self-consciousness. The various Aboriginal nationalisms are given voice not by governments but by four Aboriginal organizations, which are challenged by a fifth representing Aboriginal women.

Their presence at the bargaining table is, unlike the others (except for the northern territories), not accompanied by formal responsibilities in the amending process. They are, therefore, dependent on the governments of federalism to achieve constitutional objectives that will profoundly transform federalism and greatly complicate its future workings.

Indian, Inuit, and Métis identities have been fashioned by distinct political histories, which for status Indians and Inuit have involved idiosyncratic relations to the federal system. Only the Métis have experienced the garden-variety existence of ordinary Canadians subject to the normal application of the division of powers, until their recognition as an Aboriginal people in 1982.

Of the four nationalisms (viewing the various Aboriginal nationalisms as one), only the Canadian, with the federal government as its advocate, is harmonious with the constitutional assúmptions of federalism. Its existence flows naturally from the federal facts of a central government and the countrywide community it serves. Now, however, it is a defensive nationalism, under attack, and seeking to salvage what it can. Aboriginal nationalisms and Québécois nationalism work the constitutional machinery to strengthen their nationhood. Much of the complexity and confusion of the Canadian constitutional process is because Canadians are playing a multinational game by rules that presuppose that they are essentially a federal people. We find, therefore, much ambiguity and slippage of identity and terminology. Does the federal government speak for Canada or for the Rest of Canada? If the former, who speaks for the latter? Does the *premier ministre* of Quebec represent a province or a nation? Do Aboriginal peoples participate as nations, as supplicants, or as provinces of the future?

At the level of ordinary social observation, Canadians outside Quebec recognize that in some sense Quebec is clearly a distinct society, nation, or people. Yet viewed through the constitutional lens of federalism, Quebec is simply a province. The Canadian constitutional model adhered to by ROC allows only extremely limited official constitutional recognition to what is widely accepted as a social reality, the unique sociocultural, linguistic, historic aspects of the Quebec people. The natural assumption, however, that it is ROC's sense of the Canadian nation that sets limits to the degree of constitutional diversity that can be officially sanctioned is, somewhat surprisingly, clearly erroneous. As discussed below, the Charlottetown Accord – which was largely fashioned by federal, provincial, territorial, and Aboriginal leaders before the Quebec government came to the bargaining table – was dramatically more responsive to Aboriginal nationalisms than to Quebec nationalism. Since in most ways the differences between Aboriginals and other Canadians are already much more pronounced than between Québécois and other Canadians, and since the Charlottetown Accord potentially constitutionalized a profoundly greater diversity of constitutional status and treatment for Aboriginal peoples than for Québécois, the limited response to Quebec cannot be explained by a generalized antipathy to recognizing cultural difference or by resistance to deviations from constitutional normality. Why it is apparently easier to give constitutional recognition to Aboriginal than to Québécois diversity, using the Charlottetown Accord as an example, is tentatively answered below.

The first major contemporary attempt to find a constitutional reconciliation between Quebec nationalism, Aboriginal nationalism, incipient ROC nationalism, and the inherited pan-Canadian nationalism occurred in the post-Meech process that led to Charlottetown. In the 1960s and 1970s the constitutional challenge came from Quebec, with Aboriginals only beginning to emerge from the shadows. Although Aboriginal Canadians made major gains in the Constitution Act, 1982, much of their achievement was a promissory note that has not yet been met.

By the 1980s, the constitutional status quo was challenged by both Quebec and Aboriginal nationalisms, but their challenge occurred in discrete arenas, which avoided the necessity of producing a synthesizing response. Aboriginal issues received constitutional attention, but minimal response, in the four special Aboriginal constitutional conferences, 1983–87, in which Quebec did not officially participate. In the subsequent Meech Lake constitutional round, dubbed the Quebec round, the other Canadian provinces made constitutional gains on Quebec's coattails by insisting that the equality of provinces principle had to be followed, so that what Quebec asked for – distinct society excepted – Prince Edward Island also received. Aboriginal organizations, lacking formal veto power and being absent from the intergovernmental negotiations, were unable to duplicate the gains of provincial governments outside Quebec. Although Aboriginal organizations successfully exempted Aboriginal constitutional clauses from the distinct society's application and although they played a key role in discrediting and defeating the accord (in particular, by Elijah Harper's Manitoba role), their input is best described as constitutional guerrilla warfare.

Thus, until the post-Meech processes, responses to Quebec and Aboriginal nationalisms were separated. They came together for the first time in the Charlottetown Accord and in the events that preceded this failed effort at major constitutional reform. The four main Aboriginal organizations not only participated directly in the negotiation process but conducted their own consultations with their specific Aboriginal constituencies. Quebec, too, conducted itself as a separate actor, with the Allaire and Bélanger-Campeau inquiries, two National Assembly committees to examine sovereignty and offers of renewed federalism, and the planned Quebec referendum. As there was minimal input from Quebec and Aboriginal peoples to the Spicer Commission, the Beaudoin-Dobbie committee, and the winter 1992 public constitutional conferences, these designedly Canadian processes unexpectedly developed into vehicles for ROC to develop its own constitutional positions. There was, therefore, separate input from the three national communities before the federal dimension, including the federal government's version of Canadian nationalism, asserted itself in the final negotiation stage (with Aboriginal leaders and advisers, of course, also present).

The Charlottetown Accord, therefore, including its background and its electoral repudiation, is a historic event that illuminates the difficulties of responding to multinational realities through federalist amendment processes. It also illustrates the ambiguities and tension between Canada, as an official, constitutional actor speaking through the federal government, and ROC, whose existential existence lacks constitutionally authoritative advocates.

QUEBEC AND ROC: RECOGNITION WITH LIMITED RESPONSE

At one level of behaviour and perception, Quebec and ROC clearly see each other as separate entities and fully recognize that in constitutional politics they are responding to each other.[3] At this level, it is understood that Quebec has a national existence, that it is not a province like the others, and that it might opt for and attain independence. Simultaneously, ROC understands that it may become the reluctant inheritor of a Canada without Quebec and begins, psychologically and gropingly, to adjust to that unwelcome but not implausible future.

At a different level, Quebec is a province trapped in the workings of federalism, and ROC responds to the structure of federalism by putting on its Canada mask or losing itself in competing provincialisms. In recent decades, the inertia of federalism has triumphed over the two nations view that is especially congenial to Quebec, particularly when constitutional proposals are formulated and in the ratification process. Québécois nationalism chafes against the provincial constraints imposed by Canadian federalism. The equality of provinces norm is opposed as being incompatible with the preferred two nations view of Canada. Francophone Québécois, like Aboriginal peoples, also categorically resist any suggestion that they are part of multicultural Canada.

The powerful presence of nationalism is evident in numerous phenomena – the election of the Parti Québécois in 1976, the continuing presence of a major *indépendantiste* party, either in government or waiting in the wings to become the government, a nationalist intelligentsia, an extensive international presence, the tenacious search for formal constitutional recognition under the rubric of a distinct society, and the paraphernalia of statehood (National Assembly, "prime minister" rather than "premier") which evidence a degree of nationalist affirmation that is unrivalled in other provinces. These nationalist indicators are sustained by an unremitting concern for the survival of a distinctive people and language threatened by demographic weakness in an engulfing English-speaking continent. Quebec's sense of national distinctiveness is also fed by demographic trends – the significant decline in the Quebec anglophone community as a result of extensive emigration, a consequent increase in the francophone share of the total Quebec population, and, simultaneously, the increasing concentration of the Canadian francophone population within Quebec.

Nationalist rhetoric is part of everyday political language and is uttered by federalist Liberals with a passion almost indistinguishable from that of their Parti Québécois opponents.[4] "Quebecers," in the words of the preamble to the Act establishing the Bélanger-Campeau Commission, "are free to assume their own destiny, to determine their political status and to assure their economic, social and cultural development."[5] Rhetoric is supplemented by distinctive political and constitutional behaviour that suggests a degree of self-perceived uniqueness that goes well beyond the provincial diversities in ROC – behaviour that strains the limits of Quebec's jurisdictional status as a province. The very acronym ROC, which is used both inside and outside Quebec, imputes a singularity to Quebec's position that is implicitly recognized by Canadians outside Quebec. No one would refer to the nine provinces outside Manitoba or Nova Scotia as ROC.

Quebec repeatedly conducts itself as a national rather than provincial actor, and engages in bouts of nationalist introspection about its past treatment or preferred futures. From 1976 to 1980, Quebec introspectively prepared for its pending referendum, designed to increase its constitutional bargaining power, while Canada, acting for

ROC, readied its response to Quebec by Bill c-60 and the Pepin-Robarts task force, in which the Parti Québécois government displayed minimal interest (especially in the former). The 1980 referendum was an inward-looking exercise in national choice, self-definition, and democratically based national self-determination. Significantly, there was general acceptance by Canadians outside Quebec of the right of Québécois democratically to choose their own future. The threat of using force to keep Quebec in a Canada which its citizens wished to leave was conspicuously absent from the responses of ROC.

Revealingly, Canadians outside Quebec were clearly defined as outsiders or unwelcome intruders in the referendum as Quebec engaged in agonizing constitutional introspection. Thus, ROC was relegated to an apprehensive audience role while it awaited the referendum outcome. Later versions of constitutional introspection, the Allaire and Bélanger-Campeau reports, which examined alternative futures for Quebec, displayed monumental indifference to the Canadian dimension of the contemporary Quebec-Canadian reality. These powerful symbolic acts implicitly assumed that Québécois, defined in national terms, should decide on their future in their Québécois capacity, not their Canadian capacity. By eliminating the latter from consciousness, or at least from conscious attention, they induced Canadians elsewhere to think of themselves as ROC.

The Quebec government has deliberately and shrewdly deployed nationalist symbolism in its confrontational encounters with the Canadian government and ROC. It responded to the proclamation of the 1982 Constitution Act, following the isolation of the Quebec government in the closing days of its negotiation, by the symbolism of Quebec flags at half mast. Officially, the Quebec government rejected both the Act and its "bloody Charter" (as René Lévesque referred to it). The Quebec government subsequently wielded the notwithstanding clause across the board as a symbolic defiance of the Charter until the Parti Québécois defeat in 1985, turned inwards and retreated from intergovernmental conferences from 1982 to 1985, and declined official participation in the 1983–87 Aboriginal constitutional conferences while Quebec's constitutional demands remained unmet.

In the Meech Lake constitutional drama, the Quebec government conducted itself as the aggrieved party that had been betrayed in 1982, established its minimum demands for a return to the constitutional family, quickly ratified the Meech Lake resolution after it had gained intergovernmental agreement, and then retreated to the sidelines until the closing weeks of the three-year ratification period, as a provincially fragmented ROC struggled without success to produce the requisite unanimous positive response.

After the Meech Lake fiasco, Quebec watched or participated only minimally in the various constitutional activities and processes that produced the Charlottetown Accord, until the final meetings in August 1992. Robert Bourassa had previously asserted that he would bargain only one on one – "nation to nation" – with the federal government, thus attributing to the latter a responsibility it cannot assume, to be the representative and advocate of the interests of ROC. In the interval between Meech Lake and the Charlottetown Accord, Quebec established two National Assembly committees to examine, respectively, renewed federalism offers and sovereignty; it established a deadline of 26 October 1992 for a Quebec vote on sovereignty if a reasonable offer of renewed federalism was not forthcoming; and, in general, it conducted itself as a nation – as one of two nations – capable of opting for sovereignty by a unilateral act, following an analysis of the advantages of staying and going according to the criterion of Quebec's self-interest.

Finally, although both the Canadian and Quebec referenda were held on the same day and asked the same question, the Quebec referendum campaign was essentially a separate campaign. It was governed by Quebec referendum legislation that structured the campaign under two umbrella organizations for Yes and No, headed, respectively, by Robert Bourassa and Jacques Parizeau, the leaders of the two main parties in Quebec. As far as the accord's specifics were concerned, the Quebec campaign focused primarily on Quebec's gains and losses. The Quebec and ROC referendum debates, accordingly, were two inward-looking solitudes that did not engage each other. This absence of a common discourse, with few exceptions, was "the most important and significant single fact about the referendum debate of 1992."[6] To Guy Laforest, the very fact of Quebec's administering its own referendum confirmed the message of the earlier 1980 referendum, namely, that Quebec had a right to determine its own future by introspective actions which already indicated a psychological special status.[7] Throughout the whole period, from the Parti Québécois victory in 1976 to the present, nationalist rhetoric insistently defined Canada as English Canada or Rest of Canada and thus sought to deny the psychological presence of Canada in Quebec. The preceding are the visible manifestations of an aggressive, frustrated, underlying nationalism.

The reality and symbolism of Quebec nationalism have induced Canadians outside Quebec to think of themselves, at one level, as

ROC, and at crucial constitutional moments to realize that they are responding to Quebec in their ROC capacity. Admittedly, this recognition is muffled by the constitutional reality that ROC acts through federalism and thus through a Canadian government that represents Quebec and has been led by a Quebecker for a quarter of a century, except for the Turner and Clark interludes. While this Canada/ROC split personality runs through the events cited below, this very ambiguity contains the premise that from one perspective ROC exists and seeks to express itself in spite of its lack of constitutional clothing.

The range and diversity of ROC response to Quebec in the last decade include the following positions: (1) as the partner that concludes that an agreement is impossible and therefore goes its own way (Constitution Act, 1982); (2) as a divided party that fully recognizes that its response to the Meech Lake Accord is a response to Quebec but fails to muster a Yes response to Quebec's demands; (3) as a composite actor employing various means on multiple fronts to generate a set of offers that will entice Quebec back into the constitutional family (Spicer Commission to Charlottetown Accord); (4) as a referendum electorate that fails to support the Charlottetown Accord negotiated by its own leaders, a repudiation concurred in by the Quebec electorate for different reasons.

Widespread acceptance of a "two nations" view was evident in public discussion throughout the recent referendum campaign, in which the worst scenario was consistently portrayed as either Quebec votes Yes and ROC votes No, or the reverse, a Quebec No and ROC Yes.[8] Implicit in this analysis was the assumption that behind the eleven governments, two separate national partners were deciding whether or not they could agree with the future terms of their coexistence as proposed in the Charlottetown Accord. That Quebec might react to various negative referendum outcomes as a frustrated nation rather than just a disgruntled province was taken for granted.

The above episodes indicate that, from one perspective, ROC clearly sees itself as participating in a two-nation constitutional game. This, however, shades into the recognition that constitutionally it is both fragmented into provinces and incorporated in a pan-Canadian community which includes Quebec, and for which the federal government is the authoritative spokesperson. The latter speaks not for ROC as such, but for ROC as part of Canada. Unlike Quebec nationalism, whose encounter with Canadian nationalism is an encounter between governments, ROC nationalism neither encounters Canadian nationalism through a government of its own nor as a rival. Hence, ROC nationalism, the response of non-Québécois to Quebec nationalism, is muffled behind a Canadian nationalism that seeks to shore up the

Canadian component of the Québécois psyche. When ROC indulges its taste for complexity, it recognizes the existence of a third set of Aboriginal nationalisms that has to be accommodated (discussed below).

The triangular relationship between Quebec, Canada, and ROC is immensely complicated by the ambiguities in the self-conceptions and identities of the major actors. The Quebec government acts as the voice of a nation from the constitutional vantage point of a province. It conducts itself in terms of what it hopes to become and thus denies what it constitutionally is. At first glance, the Canadian government acts straightforwardly as the senior government of a federal system containing ten provinces and two territories, and thus as the government of the coast-to-coast community of all Canadians. This self-definition, however, presupposes a reality that is contested by Quebec nationalists, who repudiate Quebec's provincial status and who seek escape from standard Canadian citizen status, either to some special national status or to independent statehood.

Quebec nationalism elicits an incipient counternationalism in ROC, which exerts diffuse pressure on the federal government to see its conciliation task as applying not to a dozen provinces and territories but to two national peoples – Quebec and ROC. To the extent that the Quebec government succeeds in monopolizing the Quebec nationalist voice, the federal government is pushed to become a spokesperson for ROC. The latter, defined by Quebec as the coexisting national partner, and defined by the official constitutional order as nonexistent and in any event incapable of acting because it lacks an authoritative centre, is correctly diagnosed as having a split personality/identity which paralyses choice.

To a large extent, the difficulty of resolving Canada's constitutional problems results from the ambiguity that attends the behaviour, identity, and constitutional reality of these three major actors. The constitutional politics of "as if" means that the standard rules of the constitutional game, which presuppose stable realities of identity and community that faithfully reflect the existing formal constitutional order, in fact apply to a Kafkaesque-Pirandello world of things that are not as they seem. This complexity is deepened, as noted below, when Aboriginal Canadians are brought into the constitutional picture.

The major ambiguity, or identity confusion, or location between two worlds that attaches to ROC deserves further comment. To Philip Resnick, ROC, or English Canada, is the nation "that too often dares not speak its name."[9] The ambiguity of identity in the absence of a positive label runs through a recent volume on the view from outside Quebec (for example, "So long as Quebec is an integral part of

Canada, we lack a name"; "the mystery spouse – the counterpart to Quebec"; and "an entity – whatever we call it – that has no institutional form without Quebec").[10]

ROC self-consciousness is reactive. The labels and acronyms under which it operates – Rest of Canada (ROC) and Canada without Quebec (CWOQ) – have little capacity to stir nationalist passion. They appear not as goals but as by-products of someone else's activism. The development of a positive nationalist ROC self-consciousness is impeded by the absence of an official leadership that can speak for and to ROC. The holders of official office in the federal system address their citizens as Canadians and as members of provincial communities or of northern territories, but not as ROC. Prime Minister Brian Mulroney explicitly and correctly denied the capacity and propriety of the federal government's speaking for "English Canada" as such, because the federal government speaks for all Canadians.[11] As Reg Whitaker asserts, federal politicians, especially from Quebec, "have a vested interest in stifling the development of an authentic English-Canadian voice."[12] Thus, it was only to be expected that asymmetrical federalism, which received considerable support at the Halifax public constitutional conference – suggesting special powers for Quebec and a strong central/national government in Ottawa for "English Canada" – disappeared when the "provincial powerbrokers" took charge in the final negotiations.[13] "English Canada" has a much stronger existence at the level of the citizenry than in the minds of the leaders of the non-Quebec governments of federalism.

In spite of these structural impediments, ROC self-consciousness receives stimulation with every failure to reach an accommodation with Quebec and with each renewed effort to try one more time.[14] Barbara Cameron correctly notes the "remarkable" development in the post-Meech round of "distinctly English-Canadian views of constitutional arrangements." This was partly stimulated by the contagion of Quebec and Aboriginal nationalisms that "forced English Canadians to act like a national community, too."[15] A nationalist intelligentsia in ROC now openly canvasses and sometimes supports a two- or three-nation definition of Canada, or unflinchingly faces the prospect of a Canadian breakup as being advantageous for the two national communities of European origin.[16] Indeed, the slow and grudging but steady, reactive development of a separate, incipiently nationalist self-consciousness in ROC is the ultimate testimony to the powerful impact of Quebec nationalism on how Canadians outside Quebec see themselves.

ROC self-consciousness is anticipatory. It is held in reserve. It is an insurance consciousness. In a period of constitutional uncertainty, the ROC citizen lives in two worlds. The first is the inertial world of the status quo, in which Canada still exists and receives loyalty and civic attachment from its ROC citizens. It is the everyday world with deep historical roots. Yet attachment to it is no longer habitual and unthinking, for its solidity can no longer be assumed. The second world is a plausible tomorrow world, in which Quebec has departed and ROC takes ownership of the name Canada and applies it to the diminished, geographically bifurcated but more homogeneous survivor that it has become. For ROC, this world is an imagined if largely unsought future, which might emerge because continuity with the past has been broken by the Quebec national partner. Simply put, ROC exists psychologically because human beings live in the future as well as the present. Citizens naturally prepare themselves psychologically for plausible futures, both sought and unsought. At the moment, the relative balance between these two worlds is unclear, although the second future world is gaining ground.

ROC, however, is incapable of responding directly to Quebec. Nobody acts for it. It speaks through the multiple outlets of the governments of Canadian federalism outside Quebec. These governments submerge and conceal ROC's identity and sense of self behind the normative and institutional realities of a federal system with a Charter. The "ten equal provinces" view overpowers the "two nations" view when office-holding incumbents take charge. The Charter imposes a standard version of Canadian citizenship that limits deviations from the norm of equal rights. The amending formula, especially when the unanimity requirement is relevant, provincializes both the making and the evaluation of proposed amendments. When a referendum is added, as for the Charlottetown Accord, unanimity makes provincial self-interest one of the dominating criteria for the electorate.

While it was clear, following the demise of Meech Lake, that a positive response to Quebec was the core requirement of the next constitutional round, the actual response was restrained, especially given the constitutional demands of the Allaire Report and the knowledge that a referendum on sovereignty was required under Quebec legislation. The reasons for this restrained response become apparent when it is contrasted with the much more far-reaching set of proposals offered to the Aboriginal peoples of Canada. The response to Quebec was constrained by the reality that Quebec is now a province – and thus caught up in a network of norms and assumptions that derive from contemporary federalism and have countrywide application – and that its people are an integral part of the Canadian community of citizens to whom it is assumed, especially since the Charter, that a common set of rights should apply.

Significant constitutional advances for Quebec in the direction of special status are constrained by the perception that it is part of a system of provinces and that its people are part of a Canadian community of citizens. Aboriginal peoples, by contrast, are not thought of in federal terms – the constraints of provincial equality do not limit responses to their aspirations – and in some sense they already have a recognized status of being apart, which sustains policy responses that further institutionalize their apartness. The contrast between the limited response to Quebec, described immediately below, and the elaborate response to Aboriginal peoples, described later in this essay, can be understood only in the light of the profound difference in their starting points.

The Charlottetown Accord was a limited response to the heightened Quebec constitutional aspirations that developed following the defeat of the Meech Lake Accord, which had been based on Quebec's minimal demands.[17] Quebec received an initial allocation of an additional eighteen seats in the House of Commons; the guarantee of a minimum 25 per cent of the seats in the House of Commons in the future; a weak reference to the distinct society in the Canada clause, which also affirmed the "role of the legislature and Government of Quebec to preserve and promote the distinct society of Quebec" (*Consensus Report*, s. 1(2)(2)); a double-majority Senate voting rule that would require there to be both a majority of all senators voting and of francophone senators voting for bills "that materially affect French language or French culture" (*Consensus Report*, s. 12); a concession to Bourassa that provincial senators could be selected by the Quebec National Assembly; a guarantee of three Quebec seats on the Supreme Court, to be filled from a list of candidates submitted by the Quebec government; a veto on future changes to central institutions; controls on the future use of the federal spending power; provincial control over culture within the province; a significantly enhanced provincial role in manpower training; a federal commitment to negotiate an immigration agreement; a federal commitment to withdraw from a number of areas already clearly within provincial jurisdiction (*Consensus Report*, s. 30–5); and various constitutional instrumentalities that might be beneficial to future Quebec governments. In addition, the federal powers of disallowance and reservation were to be repealed, future use of the federal declaratory power would require explicit provincial consent, designated future intergovernmental agreements were to be constitutionally protected from unilateral change for periods of up to five years, and new agreements were to be negotiated with provincial governments concerning regional development and telecommunications.

Most of the proposed changes applied to all provincial governments, including all division of powers proposals and the enlarge-
ment of the category of amendments requiring unanimity. While the
overall package was far from trivial, it was very limited in the area
of division of powers, the core of Quebec's constitutional demands,
and the centrepiece of the Allaire Report.[18] Further, the pervasive
tendency to generalize changes to all provinces, thus repeating the
Meech Lake practice, suggested that in the conflict between recognition of formal asymmetry or explicit special status versus equality
of the provinces, the latter principle had once again triumphed. Even
the Reform Party of Canada was struck by the very limited nature
of Quebec's gains in terms of its major demand for more power at
the provincial level, suggesting that the distinct society clause had
been "effectively gutted" and that gains in the division of powers
were "marginal." The Reform party also noted what many other
analysts commented on, the fact that Quebec's greatest gains were in
central institutions – the Supreme Court, the House of Commons, a
double majority in the Senate with Quebec members in effect nominated by the Quebec government, and a veto with other provinces
on constitutional changes to central institutions. "The net effect,"
according to the Reform party, "instead of granting Quebec more
provincial autonomy, is to involve it more deeply in national affairs."[19]
The limited nature of Quebec's gains was underlined by the much
more generous response to the Aboriginal peoples.

CANADA AND ABORIGINAL PEOPLES:
RECOGNITION AND RESPONSE[20]

After the Aboriginal contribution to the defeat of the Meech Lake
Accord, and after the serious Oka disturbances, it was widely understood that the next constitutional agreement would have to respond
to Aboriginal demands for a constitutional recognition that would
differentiate them from standard versions of Canadian citizenship.
The understanding that there were two sides – non-Aboriginal and
Aboriginal – and that the former, the historical Canadian community,
had to respond to the separate Aboriginal nations in its midst, and
to do so from a basis of rough equality, was little short of revolutionary in the light of the Canadian past.

Although the Charlottetown Accord containing the agreement that
had been struck between Aboriginal and non-Aboriginal leaders
failed to pass in the referendum, the Aboriginal components of the
accord remain instructive. They indicate how far the leaders of the

existing eleven governments were prepared to go, and what Aboriginal leaders were prepared to accept. Further, the ongoing research and the hearings of the Royal Commission on Aboriginal Peoples will likely inject many of the accord's Aboriginal proposals into the commission's report. The Charlottetown Accord proposed a remarkable battery of recognitions and constitutional accommodations for the Aboriginal peoples of Canada. At mid-century, status Indians lacked the vote; the Inuit (then known as Eskimo) were politically voiceless and enjoyed only a superficial, romantic, postcard existence in Canadian consciousness; the Métis were, at least officially, considered to be ordinary Canadians with a somewhat unique background. No constitutional category "Aboriginal" then existed to give these three contemporary subcategories of indigenous peoples a common label and a shared constitutional identity. Further, the off-reserve status Indian population was then absolutely and proportionately much smaller than it is now (30–40 per cent of the status Indian population). The distance between the isolation and virtual invisibility of Aboriginal peoples at mid-century and their position during the Charlottetown Accord proposals of 1992 is truly breathtaking.

The extent and openness of the accord's response to Aboriginal peoples, contrasted with past treatment, both astonished and gratified academic students of Aboriginal issues. According to Radha Jhappan, a sympathetic student of Aboriginal issues, the self-government provisions "represent a historic (though imperfect) achievement for the First Nations of Canada" and "far exceed the expectations and even imaginations of most informed observers of aboriginal politics ... The accord is a magnificent coup for the aboriginal leaders."[21] According to Tony Hall, another shrewd scholar of Aboriginal affairs, the top leaders of no other country had ever before lavished so much attention on the accommodation of "Aboriginal aspirations" within the governing arrangements of a contemporary "New World State." The Charlottetown Accord, he continued, gave "concrete political form to the new thinking" associated with the re-evaluation of the "horrific legacy" of Christopher Columbus.[22] Two of the most prolific legal writers on Aboriginal matters were equally laudatory of the accord. To law professor Douglas Sanders, the accord's "Aboriginal provisions ... [were] a hallmark of tolerance and generosity."[23] Bradford Morse asserted that the "changes [proposed in the accord] ... would truly represent a major departure from our colonial history and set us on the path of restoring the mutual respect and partnership that was the foundation of our initial relationship."[24] "For off-reserve Indians and Métis in Canada," stated

Ron George, president of the Native Council of Canada, "the acceptance of these provisions represents an historic breakthrough that is comparable to the bringing down of the Berlin Wall."[25]

The accord's Aboriginal proposals sanctioned an extraordinary degree of institutional and constitutional separateness. Most important was the proposed constitutional recognition of "the inherent right of self-government within Canada," to be exercised as "one of three orders of government in Canada" (*Consensus Report*, s. 41). Within their jurisdictions, Aboriginal governments were to have the authority:

(a) to safeguard and develop their languages, cultures, economies, identities, institutions and traditions; and,

(b) to develop, maintain and strengthen their relationship with their lands, waters and environment

so as to determine and control their development as peoples according to their own values and priorities and ensure the integrity of their societies. (*Consensus Report*, s. 41)

Significantly, off-reserve urban Aboriginal populations were not to be denied versions of self-government, which would probably provide services to mixed Aboriginal urban peoples, even though they lacked a land base.

The third order of Aboriginal government was to be accompanied by separate Aboriginal representation in the House of Commons and in the revised Senate, the details to be worked out by Aboriginal peoples, their leaders, and relevant governments. Both proposals, with that for the Commons being tentative rather than definite, implied that Aboriginal peoples should be represented by their own kind, and the latter carried the additional implication that Aboriginal peoples were not part of provincial or territorial communities, since Aboriginal seats were to "be additional to provincial and territorial seats" (*Consensus Report*, s. 9). Aboriginal senators, in addition to the standard senatorial responsibilities, might have received a "double majority power in relation to certain matters materially affecting Aboriginal people" (*Consensus Report*, s. 9), thus paralleling the proposed double majority role of francophone senators with respect to bills that "materially affect French language or French culture" (*Consensus Report*, s. 12). In addition, various proposals held out the possibility of a distinctive Aboriginal relationship to the Supreme Court and potential roles in nominating candidates for the court. The federal government and Aboriginal groups were to consider "the proposal that an Aboriginal Council of Elders be entitled to make submissions to the Supreme Court when the court considers Aboriginal issues" (*Consensus Report*, s. 20). Section 53 proposed four First Ministers' Conferences on Aboriginal constitutional matters, commencing no later than 1996 and following at two yearly intervals. In future, specific Aboriginal consent to constitutional amendments that directly referred to Aboriginal peoples would be required (by a mechanism not yet determined). Aboriginal representatives were to participate on any agenda item at First Ministers' Conferences "that directly affects the Aboriginal peoples" (*Consensus Report*, s. 23). The Canada clause required the constitution to be interpreted in a manner consistent with various fundamental characteristics of Canada, one of which was that

the Aboriginal peoples of Canada, being the first peoples to govern this land, have the right to promote their languages, cultures and traditions and to ensure the integrity of their societies, and their governments constitute one of three orders of government in Canada. (*Consensus Report*, 1(2)(1)(b))

Finally, the original 1982 exemption of certain Aboriginal rights from the Charter's application by section 25 of the Charter was strengthened to ensure that nothing in the Charter "abrogates or derogates from ... in particular any rights or freedoms relating to the exercise or protection of their languages, cultures or traditions" (*Consensus Report*, s. 2). Further, Aboriginal governments were exempted from the Charter's democratic rights, which gave every citizen "the right to vote in an election of members ... and to be qualified for membership" in federal and provincial legislatures (*Draft Legal Text*, s. 24). The purpose of this exemption was to facilitate traditional practices for determining leaders – practices that would otherwise violate Charter requirements. Aboriginal legislatures were given access to the notwithstanding clause, and Aboriginal governments were to have authority to "undertake affirmative action programs for socially and economically disadvantaged individuals or groups and programs for the advancement of Aboriginal languages and cultures" (*Consensus Report*, s. 51).

The importance of these constitutional proposals was magnified by the extended coverage of the new constitutional concept "Aboriginal" in section 35 of the Constitution Act, 1982, to include Indian, Inuit, and Métis. The inclusion of the last of these was a signal political triumph for the Métis, who were thereby given constitutional leverage to press for whatever positive treatment was available to the Inuit and Indians with whom they now shared a common constitutional clause. This leverage was used to good effect in the

Charlottetown Accord Canada round, under which "for greater certainty" Métis were explicitly to be brought under the federal jurisdiction of section 91(24), a recognition that would have constituted yet another lever behind Métis demands for equal treatment in terms of perquisites and services available to Indians. Section 56 of the *Consensus Report* noted that a Métis Nation Accord was being prepared by the federal government, the five most westerly provinces (Ontario to British Columbia), and the Métis National Council, and that it would commit governments to negotiate various issues related to Métis self-government. As part of this development, the Métis were to be defined and members of the Métis Nation were to be enumerated and registered.[26] Had the accord been implemented, the Métis, who lacked explicit constitutional recognition until 1982, would by 1992 have taken several large steps to differentiate themselves from the general mass of Canadian citizens. According to Radha Jhappan, the accord signalled "great progress for the Métis peoples' claims and aspirations."[27]

To summarize, although many of the details were left to the future, the accord very clearly proposed a unique Aboriginal relation to the Canadian state. The proposed changes were to apply to an enlarged category of Aboriginal peoples – approximately one million – and they were to apply, albeit differentially, to Aboriginal peoples without a land base. Hence, different versions of this special Aboriginal constitutional regime would extend to a population larger than that of five, possibly six, of the ten Canadian provinces. This massive proposed enhancement of the constitutional/institutional accommodation and expression of indigenousness occurred in a supportive climate of guilt, diffuse support, and despair over the failure of past policies. However, the cumulative consequences of all the specific changes proposed in the Charlottetown Accord were neither publicly examined nor discussed, at least in non-Aboriginal communities.

CONSTITUTIONAL THEORY IN THE
NEGOTIATION PROCESS AND IN
THE ABORIGINAL PACKAGE

To step back from the particulars and cast a synoptic glance at the total Aboriginal package is to realize that the implementation of the Charlottetown Accord would have fostered and powerfully reinforced the aboriginality of Aboriginal Canadians. Just as children in Red Deer become Albertans by the reinforcing cues they receive from their provincial environment, and just as the experience of living under the Indian Act regime has fashioned status Indians into a distinct people who are apart from other indigenous Canadians, so the Aboriginal peoples of the future, as a whole, would constantly have been reminded of their separate status by their particularistic interactions with institutions specific to themselves. Equally, non-Aboriginal Canadians would constantly have been reminded of the unique status of the various Aboriginal peoples.

The distinctive treatment of Aboriginal peoples that would have emerged if the accord had been implemented was foreshadowed by, and indeed developed from, the unique and innovative manner of Aboriginal participation in the post-Meech constitutional reform process. The accord's elaborate recognition of Aboriginal particularity emerged from a bargaining context in which leaders of the four Aboriginal organizations were the only nongovernmental participants at executive federalism meetings that were devoted to comprehensive constitutional change which had hitherto been the preserve of elected politicians and their advisers. In an earlier breakthrough, from 1983 to 1987 Aboriginal representatives had participated in four constitutional conferences devoted to Aboriginal constitutional concerns. In the Canada round, however, Aboriginal participation extended to the whole range of constitutional issues on the table. This Aboriginal presence suggested, if only implicitly, that existing governments and their elected political leaders lacked the legitimacy to speak authoritatively for the Aboriginal peoples in their electorates on constitutional issues. Non-Aboriginal leaders, accordingly, were implicitly defined as representing only non-Aboriginal Canadians in constitutional policy making, in spite of the Aboriginal voters in their electorates.

The significance of Aboriginal possession and exercise of the federal and provincial franchise was proportionately reduced by this excision. The inference that Aboriginal advocacy and representation, at least in constitutional matters, were the responsibility of the four major Aboriginal organizations then shifted the question of representative legitimacy to the latter's right to speak for their imputed membership. The answer was not self-evident, since the Native Women's Association of Canada (NWAC) categorically denied the capacity of the Assembly of First Nations leadership to speak for NWAC members, an interpretation supported by the Federal Court of Appeal.[28]

This remarkable act of representational affirmation by government-funded Aboriginal organizations underlined Aboriginal alienation from the conventional practices of the Canadian state. Its accommodation by the first ministers leaves the conventional theory of parliamentary representation in disarray, a consequence that received virtually no attention. If Aboriginal organizations are to displace the representational role of elected legislators and ministers, even if only in constitutional matters, then the role of Aboriginal voters in federal and provincial elections becomes problematic. What logic restricts the delegitimation of non-Aboriginal representatives acting on behalf of Aboriginal constituents to constitutional matters? Further, if Aboriginal organizations become public bodies performing crucial representational roles within the state, irresistible pressure will develop to subject their internal procedures to public scrutiny and regulation. If there is to be an ongoing division of representative labour between Aboriginal organizations and elected politicians in constitutional or other matters, the boundaries should be clearly drawn and publicly known, rather than being overlooked, as in the recent constitutional negotiations.

The contemporary origins of separate Aboriginal representation at the first ministers' constitutional bargaining table date from Elijah Harper's contribution to the blocking of the Meech Lake Accord. Harper's role was jubilantly seen by Aboriginal peoples as a decisive and positive Aboriginal assertion of constitutional power. The basic post-Meech Aboriginal strategy was to minimize participation that threatened to reduce the status of Aboriginals to that of an ordinary interest group, and to fight for participatory roles that recognized their status as first nations. This meant either being treated as the equal of governments or being treated separately from other Canadians, or both.

From Meech Lake to the Charlottetown Accord, Aboriginal peoples participated only minimally in the grand national inquests by the Spicer Commission and the Beaudoin-Dobbie parliamentary committee. Their more extensive participation in the Beaudoin-Edwards committee's examination of the amending process was largely devoted to obtaining an Aboriginal right of consent, and hence of veto, to constitutional change directly affecting Aboriginal treaties, status, and rights. As the committee's report phrased it, "The underlying concept here is that of sovereign nations and government-to-government relations."[29]

The four main Aboriginal organizations held separate, publicly funded, officially recognized Aboriginal consultations with their respective constituencies which paralleled the Beaudoin-Dobbie inquiries. A separate Aboriginal public constitutional conference on Aboriginal constitutional issues was held in the winter of 1992.[30] Although these separate Aboriginal inquiries attracted little public attention, they were Aboriginal equivalents of Quebec's Bélanger-Campeau inquiry. The fact that they were undertaken as federally recognized inquiries was an advance intimation that Aboriginal peoples, by virtue of their aboriginality, had both an existing and a prospectively unique constitutional status which the consultative inquiries were to explore. Consequently, while the status of the major Aboriginal organizations was less than that of governments in the post-Meech constitutional process, it was clearly superior to that of ordinary constitutional interest groups.

To the Source,[31] the report of the parallel Assembly of First Nations' constitutional consultation of its status peoples, is the most elaborate and uncompromising of the Aboriginal reports that developed alongside the Beaudoin-Dobbie inquiry. In attributing a profound sense of cultural singularity to its people (while portraying Euro-Canadians in terms of diametrically opposed values), it is an Aboriginal version of Quebec's Tremblay Report of the mid-fifties, which portrayed French and English Canada as polar opposites.[32]

To the Source attributes virtually all the ills of contemporary Indian societies to the contaminating intrusion of Euro-Canadian values. Hence, the application of the Charter to Aboriginal self-government is considered unacceptable, because it is an instrument of an individualistic Euro-Canadian culture, whose acceptance would further the disintegration of Indian society and conflict with the desired recovery of tradition. *To the Source*, a classic example of the nativistic revivalism that is a common feature of nationalist movements, suggests that status Indians identify only minimally with the surrounding Canadian society. If future Aboriginal governments are to be informed by the philosophy of *To the Source*, they will be bastions of "otherness" conducting foreign relations with their Canadian neighbours.

The Assembly of First Nations' request to have the reserve votes of status Indians counted separately – a request granted by the chief electoral officer – further underlined the apartness of status Indians from the Canadian community. It suggested that the status-Indian vote would be a response not to the whole package but to its Aboriginal components. It implied that if the status-Indian vote and the Canadian vote went in opposite directions, the latter results might not be conclusive with respect to the Aboriginal package. According to Ovide Mercredi, chief of the Assembly of First Nations, an Indian rejection should trigger further negotiations. The same thesis of the need for a double majority or a separate Aboriginal vote count was advocated for the proposed Quebec referendum on sovereignty.[33]

The desire for a separate status-Indian vote was a logical response to a constitutional package whose Aboriginal contents had been shaped by Aboriginal inputs and which proposed a very high degree of institutional differentiation of Aboriginal peoples from other Canadians.

A number of Indian First Nations carried the logic of separate status further by boycotting the referendum, which they saw as incompatible with their treaty relations with the crown. For them, the accord's goal of resolving Aboriginal/non-Aboriginal constitutional differences foundered on a referendum process that presupposed a commonality of Canadian and First Nations citizenship, which they denied.[34] Professor Tony Hall, noting the number of band governments that prevented the setting up of polling stations, stated: "This decision reflects a strong current of opinion among many First Nations people that their participation in the vote, no matter which side of the question they took, would be inconsistent with the distinct constitutional status of Indian societies in Canada."[35] The same logic lay behind the suspicions many status Indians had earlier held about Prime Minister Diefenbaker's 1960 extension of the franchise to their people – the fear that acceptance would be a form of assimilation that would eat away at their distinct status.

Had the accord been fully implemented, Aboriginal peoples would have experienced a profound degree of institutional and constitutional separateness. They would probably have voted separately from other Canadians on separate Aboriginal rolls for Aboriginal candidates for the House of Commons. They would have had separate Aboriginal representation in the Senate, clearly indicating that they were not thought of as members of the provincial communities. To varying degrees (the Inuit in Nunavut excepted), they would have been directly linked to a third order of government responsive to Aboriginal citizens separated out from the general community. Accordingly, they would have experienced the jurisdictional impact of federalism in a markedly different fashion from other Canadians; the impact of the Charter – a key symbol of citizenship for many Canadians – would have been greatly attenuated; the Métis would have been brought under the section 91(24) jurisdiction of the federal government and, like status Indians, would have become a legally defined community with specific criteria for inclusion in and exclusion from its official membership roster. Consequently, a new category of non- or unrecognized Métis would have emerged to trouble future policy makers.

The extensive differential constitutional and policy treatment proposed for about one million Aboriginal Canadians received negligible public discussion in the non-Aboriginal community. Discussion concentrated on Aboriginal self-government, for which details were sparse, at the expense of a larger focus on the potential cumulative consequences of the overall battery of proposed changes. The following concerns do not appear to have been addressed:

1 If Aboriginal peoples are progressively differentiated from other Canadians by a spate of reinforcing specific constitutional arrangements, what sense of shared Canadian citizenship will develop within the Aboriginal and the larger Canadian community? If a sense of shared citizenship is severely attenuated, will the governments of Canadian federalism, responsive and responsible to non-Aboriginal majorities, be willing to support the flow of funds that impoverished Aboriginal peoples and their governments will require for decades to come? Can generous financial arrangements be sustained for an indefinite future simply as entitlements, unsupported by a fellow feeling of shared citizenship?

2 What theory of representation lies behind the following proposals?
   a Representation of Aboriginal peoples will be specifically provided in both houses of the federal parliament.[36] The Aboriginal senators are to have the "same role and powers as other Senators, plus a possible double majority power in relation to certain matters materially affecting Aboriginal people" (*Consensus Report*, s. 9). The specification and strengthening of Aboriginal parliamentary representation, however, coincides with a prospective reduction in the application of federal (and provincial) legislation to Aboriginal peoples when the constitutionally entrenched third Aboriginal order of government takes shape. Thus, Aboriginal peoples, to varying degrees, were to be progressively removed from federal government jurisdiction at the same time as their representation in the federal parliament was to be enhanced.

   b "Representatives of the Aboriginal peoples of Canada should be invited to participate in discussions on any item on the agenda of a First Ministers' Conference that directly affects the Aboriginal peoples" (*Consensus Report*, s. 23). Does this imply that the federal government – with specified Aboriginal representation in both houses, possibly with Aboriginal members on the government side of the House, and conceivably with Aboriginal members of the cabinet – has no legitimacy on issues that directly affect Aboriginal peoples?

   c There should be "Aboriginal consent to future constitutional amendments that directly refer to the Aboriginal peoples" by means of an Aboriginal consent mechanism to be worked out (*Consensus Report*, s. 60). Does this imply that non-Aboriginal governments do not speak for Aboriginal peoples on these issues? Or perhaps that they speak for the Canadian component of Aboriginal Canadians? If the latter, what is this Canadian component? Is it the residual and varying federal and provincial jurisdictions that will continue to apply to Aboriginal peoples in matters that have not been taken over by Aboriginal governments?

Are Canadians to assume that in the same way as non-Aboriginal Canadians have federal and provincial identities, Aboriginal Canadians are to have three constitutional identities derived from their coexisting membership in three constitutionally recognized communities? If this is the case, each of the three orders of government will represent a distinct component of the multiple identities and community memberships of Aboriginal Canadians, who are simultaneously members of Canadian and provincial communities, as well as being an Aboriginal people. Contemporary Aboriginal nationalists pay little attention to this criterion for a well-functioning constitutional order with three levels of entrenched government, each of which will have some jurisdiction over Aboriginal Canadians.

The multiplication of what appear to be ad hoc responses to the question of Aboriginal representation in Parliament, in the amendment process, and at First Ministers' Conferences at the same time as the accord was giving birth to a triple-decker federalism produced disconnected, confusing, and contradictory representation proposals. The failure to confront these apparent contradictions would doubtless have damaged future Aboriginal/non-Aboriginal relations had the accord's various loose ends been worked out and implemented in terms of their varying intents. Perhaps the incoherence in Aboriginal representation that would follow from the combined third order of government, representation in both houses of Parliament, and executive federalism roles would have been viewed as an endearing anomaly, justified by the legacy of injustice it sought to rectify. Anomalies, however, are not self-explanatory. They, too, must be defended by rationales that can be contested. The basic contradiction is between the view that Aboriginal nations as such are to have direct access to and/or membership in the representative institutions of the Canadian state, including First Ministers' Conferences and amending processes, and the traditional assumptions of a parliamentary federalism based on countrywide and provincial communities of individual citizens, whose representation springs from federal and provincial electoral competition based on a virtually universal franchise.

WHY THE QUEBEC-ABORIGINAL
DIFFERENCE?

The possibility of there being a more broad-ranging, sensitive, and far-reaching response to Aboriginal nationalism than to Québécois nationalism was indirectly signalled by the initial federal government proposals, *Shaping Canada's Future Together: Proposals.* In the introduction, the need to respond to Aboriginal Canadians was cited ahead of the need to respond to Quebec, and the opening chapter devoted nearly twice as much space to Aboriginal as to Quebec's constitutional requirements.[37] Senior Quebec civil servants were frustrated, annoyed, and disbelieving when the realities in the accord confirmed these anticipations that Aboriginal gains would be markedly superior to those offered to Quebec, a comparison that was doubly wounding because Quebec poll respondents were twice as likely as Canadians in general to dislike the Aboriginal self-government proposals (19 per cent to 10 per cent).[38]

According to Quebec officials, the Aboriginal peoples were the "big winners," making gains they could not have hoped for only a few months earlier. Their inherent right to self-government surpassed in significance and impact Quebec's distinct society recognition. Their achievement of a third order of government underlined the failure of Quebec, constrained by the equality of the provinces principle, to attain asymmetrical status. The Aboriginal peoples' future right of veto on amendments referring directly to Aboriginal peoples was described as an important power that Quebec had never been able to obtain. Finally, Quebec officials feared that the implementation of the Aboriginal gains, most of which were general agreements in principle, would monopolize government attention for years to come and thus make it difficult for Quebec to achieve additional constitutional changes.[39] Nationalist academics were equally disturbed and irate. Guy Laforest, for example, bitingly contrasted the accord's generous response to Aboriginal nationalism with its insensitivity, as in previous constitutional debacles, to Quebec's national aspirations.[40] While official explanations for this differential response to Quebec and Aboriginal demands are lacking, the phenomenon is so remarkable that speculation on its causes is worthwhile.

Some of the differences can be attributed to the presence of Aboriginal negotiators at the bargaining table that produced the Charlottetown Accord, contrasted with Quebec's absence prior to the penultimate stage. Further, Aboriginal negotiators were able and effective, and had positive public images, especially Ovide Mercredi.

The contrast between the Charlottetown Aboriginal package and the minimal Aboriginal Meech Lake gains – protection of their constitutional clauses from the distinct society – when they were not part of the bargaining group provides supporting evidence that presence is better than absence. On the other hand, Quebec was not only present in the bargaining that led to Meech Lake, but it set the agenda in what was described as the Quebec round – and still received less than Aboriginal peoples gained in the 1992 accord. Further, although physically absent, Quebec was a brooding presence throughout the post–Meech Lake constitutional process, either through the proxy of the federal government or by covert communications, or simply because the urgency that drove the entire process came from the looming Quebec referendum. The presence of Aboriginal negotiators in the pre-Charlottetown process partly explains why they did better than they had at Meech Lake, but it has only limited relevance to why their Charlottetown gains were greater than those offered to Quebec either at Meech Lake, with the Quebec government present, or in the Charlottetown package, with the Quebec government largely absent. Whether Quebec's physical absence throughout most of the post-Meech process diminished Quebec's gains is a moot point. It is, however, clear that by the time Quebec explicitly joined the negotiations in August 1992, further Quebec gains were inhibited by the complex interdependence of the deals that had already been struck.

An easily overlooked explanation for the public's acceptance of the Aboriginal-Quebec difference is ignorance. The components of the Aboriginal package were not brought together for easy examination of their likely overall impact. Attention was directed almost exclusively to Aboriginal self-government, which was relatively undefined and thus not amenable to rigorous examination. The potential cumulative impact of the Aboriginal components was not only ignored in the public debate but does not appear to have been considered seriously in the private discussions that led to the accord. In some part, this was due to the frantic pace dictated by the looming Quebec referendum, supplemented by the fragmentation of the 1992 spring and summer bargaining process into subgroups – factors that concealed the big picture. In addition, first ministers and their advisers could put off asking the big questions because the details of virtually every part of the Aboriginal package were to be worked out in the future. The direction, however, was clear – towards a third order of Aboriginal government and a distinct Aboriginal role in or in relation to virtually every major institution of the Canadian state: Senate,

House of Commons, amending formula, First Ministers' Conferences, the Charter, and, somewhat less clearly, the Supreme Court.

The logical question to which these parallel relationships led – What degree of institutional differentiation of a people is compatible with the nation-state form? – was never asked. Would the consistent departures from a common citizenship and from a common relationship to the Canadian constitutional order that would flow from implementation of the Aboriginal proposals be threatening to the flow of sympathy and empathy that should exist between members of the same political community? At what point do good fences cease to make good neighbours and instead make strangers of fellow citizens? Analogous questions, of course, also applied to Quebec, but here the questions were not new. A well-developed discourse was at hand to address them, which Pierre Trudeau ensured was vigorously employed.[41] By contrast, the developing Aboriginal constitutional discourse drove inexorably towards enhanced, positive differential treatment for Aboriginal peoples,[42] for which self-government was an encompassing codeword. Fifty years ago, such aspirations would have been routinely scorned by non-Aboriginals as both unattainable and undesirable because of a taken-for-granted cultural backwardness or low levels of civilization of Aboriginal peoples. Even the issue of size has virtually disappeared as an acceptable rationale for non-Aboriginal opposition to self-government. "Nation" is now routinely employed as a self-description by small Indian bands of several hundred people. Five of nine recent Indian band name changes added "nation" to the band's self-description.[43]

Additional backing for the more positive response to Aboriginal Canadians came from liberal guilt and, among the intelligentsia, from the political correctness imperative. According to Richard Gwyn, with the exception of Quebeckers, who were introspectively obsessed with their own minority status, "all Canadians appear to agree ... that a debt of guilt is overdue to be paid to Indians and Inuit."[44] By 1991–92, this was supplemented by memories of Elijah Harper and Oka and the recognition that Aboriginal support for the overall Canada package was politically essential. Douglas Sanders has noted the extreme reluctance of political leaders to appear to oppose – or even to ask tough questions about – Aboriginal self-government, an inhibition that Bryan Schwartz had previously observed at the four Aboriginal constitutional conferences from 1983 to 1987.[45] Recurring assertions by the accord's non-Aboriginal opponents, such as Judy Rebick of the National Action Committee on the Status of Women and Sharon Carstairs, the then leader of the Manitoba

Liberal Party, of their strong support for Aboriginal self-government confirm the Sanders and Schwartz thesis.[46]

In any event, from the ROC perspective, Quebec and French Canada have already been accorded a generous response – by federalism, by the Official Languages Act, by the language clauses of the Charter, by the virtual monopolization of the office of prime minister in all but one of the past twenty-four years, and by the perception that Quebec has been an excessively favoured recipient of federal bounty. ROC did not view Quebec as an exploited, impoverished community whose plight elicited sympathy, but saw it as a fully integrated, thriving provincial member of the established system.

The Aboriginal status quo, however, was not defensible, with its ubiquitous indications of social malaise, poverty, and marginality. The impetus this provided for the acceptance of radical change was the basic premise behind Thomas Courchene and Lisa Powell's advocacy of a First Nations province: "The time for self-determination and self-government is clearly at hand. The old ways have not worked. [A First Nations province] ... would clearly be a quantum leap, for both aboriginals and non aboriginal Canadians. There are no guarantees ... [but] we have no choice but to vere [sic] boldly in a new direction."[47]

Further, in a constitutional sense, Aboriginal Canadians, unlike Quebec, have not been full members of the Canadian community; they have been on the periphery of the Canadian sense of self. A long history of neglect of the forgotten people, as Métis and Inuit were often called, and of exclusion from the franchise, the symbol of citizenship, as was true of status Indians until 1960, meant that Aboriginal peoples were not part of the "we" community of Canadian citizens; rather, they lived alongside it or, in the case of status Indians, were subject to it. Aboriginal peoples have been in waiting and thus are logically thought of as being in transition. This was most explicitly the case for status Indians, historically viewed as wards or children, who were being prepared for citizenship in some distant tomorrow by the residential schools and the tutelary administration of the Indian Affairs Branch. Given this context of understanding, it was not irrational for voters outside Quebec to be seven times more likely to cite "Quebec got too much" as their main reason for voting No than to cite "Too much was given to aboriginals" (27 to 4 per cent), even though the latter were treated much more generously than the former.[48]

The contemporary momentum behind having an Indian status that is permanently differentiated from that of other Canadians derives from the vehement rejection by the Indian people of the assimilationist philosophy of the 1969 federal government white paper on Indian policy. Indianness was not to be a transitional status or a way station on the path to undifferentiated Canadianness; from the time of the rejection of the white paper, it was a presumptively permanent condition. This change of constitutional goal for the status-Indian community inevitably spilled over to the Inuit who, constitutionally if not legislatively, were Indians, and to the Métis who had long struggled to catch up to the constitutional recognition accorded their indigenous brethren. The defeat of the white paper is therefore a seminal event, because it blocked one line of development – the non-recognition of difference and of historical priority – and virtually ensured that differential status for Indians, logically extended to all Aboriginals, would survive in new forms that would evolve from future constitutional politics.

From the Aboriginal perspective, a constitutional and institutional recognition of difference represented continuity. As Monture-Okanee and Turpel argue in their advocacy of a separate Aboriginal justice system, "Aboriginal peoples, [who are] both different and separate, simply cannot be considered as part of Canadian society ... We are not necessarily culturally, linguistically or historically part of Canada or Canadian legal and political institutions. We are ... set apart by our cultures, languages, distance and histories." This Aboriginal difference merits recognition because the fact of being "First Peoples distinguishes us from any other 'group' or 'minority' in Canada" and justifies special constitutional status. The Aboriginal desire for separate treatment is given further impetus by "centuries of mistrust ... [based] ... upon the centuries of ill-founded approaches to aboriginal-Canadian relations."[49]

Accordingly, from both Aboriginal and non-Aboriginal perspectives a separate Aboriginal institutional and constitutional path appeared more as a given than as a departure from a hitherto applicable norm or practice. For non-Aboriginals, a proposed third order of government and the battery of additional differentiating arrangements noted above were intellectually and psychologically less threatening and easier to digest when viewed as continuing if updated expressions of a historical pattern of different treatment. Recognition of separate Aboriginal roles and governments does not tear asunder an established relationship among equals. It can be viewed as a progressive revision of a parallel relationship, or the ending of paternalism, or as incorporating Aboriginal peoples as full participants in the Canadian polity, or as derived from unique histories and ancient legal entitlements. For example, David Bercuson and Barry Cooper – who advocate a parting of the ways between Quebec and ROC because of the harm they consider the former's presence in Canada does to liberal principles – identify Aboriginal Canadians as "one exception to our general principle of citizen equality ... [for] they were Canada's first inhabitants and they entered into direct legal relationships with the Crown under the terms of which they surrendered their aboriginal title to the land in exchange for reserves, cash, and other considerations. Thus, it would be a violation of both law and moral standards to apply the same legal and constitutional status to them as to other Canadians."[50]

To some degree, also, the extent of the unique future constitutional status of Aboriginal peoples was concealed by the concept of a third order of government, with its reassuring implication that Aboriginal peoples were to become part of the Canadian constitutional system, in harmony with traditional, characteristic, federal ways. Thus, dramatic change was veiled behind the skilful use of common terms. It was, therefore, misleadingly easy to view a third order of government as a straightforward add-on, and thus to pay negligible attention to its actual departure from Canadian constitutional traditions. A third order of entrenched Aboriginal government is not simply more of the traditional federalism game; it is the onset of a different game, in the same way that a three-team hockey game is qualitatively different from the traditional two-team game.

Not only is a three-order federal system qualitatively different from the traditional two-order system by virtue of its complexity, but the Aboriginal third order would be qualitatively different from the provincial second order. The third order of government was to apply to specific, listed populations of legally defined individuals (Nunavut excepted), in marked contrast to open provincial communities subject to pervasive mobility into and out of their ranks. Even had this significant difference been publicly noted and discussed, the non-Aboriginal reaction might have been supportive. Psychologically, an elaborate constitutional recognition of Aboriginal difference is much less disturbing to the non-Aboriginal ROC sense of Canadian peoplehood, which historically marginalized Aboriginal people, than a much smaller response to Quebec, which is viewed as a full member of the Canadian community. (Within Quebec, however, the tension between Québécois and Aboriginal nationalisms, with the former fearing that the latter might successfully appeal to the same principles of national self-determination that the Québécois French-speaking majority employs, is deep and serious. The presence of rival nations on Quebec soil is not only an unwelcome, unassimilable alien presence, but it is a potential threat to Quebec's territorial integrity.[51]

Space limitations prevent the fuller exploration of this issue beyond footnote references.)[52]

Since ROC nationalism dresses itself in the guise of pan-Canadian nationalism, its sense of self includes Quebec. As long as this correlation continues, ROC cannot act as an independent constitutional participant and cannot extricate itself from its pan-Canadian, countrywide sense of community; accordingly, in officially responding to Quebec from a Canadian rather than ROC perspective, it is responding to itself rather than to a discrete external party that is detached from its own sense of community identity and membership. Consequently, ROC, speaking through the other governments of Canadian federalism and wearing its Canadian hat, seeks to minimize differential treatment for Quebec, for that would necessarily rearrange ROC's sense of its Canadian self. Further, the Quebec goal of asymmetrical status, with its corollary of a weaker federal government presence in Quebec, and a weaker Québécois attachment to a pan-Canadian nation, is viewed by ROC as an undesirable diminution and weakening of the Canadianism of Québécois, not as a liberation from a constraint that prevents Québécois from being truly themselves. By contrast, the historical outsider status of Aboriginal peoples, who have not been part of the "we" Canadian community, allows a more flexible range of policy responses.

The response to Quebec in both Meech Lake and the subsequent Charlottetown Accord was constrained by the equality of the provinces principle. In the former, it meant that what Quebec received (distinct society excepted) had also to be given to the other provinces. This equality principle was the most important factor in the opposition of Clyde Wells to the Meech Lake Accord. In the *Consensus Report on the Constitution* (the Charlottetown Accord), with Meech Lake in mind, respect for the equality of the provinces principle is reiterated like a reassuring mantra on page after page. According to Roger Tassé, former deputy minister of justice and participating constitutional consultant in the pre-Charlottetown negotiations, it "is a theme that weaves its way through the entire set of proposals ... Of the current proposals on the division of powers, none singles out Quebec for special powers or a unique authority. In every case, the proposed transfer of power has been made available to all the provinces."[53] The equality of the provinces principle is explicitly affirmed in the Canada clause and in the composition of the reformed Senate. The provincial equality principle, however, had no application to the third, Aboriginal order of government.

A version of the equality of provinces norm could have applied to the proposed third order of Aboriginal governments in two separate ways. Their anticipated jurisdiction could have been modelled on the existing provinces. Instead, however, it was understood that the jurisdictional powers of self-governing Aboriginal peoples could be drawn from jurisdictions normally possessed by either federal or provincial governments, thus differentiating them from existing provinces. Second, in spite of the difference in the content of their jurisdiction from that of provinces, an equality norm could have been applied to prospective Aboriginal governments within the third order. This, however, was not even considered. In the language of the accord, "self-government negotiations should take into consideration the different circumstances of the various Aboriginal peoples" (*Consensus Report*, s. 46).

Even to describe the probable variations within the Aboriginal order of government as asymmetrical is misleading, for the concept implies a norm from which there are isolated departures. However, the variation in the jurisdictional powers wielded by Nunavut, as a future quasi-province with an overwhelming Inuit majority, compared with the limited powers to be wielded by Aboriginal people in metropolitan Winnipeg is sufficiently profound to become a difference in kind. In practical terms, these variations are appropriate responses to the diversity of situations in which Aboriginal people are located. Theoretically, however, they nevertheless raise constitutional questions. Logically, the potential variations of jurisdiction that will occur amongst the diversely situated Aboriginal communities raise the same constitutional issues that concern opponents of significant asymmetry within the second order of government – such as the role and status of MPs from provincial communities whose governments wield powers that for other Canadians are handled by the federal government. Analogously, the propriety of Aboriginal MPs representing Aboriginal people influencing policy and legislation that would not apply to their Aboriginal constituents raised the same constitutional issue, but it was not addressed.

The proposal by several non-Aboriginal scholars that the diverse aggregation of self-governing Aboriginal peoples be constituted as one province would overcome these concerns (assuming that such a province did not have "special status") and would have the tremendous virtue of familiarity and continuity.[54] This provincial proposal, however, appears to lack even minimal support from Aboriginal peoples.[55]

Analysis of the Canada round suggests that the equality of the provinces norm is a very specific norm of club membership which applies only to existing provinces. Hence, no version of the provincial equality norm had any application to, or was even considered for, future Aboriginal governments. Further, the accord was explicit that equal provincial rights would not automatically be available to future new northern provinces, which accordingly would lack some of the basic attributes of provincehood held by the other ten. Although the provisions for the creation of new provinces were significantly eased, such provinces could only become full participants in the amending formula with the unanimous consent of the other eleven governments, and they would only be entitled to equal provincial representation in the revised Senate with unanimous agreement.

The equality of the provinces norm, which applies to existing club members, is perfectly compatible with the visiting of negative inequalities on future members. That new members should be lesser members can be accepted with equanimity by old members. The same principle of privileging first arrivals was used when Manitoba (1870) and, later, Saskatchewan and Alberta (both 1905) became provinces. The federal government retained control of their natural resources for nation-building and development purposes until they were given to the provinces in 1930. What is rejected by those already in the club is granting an existing member more status or powers than other club members have, and admitting new members on equality terms if this might disadvantage those who are already full members. Had Aboriginal peoples sought province status both by name and in terms of jurisdictional powers and other standard perquisites, they would doubtless have encountered much greater resistance than they did when setting up their own third-order club. Conversely, had Quebec been seen as a political unit other than a province, with a distinctive constitutional designation, and had it been viewed as existing alongside rather than as a standard member of the provincial order, the response to its constitutional aspirations might have been more generous.

The flexible response to Aboriginal peoples derived from the perception that neither historically nor prospectively (a future Nunavut excepted) should they be thought of in provincial terms. Indicative of the Quebec/Aboriginal difference is the fact that the limits imposed on Aboriginal self-government appear to have been ad hoc responses developed hastily by policy makers who lacked guidance and historical precedents in their novel situation. The Canada clause statement that the third order of Aboriginal government was "in Canada" (*Consensus Report*, s. 1(2)(1)(b)); the provision that Aboriginal laws or assertions of authority "may not be inconsistent with those laws which are essential to the preservation of peace, order and good government in Canada" (*Consensus Report*, s. 47) (this, incidentally, was not the traditional s. 91 POGG); the attempt by

Bourassa to protect Quebec's territorial integrity by the provision that the self-government clauses "should not create new Aboriginal rights to land" (*Consensus Report*, s. 44); and the convoluted attempts to deal with the Charter issue – all these suggest policy making on the run.

The seeming irrelevance of the equality of the provinces norm for Aboriginal peoples contrasted markedly with the salience of the issue of the equality of citizens, which generated a vigorous debate about the Charter's application to Aboriginal self-government. Once the concept of inherent rights had been accepted, the controversy over Aboriginal self-government concentrated on the Charter of Rights and Freedoms. The negotiating governments and non-Aboriginal public opinion were advocates of the Charter's application to Aboriginal governments, a demand powerfully supported by the Native Women's Association of Canada.[56] The main resistance came from the Assembly of First Nations, whose constitutional document, *To the Source*,[57] was unrelentingly hostile to the Charter and whose constitutional adviser, Mary Ellen Turpel, had previously written a passionate critique of the Charter's application to Aboriginal peoples.[58]

The sensitivity of the issue was evident in the obfuscating ambiguity of its treatment in the Aboriginal package. Non-Aboriginal defenders of the accord reiterated the Charlottetown Accord statement that "the Canadian Charter of Rights and Freedoms should apply immediately to governments of Aboriginal peoples" (*Consensus Report*, s. 43). This apparently wholehearted allegiance to the full application of the Charter norm to all Canadians presumably reflected the remarkable Charter support in Canadian constitutional culture, especially in English Canada, where the Charter has become a key symbol of civic identity. As already noted (see above, p. 41), the Charter's application was significantly eroded by various exemptions that were available only to Aboriginal peoples, along with the standard availability of the notwithstanding clause to legislatures. Had the accord been implemented, the precise effect of these Charter-weakening constitutional clauses would only have become clear in future jurisprudence. Some legal scholars, however, were convinced that they would have severely reduced the applicability of the Charter.[59] That, after all, was their intent.

The difference in the accord's treatment of the prospective application of the Charter in Quebec and to Aboriginal self-government is again instructive of the differential application of constitutional norms to the two aggressive nationalisms. For Quebec, the Charter – and indeed the whole constitution – was to be filtered through the interpretive lens of the specifications for a distinct society (which "includes a French-speaking majority, a unique culture and a civil law tradition"). These specifications were not in the Meech Lake Accord, and they are generally considered to have weakened the clause. The original section 25 Aboriginal non-derogation clause in the 1982 Charter, by contrast, is not simply an interpretive clause but is a categorical protection: in its pre-Charlottetown Accord form, Charter rights and freedoms "shall not be construed so as to abrogate or derogate from any aboriginal, treaty or other rights or freedoms that pertain to the aboriginal peoples of Canada." The Charlottetown Accord would have strengthened this protection. Thus, had the accord been implemented, Quebec's protection from the Charter would have been slightly enhanced by the addition of a weak interpretive clause, while the protection of Aboriginal peoples, already stronger than Quebec's, would have been significantly supplemented by the strengthening of what was already a broadly worded imperative statement.

Thus, the Charter would have had much less applicability to Aboriginal governments than to Quebec. Again (although perhaps not so dramatically as with the equality of the provinces norm), Aboriginal peoples were defined as being on the periphery of a fundamental constitutional norm for other Canadians. Thus, it was apparently assumed that ROC would accept the non-application of the Charter's democratic rights to Aboriginal governments (the right to vote and to be qualified for membership in a legislative body), when these same Canadians outside Quebec had reacted viscerally to Quebec's use of the notwithstanding clause to protect French-only outside commercial signs – presumably, a far smaller violation of Charter rights. By inference, the historic outsiderness of Aboriginals facilitated a continuing differentiation. The accord's philosophy suggested that Aboriginal constitutional evolution should appropriately foster and even strengthen the original separateness that Aboriginals brought to the bargaining table.

To sum up, why was there this differential response to Québécois and Aboriginal nationalisms? The response to Quebec was constrained by the provincial equality principle, by the fact that Quebec was viewed as a fully functioning member of an ongoing system with its own norms, by the corollary that Quebeckers were included in ROC's Canadian sense of self – the disruption of which would be psychologically destabilizing – and by the fact that opposition to any extensive special status could draw sustenance from the existing, theoretically developed federalist discourse, which was championed by former Prime Minister Trudeau and widely held outside Quebec, and which pervades much of the 1982 Constitution Act.

In contrast, a third order of Aboriginal government, viewed as existing outside or alongside the norm of provincial equality, and the various supplementary recognitions of aboriginality, did not require ROC to retreat to a diminished sense of self.[60] The geographical isolation of the Inuit, the distinct constitutional, administrative, and policy regime that has historically been applied to status Indians, and the incorporation of Métis into a category given its meaning by Indians and Inuit, psychologically distanced Aboriginal and other Canadians from each other. Thus, the historical civic marginality of Aboriginal peoples facilitated the further elaboration of differential treatment that was proposed in the Charlottetown Accord. Indeed, the new differentiation could be described, in a phrase of the Assembly of First Nations, as "closing the circle," as bringing Aboriginal peoples as such into the constitutional family. This definition of "closing the circle" by constitutionally sanctioning difference rested on the tacit acceptance that the most powerful discourse opposed to continuing differential treatment had been repudiated with the demise of the assimilationist 1969 white paper. By contrast, in the case of Quebec, a province and people viewed as already being in the system, the constitutional recognition of extensive additional differentiation was once again resisted, on the grounds that the circle had already been closed.

The perceived direction of movement, therefore, which depends on what is considered to be the starting point, is crucial. As historical outsiders, Aboriginal peoples can be allowed a continuing degree of differentiation that is not available to the Quebec partner, which is already viewed as in the system by those who ultimately determine the permissible limits of change. Given the opposition of Premier Clyde Wells to the Meech Lake package, it is perhaps appropriate that the Quebec experience confirms the Newfoundland aphorism that you can't get there from here – where "here" is provincial status, and "there" is special constitutional recognition of Quebec as a nation within Canadian federalism. Aboriginal peoples, starting from a different and more distant "here", encountered less resistance on a longer journey to their "there."

CONCLUSION

The preceding analysis of the Charlottetown Accord as the setting for an encounter between the multinational nature of contemporary Canada and federalism supports, without confirming, the following generalizations.

Federalism and a multinational definition of Canada are a poor fit. The sociological reality and self-perceptions of the Québécois as a nation can receive only limited constitutional expression as long as, constitutionally, Quebec is a province. The limited manoeuvrability available in responding to Quebec is a by-product of its provincial status and the contemporary federalism norms that attach to that status. These norms are powerfully embedded in the mentalities of all other government leaders. The central cue transmitted by the formal amending process to governments and citizens outside Quebec is that any proposed constitutional response to Quebec's aspirations is to be evaluated by federalist criteria. Accordingly, an inflexible response is, in a sense, routinized by the provincial equality principle.

If federalism makes it virtually impossible to treat Quebec as a nation entitled to jurisdictional and status perquisites not available to other provinces, it also muffles the voice of Rest of Canada, or English Canada. Officially, ROC has no existence. Its sense of self as a distinct people, as a legitimate constitutionally recognized community, is not constantly reinforced, as provincial peoples are, by institutions that confirm its existence. Its identity, therefore, is diffuse, incoherent, ambiguous, and unstructured. Although an intelligentsia now addresses ROC as a prospective national actor, the routinized messages that daily bombard the potential citizenry of ROC either fragment it into competing provincialisms (and territorialisms) or submerge it in the pan-Canadian community that includes Quebec and is served on a countrywide basis by the federal government.

The inability of ROC to conduct itself officially as a nation undermines the possibility of treating Quebec as a nation. Bourassa hoped to bargain with Canada one on one, nation to nation. Instead, the constitutional politics of federalism reduced Quebec to the status of a province, to the extent that the Charlottetown Accord, particularly in the area of the division of powers, was governed by the equality of the provinces principle. The logical dynamics of federalism, which muffle and suppress nationalist behaviour by ROC, necessarily denationalize Quebec. It is easier for the provincialism of ROC to force Quebec back into a provincial mould than for the nationalism of Quebec to extricate ROC from its provincialism and pan-Canadianism, and make it a national partner with whom nation-to-nation bargaining can take place. This is so even though at one level ROC citizens do see themselves as a nation, and specifically see themselves as the nationalist inheritors of what remains if Quebec should leave. This recognition, however, is frozen out or left behind when federalism's office holders confront Quebec wielding an amending formula that is an instrument and reflection of federalism.

In dramatic contrast to Quebec and ROC, constrained by federalism's norms, Aboriginal nationalism has much more latitude to express itself in highly particularistic constitutional and institutional arrangements. The control by comparison with other provincial realities that limits what Quebec can achieve does not apply to Aboriginal peoples. They are in a sense outside federalism as long as they do not conceive their future in provincial terms. Thus, the norms that automatically apply to provinces do not apply to the prospective units in a variegated Aboriginal third order of government. In addition, psychologically Aboriginal peoples are not viewed as standardized members of the Canadian community. Historically they have been outside it – isolated by geography as the Inuit were or by distinctive constitutional and policy treatment as status Indians were, including exclusion from the franchise until 1960, or by marginalization as the "forgotten people," as Métis were. Accordingly, positive differential treatment for Aboriginal peoples in the future rests on negative differential treatment in the past.

If, therefore, Aboriginal and Québécois nationalism are judged by their capacity to achieve constitutional special status, a clear advantage resides with the former. This advantage, however, comes at a price – the troubling message that, from a Canadian perspective, Aboriginal Canadians are not fully "one of us." The willingness to sanction special constitutional and institutional treatment derives from an absence of fellow feeling. A little special status for Quebec is much more disturbing to ROC's Canadian sense of self than a much more potent special status for Aboriginal peoples is. A sympathetic willingness to accord a special place for Aboriginal peoples may be the positive side of a Janus-faced reality, whose negative side is a relative indifference to the fate of peoples who are "them" not "us."

The process leading up to the Charlottetown Accord, the accord itself, and the referendum that was its downfall were separately, and even more so jointly, unique phenomena. Possibly this paper has extracted more meaning, messages, and lessons from Charlottetown than that complex event, no matter how rich, can sustain. After all, the Meech Lake fiasco was a response to the "lessons" of the flaws in the substance and the making of the 1982 Constitution Act. The Charlottetown Accord, consigned by the referendum electorate to the overflowing graveyard of failed efforts at constitutional reform was, in its turn, both in process and substance a response to the "lessons" of why Meech Lake went wrong. Since the lesson of the attempt to find lessons from 1980–82 and from Meech Lake is that real lessons are elusive, this paper and its author may join the distinguished company of past interpreters who have been outfoxed by a murky reality. The reader and the unfolding future can and will decide.

2 Deliberating a Constitution: The Meaning of the Canadian Referendum of 1992

ALAIN NOËL

On 26 October 1992, 54 per cent of Canadians outside Quebec, 57 per cent of Quebeckers, and 62 per cent of voters on Indian reserves refused to give a mandate allowing the federal and provincial governments and Aboriginal representatives to renew the Canadian constitution "on the basis of the agreement reached on August 28, 1992," in Charlottetown, Prince Edward Island.[1] What did this negative vote mean? Why did Canadians, Quebeckers, and Aboriginal peoples massively reject an agreement that seemed out of reach just a few weeks before, one that was approved by all parties to the negotiation, supported by the three major Canadian political parties, and backed by business, by the English-Canadian labour movement, and by many other groups? What are we to make of this popular veto on constitutional reform? Does it have a meaning other than negative? Does it contain an unambiguous message for politicians who would still dare to try and reform the Canadian constitution?

At the end of the campaign and in the immediate aftermath of the referendum, many observers emphasized what they saw as a crisis

I am grateful to the professors and students associated with the North American Studies Program of Colorado College, and particularly to Curtis Cook, for their hospitality. I also thank Stéphane Bernatchez, André Blais, Stéphane Dion, Alain-G. Gagnon, Pierre Martin, Ted Morton, and James Tully for their helpful comments on the first draft. Finally, I wish to acknowledge the financial support of the Social Sciences and Humanities Research Council of Canada and of the Fonds FCAR.

of legitimacy. From their point of view, the No vote expressed an unprecedented breach between Canadians and their political leaders. In English Canada in particular, voters were portrayed as disillusioned, distrustful, and highly critical of politics and politicians. Even Ovide Mercredi, the chief of the Assembly of First Nations, seemed unable to rally his own community. In Quebec, the popular distrust of politicians appeared less acute since the elites themselves split into two fairly even camps. The No victory nevertheless represen‚ ‾ strong rejection of Robert Bourassa's constitutional str‚ sibly a general expression of political dissatisfaction.[2] we were told, often turn into more or less rational ‚ popular anger, largely unrelated to the official object tation. Evoking the French referendum on Maastricht cians on the Yes side suggested, towards the end of t‚ that consulting the population was perhaps a mistake, a country as diverse and complex as Canada. We ha‚ replied Prime Minister Brian Mulroney and Ontario P Rae, admitting in the same breath that the process had badly.[3]

Underlying these arguments about the motivations ‚ torate was the idea that the No vote proved somehow point. Uninformed, moody, inattentive to the issues at stak of Canadians would stand less as a judgment on the pro stitutional package than as an ill-defined, negative feel political leaders. A related interpretation, also proposed l vote was even out, associated the decision of Canadians to ‚ lack of generosity or vision. Intolerance, we were told, m‚ No vote. Two days before the referendum, a *Globe and ‚* portrayed the seven-person Canada Committee as "th‚ angels of 'Yes,'" condemned to fight an uphill battle against ality and anti-Quebec feelings. A *Maclean's* end-of-campaig‚ ‚urvey suggested in a similar vein that the referendum demonstrated that little was "to be gained by arguing for a better understanding of the needs of others" against "parochial concerns" that were "based more on emotion and hyperbole than on reason."[4] Three overlapping observations supported these pessimistic conclusions. First, it was suggested that the No forces tapped "into the underground rivers of prejudice, racism and loathing for the political process"; second, that they played "a zero-sum game of self-interest" at the expense of "the community's good"; and third, that they were led by strange bedfellows, who had nothing in common besides an interest in defeating the proposed, and probably any, agreement.[5] Disappointed with the results, pundits were quick to blame Canadian voters.

Without denying that prejudices, self-interest, and political calculations played a role, I think that a different, more positive, and more satisfying interpretation is possible. What if Canadians had voted No simply because they disapproved of the proposed constitutional package? After all, a *Maclean's*/Decima poll conducted on referendum day suggests that most voters based their decision not on their views of politicians but on the substance of the agreement as they perceived it.[6] At 74.9 per cent, the turnout was high, in line with the standard federal election rate. "Canadians," noted Graham Fraser, "took their civic duty as decision-makers extremely seriously, poring over documents, questioning the details and voting in massive numbers."[7] If these indications are valid, there may be more to the vote than an outburst of dissatisfaction, and it may be possible to discern a positive meaning in the outcome of 26 October 1992.

In this chapter, I want to argue that democratic deliberation played a role in helping Canadians make up their minds about the Charlottetown agreement and that this deliberation affirmed a few decisive principles, embodied into meaningful but incompatible conceptions of justice. In other words, Canadians discussed the constitutional proposal with a good degree of honesty; and a majority – or, more precisely, different majorities – decided to vote No because they thought the agreement violated principles they considered important, not only for themselves but also for Canada as a community.

I do not have access to the opinion data necessary to demonstrate this interpretation beyond any doubt, but I think it fits the evidence and makes sense of what happened better than the pessimistic interpretations outlined above. Recent developments in political science suggest that voting decisions involve rather sophisticated processes, which are more akin to democratic deliberations than what students of rational choice and public opinion used to expect. Informed by these findings, I think it is possible to reassess not only the early interpretations of the referendum but also our general understanding of the never-ending Canadian constitutional debate. Indeed, if Canadians deliberate the country's defining contract with honesty, on the basis of diverging but legitimate conceptions of justice, it means that we can be cautiously optimistic about the outcome. A stable and satisfying solution may be long to come, but in the end it has some chances of reflecting meaningful principles. The Canadian constitutional crisis will not be, can no longer be, settled through confusion, deception, or superficial tinkering.

The first part of this chapter introduces the notion of democratic deliberation in the context of Canadian politics. Long a core concept of political philosophy and political science, democratic deliberation gradually gave way, especially after the 1950s, to concepts such as self-interest, political attitudes, and individual preferences. This conceptual evolution engendered a pessimistic view of politics that proved very influential in the study of Canadian politics. In the first part of the chapter, I question this view and try to recast the Canadian constitutional debate as an instance of democratic deliberation. The second part applies the general argument to the referendum campaign, to present it as serious, coherent, and fundamentally deliberative. The third part moves back in time to explain the different conceptions of justice that competed during the campaign. The final part discusses possible developments, in the light of these conceptions of justice. The conclusion comes back to the concept of democratic deliberation, briefly discusses its relationship to the more familiar notions of political interests and strategies, and suggests a cautiously optimistic view of the coming years.

DEMOCRATIC DELIBERATION

In an excellent essay published in the *Globe and Mail* the morning after the vote, Thomas J. Courchene, professor of economics at Queen's University, wrote that the No victory signalled the end of a political order, "the demise of the two-founding nations/elite-accommodation approach to governing the federation." For Courchene, the Charlottetown agreement represented an "incredible balancing act," a "comprehensive constitutional compromise" that embodied the "genius" of Canada's elite-accommodation system. Its rejection by voters marked the end of this system and the triumph of a new, more democratic but less generous political order: "We have become a nation of uncompromising special interests," concluded Courchene, "bent on looking inward and engaging in a negative-sum, redistributional game over entitlements, powers and transfers."[8] The contrast outlined by Courchene was clear: on one hand, the old order, not so democratic but favourable to parliamentarism, federalism, and compromise; on the other, the new one, democratic but destructive of Canada's unity, always a fragile outcome, easily undermined by the narrow, uninformed, and interested demands of the masses.

Courchene's lament for the old Canadian order did not simply represent the disappointment of an intellectual close to the Ottawa inner circle. It reflected as well the picture of the country that Canadian political scientists have drawn over the years. In this respect, three empirical concepts predominated: the notion of an absent mandate from the electorate, the concept of executive federalism, and the understanding of Canada as a consociational arrangement. These concepts had both a descriptive and a normative function. As descriptive tools, they produced the image of the old order saluted by Courchene; as normative ones, they legitimated this same order and predicted dire consequences should it come to fail.

The political scientists responsible for the 1974, 1979, and 1980 National Election Studies entitled their last book *Absent Mandate*. From their point of view, the ethnic, linguistic, and regional divisions of Canada produced a brokerage party system that defined "national problems in the vaguest and most general of terms" and made it impossible for citizens to express a substantial public judgment, let alone to give governments a mandate.[9] Campaigns did not matter much, and votes expressed either a range of idiosyncratic preoccupations or a general discontent about the political system. In this context, Canadian voters could hardly be expected to deliberate on something as complex as a constitutional agreement. If voters failed to produce clear mandates, then leadership rested in the hands of governments.

The need for more than "relatively" autonomous states was captured in a second notion, just as central to Canadian political science – executive federalism. Coined by Donald Smiley in the early 1970s, the concept was used to describe "the pattern of relations between two powerful orders of government locked into a kind of competitive interdependence orchestrated by their central political and bureaucratic officials."[10] This power game, added Alan Cairns, remained at a good distance from the preoccupations of ordinary Canadians. Like the absent mandate notion, executive federalism portrayed popular participation as essentially remote and amorphous.[11]

Not perfectly open and democratic, the Canadian political process had at least the advantage of being stable, tolerant, and conducive to compromise. A third, much-discussed notion, the comparative concept of consociationalism, suggested that the primary advantage of a disconnected citizenship and of executive federalism was that together they facilitated accommodations between the different ethnic and linguistic groups of a complex, segmented country. Canadian political scientists, noted Garth Stevenson, expressed doubts about the applicability of Lijphart's full model to Canada but nevertheless retained the model's emphasis on the importance and usefulness of centralized elite bargaining.[12] For a country like Canada, they usually argued, the best solution was to trust elites, which alone were able to reach the necessary compromises, at a distance from their less enlightened, less tolerant constituents.[13]

Threatened by popular discontent and weakened by the arcane jurisdictional conflicts of politicians and bureaucrats, Canada in its standard image appeared at least manageable, not a minor achievement for a young bilingual and bicultural country. Normatively satisfying, this standard image also rested on good theoretical, historical, and comparative grounds. The notion of an absent mandate, for instance, was in tune with much of the international research on electoral behaviour, which "painted a rather dismal picture of the public spirit of the average citizen and more generally of his ability to live up to the classical democratic ideals of the informed, rational, and disinterested voter."[14] Likewise, the concept of consociation originated in the comparative study of segmented societies, where it had helped solve important puzzles about democratic governance. Finally, the idea that Canada remained to a large extent the affair of the elites seemed fit for a country that had never affirmed popular sovereignty.[15]

But the country changed. The 1988 federal election, centered on the free trade agreement with the United States, raised questions about the absence of mandates in Canadian elections; the post-1982 politics of the Charter signalled the end of old-style executive federalism; and the failure of the Meech Lake Accord marked the limits of consociational arrangements in an open polity.[16] Political science changed as well. In the 1980s, the conventional understanding of democracy as a self-interested confrontation of naked preferences was challenged from various sides, notably by political philosophers and electoral behaviour specialists. Dissatisfied with the adversarial model of democracy, many political philosophers rediscovered the discipline's traditional concern for the community, the public interest, and democratic deliberation.[17] Likewise, students of political behaviour increasingly challenged the conventional accounts of public opinion and voting as incoherent, selfish, or simplistic, and entertained the possibility that ideas, political principles, and electoral campaigns matter.[18]

Canadian political scientists were not insensitive to these empirical and theoretical challenges. Charles Taylor, for instance, pioneered the communitarian discussion of politics and applied it early to the Canadian constitutional debate.[19] Alan Cairns, on his part, was born again, in what he himself called a second "incarnation," to fight a state-centric understanding of federalism that still haunts us.[20] Most impressive was the 1988 Canadian Election Study, which offered a picture of Canadian politics dramatically different from that of the "absent mandate" years. The 1988 study, observed Richard Johnston,

André Blais, Henry Brady, and Jean Crête, "revealed the capacity of Canadian voters to deliberate, to behave remarkably like actors who rarely appear on the stage of voting research: *citizens*."[21]

The old image of Canadian politics nevertheless kept much of its appeal, particularly in normative terms. While many political scientists came to acknowledge that Cairns was right when he presented the Charter as a democratizing innovation, they rarely shared his optimism about the consequences. One can contrast Cairns's satisfaction with the idea that "constitutional politics is never-ending" with Peter Russell's contention that "if there are any among us who want to keep this soap opera going, they must be mad!"[22]

Courchene's argument, outlined above, is typical of this ambivalence: it acknowledges the new reality depicted by Canadian political scientists but evaluates it with the tools provided by the old perspective. Yes, Courchene admits, in the process we gain popular sovereignty, but this achievement spells the end of compromise and accommodation. The new politics of participation announces endless conflicts over partial claims and counterclaims.

If, however, the old image of Canada's political order no longer holds as a description of reality, it is probably obsolete as a normative instrument as well. When voters fail to deliberate, when federalism remains essentially a power game between governments, and when elite accommodations alone make the country work, then, of course, a democratization of the constitutional debate appears perilous. If, however, voters act as responsible citizens, are concerned by rights, and stand ready to discuss their different conceptions of justice, then the politics of constitution making becomes what Alan Cairns now makes of it: a formidable learning opportunity.[23] The debate between the pessimistic and the optimistic views of the current situation is to a large extent empirical, and it cannot be settled easily. Since the referendum has been used repeatedly to affirm the pessimistic, old-order viewpoint, it seems worth re-examining it as an instance of democratic deliberation.

What does democratic deliberation entail? First, to borrow from Jon Elster, it presumes that the political forum is not a market. Political decisions do not simply express private, isolated preferences; they result from open discussions over complex public issues.[24] Citizens deliberate because no single proposal prevails, no solution appears universally acceptable. A universally accepted truth, notes Bernard Manin, does not require persuasion. On the contrary, when nobody can be confident about the outcome of a given measure, individuals tend to be uncertain about their own views. They stand open to deliberation and are willing to discuss, learn, and be convinced.[25]

Thus, the primary characteristic of genuine deliberation is to allow meaningful movements in public opinion, following a discussion of the options. Democracy, notes Robert Dahl, is not simply the rule of public opinion; it involves "discovering what is best for oneself or others" and "requires far more than announcing one's raw will or surface preferences."[26]

Uncertainty about the outcome makes deliberation necessary, but it also makes it difficult. The outcomes of important political reforms remain uncertain precisely because the implications are so numerous and far-reaching that a utilitarian, rational assessment appears impossible. When a situation becomes impossible to evaluate in terms of individual or social costs and benefits, major political innovations require a leap of faith, a willingness to accept the risks and the costs of untried formulas. Such a motivation can only be sustained by the conviction that justice is well served by the proposed changes. "The main political reforms of the last century," observes Jon Elster, "have not been supported by instrumental considerations. Rather, they have been carried by social movements anchored in a conception of justice." The situation is akin to John Rawls's original position. Unable to predict their own fate, individuals tend to support reforms that appeal to clear conceptions of justice, but stand wary if they are "asked to participate in a large-scale experiment of no intrinsic value and highly uncertain extrinsic value." Technocratic "blueprints for Utopia," concludes Elster, usually remain "non-starters."[27] The role played by conceptions of justice thus constitutes the second characteristic of democratic deliberation. Genuine deliberation involves more than unjustified demands for entitlements; it implies that demands must be cast in specific conceptions of justice.

Finally, in any debate, only a few conceptions of justice compete for attention. If the aim of a debate is to determine individual and collective preferences about potential reforms, the choice must necessarily be restricted to a few options. Deliberating about every conceivable idea would be impossible and unproductive.[28] Serious public debates are not open discussions about anything and everything. "Because only a very limited number of changes have any significant chance of succeeding," notes Michael Harrington, the different sides "explore a relatively narrow range of possible futures and, when they are serious, respond to the same reality in fundamentally different ways."[29] Thus, democratic deliberation involves not only movements of opinion in accordance with conceptions of justice, but also the narrowing of the debate towards a small set of alternatives. This gradual construction of a few diverging conceptions can be seen as a third important characteristic of deliberation.

Difficult to establish beyond doubts, the presence of genuine democratic deliberation can be signalled by meaningful opinion movements, by explicit references to conceptions of justice, and by the emergence of a clear and limited set of alternatives. By contrast, the "rational" politics of self-interest display exogenous preferences that are impervious to arguments, motivations that are primarily economic, and amorphous, fragmentary, and shifting conceptions of the political community.[30] In the next sections, I shall argue that the Canadian referendum had more to do with deliberation than with uninformed, narrowly economic voting.

THE CAMPAIGN

When the Charlottetown agreement was signed in August 1992, polls indicated an overwhelming public support all across Canada, except in Quebec. Even in Quebec, the margin between the pros and the cons was sufficiently small and the number of undecided voters sufficiently high to expect a Yes victory, assuming that, in the end, undecided voters would rally to the more conservative, safer side. At the time, remembered a senior advisor to the prime minister at the end of the campaign, "the referendum seemed like a formality ... It looked as if it would be 'Come and sing in the streets with us.'"[31] Soon, the tide turned and it rapidly became obvious that a Yes victory in every province would be difficult to achieve. On 26 October the No prevailed everywhere except in Newfoundland, Prince Edward Island, New Brunswick, and, by very little, in Ontario.

What happened? Allan Gregg, a pollster close to the Conservative party, argued after the campaign that cynicism and ignorance prevailed over fairness and reason. "When you put these two things together," he said, "ignorance and cynicism – it created a veneer through which logic could not penetrate."[32] It may be true that citizens remained uninformed and cynical, but if these factors proved so important, one wonders why they did not play at the outset of the campaign. Were Canadians better informed when they so overwhelmingly approved the news of an accord? Did they, for a moment, support Prime Minister Brian Mulroney?

Although rare in conventional elections, such opinion reversals are common in referendums, and most times they favour the No side. Assuming that deliberation matters little, political scientists usually attribute these reversals to bandwagon effects, conservatism, or voter confusion and alienation. A recent comparative study of the short-term dynamic of referendums shows, however, that opinion shifts do not always favour the side that appears to be leading, are not always conservative, and do not simply respond to the doubts and uncertainties raised by the opposition. The authors of this study, R. Darcy and Michael Laver, try to reconstruct the conventional account by arguing that, to move the electorate towards a negative vote, groups and parties opposed to an initiative must not only raise doubts but must also count on the withdrawal of the elites favourable to the Yes side. For them, when a "widespread elite consensus" favours the Yes, this option should prevail; a reversal occurs only if "an increasingly ugly campaign, fought using techniques that often break the established rules of the game" forces these elites to withdraw and to concede the victory to their opponents.[33] Darcy and Laver's reconstructed explanation seems unhelpful, however, in accounting for the Canadian referendum. In English Canada in particular, it is difficult to speak of elite withdrawal in the wake of an ugly campaign. Brian Mulroney may have avoided some regions of the country, but there were enough politicians, intellectuals, and business and labour leaders to stand in his place. In simple spending terms, the $5 million media budget of the Yes committee far outweighed the resources of the No side.[34] As for Quebec, the leaders debate showed an aggressive Robert Bourassa trying with some success to correct the image of a premier who had "caved in." Bourassa did not succeed, but he never withdrew from the campaign. The French referendum on Maastricht points in the same direction: a united and unflinching commitment of the elites on the Yes side did not suffice to prevent an important opinion reversal.

Perhaps negativism alone did the job. Although Darcy and Laver find examples of referendums where simply raising doubts did not work, negative campaigning often seems to be a winning referendum strategy.[35] The problem in this case, and in the Maastricht case as well, is that negative arguments were presented by both sides. Costly economic and political consequences could be associated with both possible outcomes.

An alternative way of looking at the question is to consider the arguments offered by each side. According to Thomas E. Cronin, who echoes Elster in this instance, "voters will support the status quo unless they are given clear arguments for changing it."[36] What were the main reasons for voting Yes? Three types of argument were offered: positive, general arguments stressing compromise, accommodation, and Canadian unity; positive, specific arguments emphasizing gains for various constituents, be they Quebeckers, westerners, or Aboriginal peoples; and negative arguments, announcing major economic and political difficulties should the No side win. The first type of argument predominated early in the campaign, as long as the Yes side dominated sufficiently to portray No votes as almost un-Canadian. Even Preston Manning, leader of the Reform party, hesitated before embarking on a negative campaign. As the No side grew stronger, and as Canadians demanded information and specific details, this general argument faded, leaving only its weaker version, the idea that a deal offered at least an end to Canada's constitutional odyssey, a relief from chronic constitutional fatigue. The two other types of argument then took over, and they spelled trouble for the Yes campaign. In a complex game of multifaceted self-definition and of competing conceptions of justice, the outlining of the specific gains of any collective identity risked antagonizing another collective identity. To avoid this quagmire, the Yes side rapidly turned to negative campaigning, forgetting it had to give voters a positive reason to approve what one political scientist aptly called "the single biggest change in national political institutions since Confederation."[37] As a political strategist noted, the Yes supporters ended up unable to make a clear case for change. Either they condemned the No side and predicted a disaster if it won, or they lost themselves in the details of the Charlottetown agreement.[38]

On the other side, the players were more diverse and divided, but the arguments also boiled down to a few ideas. The No forces denounced the incomplete and open nature of the agreement, criticized its contradictions and inequities, and stressed the legitimacy of a No vote. In Quebec, where an important part of the population supports independence or sovereignty association, the No vote did not need to demonstrate its legitimacy. Elsewhere, the intervention of Pierre Elliott Trudeau, the opposition of Judy Rebick, president of the National Action Committee on the Status of Women, and the hesitations of Elijah Harper, a pivotal Manitoba native politician, helped to make a No vote honourable. For all No campaigners, visions of a blank cheque and of particular losses also proved important. Most central, in my opinion, were the tensions left unresolved by the Charlottetown agreement.

For all its complexity, the Canadian constitutional debate involves no more than a few contending ideas. Alan Cairns has summarized these ideas as calls for three equalities: the equality of citizens, the equality of provinces, and the equality of two nations.[39] Now that Aboriginal Canadians are recognized as peoples with an inherent right of self-government, we should probably speak of four equalities. The Charlottetown agreement constituted an ambitious attempt to incorporate these four ideas of equality in the constitution. But it was also the product of hard and rapid bargaining, and it acknowledged the various conceptions without resolving the contradictions between them. The product was a document that could appeal to no clear conception of justice. While it was perhaps honourable, the final compromise did not rest on a solid, principled justification. This lack of foundations explained, better than anything else, the opinion reversal that occurred all across the country.

CONTENDING CONCEPTIONS OF JUSTICE

If Canadians evaluated the Charlottetown agreement on the basis of one of their four contending conceptions of justice, they could not find it satisfactory. For Charter Canadians, who are committed to citizen equality, and were best represented by former Prime Minister Trudeau, the Canada clause alone, with its recognition of Quebec as a distinct society and its acknowledgement of various collective identities, was enough to make them reject the agreement.[40] For those committed to provincial equality, such as Preston Manning and the Reform party, "the less-than-2-E Senate" failed because it did not "satisfy aspirations for regional equality."[41] For Aboriginal peoples, opposition stemmed to a large extent from the incomplete character of the accord and from the absence of a clear definition of self-government.[42] Finally, in Quebec, the No side contrasted the proposed constitution to the consensus established at the Bélanger-Campeau Commission on Quebec's political and constitutional future, a consensus built around demands for a recognition of Quebec as a distinct society, for changes in the distribution of powers, and for a fair representation of Quebeckers in central institutions.[43]

Of course, voters did not always refer to these principles explicitly, and they often remained uninformed about the specifics of the agreement. No one would deny that many votes rested on less than enlightened rationales. Yet the principles behind the most articulate objections made voting No legitimate. Had the No vote simply been a knee-jerk reaction against Quebeckers, Aboriginal peoples, or Brian Mulroney, it would have had difficulties making progress in public opinion.

"The overriding argument for democracy," argues Jon Elster, "is that it makes certain arguments impossible to state in public, whereas others become endowed with almost irresistible power." He adds that "grumblings" about the short-term costs of various reforms may be justified, but that once strong arguments have prevailed, ill-founded complaints cannot "amount to more than a rearguard action."[44] In the 1992 referendum, grumblings were heard about Quebec, cereal boxes, and "Ovide Wednesday."[45] Legitimate stances, however, backed up each complaint, with a logical consistency unavailable to the Yes side. Not only did the various No camps appeal to a clear conception of justice but they could even refer to the contending conceptions. The Reform party, for instance, explained to its supporters that the Charlottetown Accord failed to achieve not only provincial equality but also the equality of citizens and a settlement acceptable to Quebeckers and Aboriginal peoples.[46]

The conceptions of justice evoked by the No side appealed to Canadian voters because they had both internal consistency and an enduring character. Each conception predated the Charlottetown Accord and stood as an established vision of Canadian politics. Following the Meech Lake debate, Alan Cairns, Peter Russell, and many others underlined the near-impossibility of accommodating visions of the country that had become as entrenched as they were divergent.[47] In his June 1991 presidential address to the Canadian Political Science Association, Peter Russell explained how difficult it would be to reconcile Quebec's search for a special recognition with principles as strongly held as individual equality, provincial equality, and national uniformity.[48]

The negotiations of August 1992 did not produce this reconciliation. They constituted what, in French, is called *une fuite en avant*, the process by which one does more of the same and thus adds to a problem in the vain hope of escaping it. Canadian political leaders tried an escape with the only vehicle they really knew, old-style executive federalism. Among themselves they compromised, and in the enthusiasm of the moment they assumed that Canadians had forgotten the old visions that had appeared so insuperable just a few months before. In the campaign, however, these visions came back with a vengeance, more explicit than ever now that popular sovereignty was fully acknowledged.

Consider, for instance, the question of duality, the contradiction between the "two nations" and the individual and provincial equality conceptions of justice. From at least the early 1960s, when the Royal Commission on Bilingualism and Biculturalism toured the country searching for a solution to the Canadian constitutional crisis, this antinomy has been at the centre of Canadian politics. In the 1988 electoral campaign, the contradiction was still so important that the three federal parties carefully avoided mentioning the constitutional question.[49] The referendum tackled the question directly, with no clear argument to resolve what may well be the deepest of all Canadian political cleavages. For the Yes to win, Canadians would have had to rank quiescence and stability higher than their long-held visions of the country.

SHOULD CANADIANS QUIT OR DELIBERATE FURTHER?

Given the political conceptions of Canadians, the No victory was not surprising. On three counts, the outcome demonstrated a capacity and a willingness to deliberate: public opinion moved; it did so in response to arguments anchored in conceptions of justice and not simply out of economic or narrow concerns; and in the end it produced an outcome that was meaningful, an affirmation that the principles that were at stake before the Charlottetown agreement are still alive and well.

Like the defeat of the Meech Lake Accord, the referendum result signalled the victory of Trudeau's vision in English Canada and its failure in Quebec. Citizen equality and the denial of duality founded, to a large extent, the English-Canadian No vote; the request for a more explicit acknowledgement of duality justified the No of Quebeckers. Now that these two contending visions have been forcefully reaffirmed, what more can be done? For some, the best and the only available option is to quit, to stop what they see as a vain existential debate over mere symbols. Asked through a poll the week after the referendum, 69 per cent of Canadians in English-speaking provinces and 55 per cent of Quebeckers agreed, saying that a five-year moratorium on constitutional talks would be a good idea.[50] Others think that we should, that we must, continue the discussion.

The argument for quitting takes the referendum as the most eloquent demonstration that agreements are impossible over questions that remain essentially symbolic, and contends that much can be achieved through conventional politics.[51] But visions of a country are not merely symbols that can be set aside when people disagree. The 1988 Canadian Election Study shows how, for Canadian parties, these contending visions represent crucial issues, the stuff of political life and death. Given the strength of both the Reform party and the Bloc Québécois, two parties that have a vested interest in keeping the constitutional debate alive, and the proximity of a federal election, a closure is unlikely. Likewise, Aboriginal claims will not easily be satisfied without reopening other questions. Finally, in Quebec, public opinion remains almost evenly divided between people in favour and opposed to sovereignty, with a good number of undecided voters in the middle.[52] The argument for quitting, admits Thomas Courchene, requires faith in "the heroic assumption that the 'No' vote in Quebec is sufficiently cathartic and/or symbolic so as not to lead immediately to a secessionist initiative."[53]

Of course, continuing to deliberate appears just as heroic. What more can be said to convince anyone to move towards a compromise? In any case, what compromise can there be? The best argument for more democratic deliberation consists in underlining the limitations of the referendum episode. The campaign allowed Canadians to deliberate, but only on a fully determined arrangement, based on a patchwork of visions that no one could find appealing. It was, wrote Duncan Cameron, akin to the "old Gaullist trick: my way or the highway."[54] The referendum, and the hard bargaining that led to it, could not replace a genuine national deliberation over what Canada should be, something like a constituent assembly or a "democracy round."[55]

The referendum campaign proved deliberative in the sense that it constituted more than an expression of ignorance and cynicism; voters entertained various considerations and assessed a complex proposal in the light of their own conceptions of what is good and fair, for themselves and for the community. The process, however, stopped short of a deeper form of deliberation, one in which prevailing understandings and existing conceptions of justice could be questioned, modified, or reconstructed. Deliberating, explains Bernard Manin, involves more than discovering an individual's or a collectivity's preferences: "The parties are not satisfied with presenting various and conflicting theses; they also try to persuade each other. They argue."[56] The process does not guarantee that a single proposal will prevail or a compromise solution will emerge, but it reshapes the options and, more important, it lends legitimacy to the outcome that is eventually chosen by a majority.

In the winter of 1992, the Beaudoin-Dobbie joint parliamentary committee on Canadian unity held five national conferences that resembled "mini constituent assemblies."[57] For all their imperfections, these conferences, which brought chosen representatives from all walks of life, came perhaps as close as we have ever seen to the deliberative opinion polls advocated by American political scientist James S. Fishkin. For Fishkin, the aim of such polls is to allow "a representative microcosm of the mass public to become deliberative" in order to reach decisions that can become national recommendations.[58] Although not perfectly representative, the Beaudoin-Dobbie conferences nevertheless produced remarkable results.[59] "This was indeed a surprise," noted Peter Russell, "for a country grown accustomed to constitutional disasters."[60] The English-Canadian participants, in particular, moved more than expected and accepted the idea of asymmetrical federalism and the recognition of Quebec as a distinct society. The Beaudoin-Dobbie process, however, soon gave way to old-style secret bargaining. The natural trade-off between asymmetrical federalism and Senate reform was discarded and was replaced by concessions which nobody ever demanded and nobody could justify on the basis of principles, such as the 25 per cent guarantee for Quebec in the House of Commons.[61]

If the spirit of the 1992 conferences and the approach that produced this spirit were reanimated, pursuing national deliberations could make sense. The game, however, is very advanced: grievances have accumulated and positions have hardened. In eighteenth-century republican thought, democratic deliberation was understood as a means of transcending particular interests and finding the common good: if "representatives could free themselves from the passion of particular interests, if institutions were properly designed, and if the process of deliberation were sufficiently unhurried, unanimity would prevail – the process would have converged to the true general will."[62] The notion of a unique and converging general will, however, does not seem plausible any more, and when Bernard Manin defends deliberation, he does not keep this aspect of the republican tradition. Deliberation may lead to the "broadest agreement possible at a particular time," but it also leaves many conflicts unresolved. Indeed, insofar as it heightens the parties' awareness of their identities and differences, a deliberative process may even exacerbate conflicts.[63]

Deliberation makes justifications necessary and, as such, it constitutes a central component of political debates. References to the common good, however, do not erase interests, any more than the interplay of interests makes principled arguments meaningless. If interests played no role in deliberations, if all were simply interested in finding the common good, there would be little need for ethics; on the contrary, if moral claims were pure rhetoric, they would play no role in political conflicts. Political controversies, argues Laura Stoker in a recent article, involve both conflicting interests and "competing claims" about common purposes. The purpose of deliberation is not to transcend conflictual interests but rather to give them a public meaning, to recast limited claims in terms acceptable to the community so as to reach a good and legitimate arrangement.[64]

CONCLUSION

For years, English Canada has tried to avoid the Quebec issue, with the help of Trudeau's vision of a simple, majoritarian, and individualist country.[65] Trudeau's success suggests that avoidance strategies which deny the demands for recognition of both Quebec and the

Aboriginal peoples may work for a few years. In the long run, however, it is hard to see how something as central as the constitutional question can remain unaddressed.

In purely strategic terms, the problem has no stable solution. With known and sufficiently balanced relations of force, a fundamental institutional disagreement cannot be solved by the unilateral imposition of one party's solution. A party may prevail in the short term, but it cannot expect its solution to prove unchallenged and durable. Superficial compromises will prove just as unstable. When a prolonged standoff and the pressure to find a modus vivendi yield temporizing solutions based on past institutions or on institutional expedients, the initial conflict remains and is bound to continue.[66]

The end of the referendum campaign marked a pause in the Canadian debate. In their comparative survey of referendums, David Butler and Austin Ranney concluded that for a government, "a 'favorable' outcome did not necessarily require a resounding 'Yes' or 'No' on a particular measure." The government, they added, "may not care very much how the measure fares but may care a great deal about shunting off responsibility for the decision."[67] Quebec Premier Robert Bourassa faced difficult choices before the referendum was announced. Either he could renege on his commitment to hold a referendum, and consequently be perceived as dishonest, or he could hold a referendum on sovereignty that he did not want, fearing it would end up about fifty-fifty.[68] The revelations made during the national referendum damaged his reputation as a negotiator, but the campaign nevertheless left him relatively strong, both in his party and in public opinion.[69] Most important, through all this procedure Bourassa evaded a commitment made as a result of a wide consultation, and he pushed aside, for a while, a debate on sovereignty. He may not have wanted much more out of a federal referendum. The point of view of the federal government may not have been very different. A deadline was removed, and the dangerous politics of constitution making gave way, for a few months at least, to the less treacherous politics of social and economic governance.

The fundamental debate, however, was only postponed. At the end of the campaign, two scenarios seemed likely. The first saw a weak or minority federal government forced by the Bloc Québécois or the Reform party to reopen the constitutional debate. The second made a Parti Québécois victory in Quebec signal the beginning of a new debate over the fate of the country. In either case, the main constitutional options were bound to be re-examined, most likely as a result of political changes in Quebec.

The positive attitude of Canadians at the beginning of the referendum campaign and the remarkable evolution of opinion that followed suggest not that Canadians are ignorant and cynical, but rather that they are still open, still willing to consider innovative proposals and to deliberate. Like citizens anywhere, Canadians have multiple, often conflicting, opinions on political issues.[70] Quebeckers, in particular, appear uncertain. Facile commentaries have often attributed this ambivalence to a calculated determination to have the cake of independence and eat the benefits of federalism too. While such a calculus is certainly not absent, something more fundamental seems at play: most Quebeckers still struggle with two overlapping collective identities, and they have difficulties forsaking either one.[71] In such a situation, deliberation takes its deeper meaning. Deliberating, then, means finding out through interior deliberation and dialogue with others what one really wants.[72]

As a deliberation process, the referendum constituted a learning opportunity for Quebeckers, and Parti Québécois leader Jacques Parizeau rightly pointed that superficial references to economic risks and uncertainties, a staple of Quebec political discussions in the past, had lost much of their efficacy now that they were shown to be unfounded.[73] For Quebec nationalists, the campaign was also an occasion to regroup and prepare for upcoming political battles.[74] The status of Quebec, however, still has to be determined. Because Quebeckers cannot possibly abandon their demand for recognition, only two stable solutions seem possible.[75] Either Canadians accept that there are many ways of being a Canadian and work to redesign the country accordingly, or else Quebec and English Canada part ways and create new states. Then again, the question of diversity will still have to be addressed by each side, this time to meet the demands of Aboriginal peoples.

COMMENTS ON ALAIN NOËL'S ESSAY
F.L. MORTON

I want to begin my comments on Alain Noël's fine paper with an anecdote. It concerns an interview with Joe Clark conducted by Peter Brimelow in 1976. Brimelow was then a junior reporter for the *Financial Post* – he has since gone on to become a senior editor with *Forbes Magazine*. Joe Clark was then a junior member of Parliament from High River, Alberta, a small farm community south of Calgary, and he too went on to bigger and better things, becoming leader of the Progressive Conservative Party and prime minister of Canada, and then holding several important cabinet posts in the Mulroney government, the most recent of which was minister of constitutional affairs. For the past year and a half, Joe Clark served as Brian Mulroney's principal negotiator, superintending the process that culminated in the Charlottetown Accord.

To return to the 1976 interview, Brimelow asked Clark what he thought about recent proposals for freer trade with the United States. Clark became flustered, stood up, closed the door, and asked Brimelow to turn off his microphone. "To tell you the truth Peter," Clark confessed apologetically, "I really don't know." Brimelow was shocked; the question of free trade with the United States has been one of the major foreign policy issues for Canada since 1867. For someone who aspired to be and soon was to be the leader of the Tory party not to have even an opinion was nothing short of astounding. Clark sensed Brimelow's astonishment and tried to explain: "To tell you the truth, when I got into politics I was told I had to make a choice. I had to either learn economics or I had to learn French. I chose to learn French."

There is both a comic and a serious side to this anecdote. The comic side – besides Mr Clark's distinctive French accent – explains why many Canadians shuddered the night of the referendum when, as it became clear that the referendum was going to be defeated, one politician after another marched up to the television microphones and said, "Well, the constitution is over, so we are going to turn our attention to the economy." This really frightened people. These men had just made a shambles of the constitution, and now they were going to turn their talents to the economy. The serious side of this anecdote shows the shadow that Quebec nationalism (and the possibility of Quebec separatism) has cast over the present generation of political leaders in Canada. Bilingualism was the pan-Canadian policy that was somehow supposed to unite the nation. This new Canada was to be a bilingual nation that would satisfy Quebec nationalist aspirations at the federal level while protecting the anglophone minority within Quebec. To many, the defeat of the Charlottetown Accord represents the failure of this policy and a personal defeat for Joe Clark and the generation of Canadian political leaders who chose to learn French rather than economics.

Turning to Professor Noël's paper, I agree with most of what I understand to be his basic thesis – that one can understand the Charlottetown Accord as essentially a process of democratic deliberation over competing principles of justice; this perspective is contrasted with economic or interest-group models, which portray referendums as simply the expression of self-interest and private preferences. I agree with Professor Noël that the accord can be understood as embracing what he calls the "four principles of justice" or the "four principles of equality," namely, the equality of individual citizens, the equality of the provinces, the equality of the two founding nations (French and English), and the equality of the first peoples (Aboriginals). Most of the details in the complex compromises that constitute the accord can be traced to some accommodation of these four principles. I agree that these principles, or competing visions of justice, predate the Charlottetown Accord and that they were recognized but not reconciled by it. Finally, I agree that the failure to reconcile these principles contributed to the defeat of the accord, in part because it gave the high ground of principle to the opponents and reduced the Yes side initially to vague appeals to patriotism and subsequently to threats of economic disaster should the accord be defeated. By contrast, the No side presented itself as representing principle. Preston Manning and the Reform party could demand, "Where is the equality of the provinces? Where is the effective, equal, elected Senate?" The Parti Québécois and Bloc Québécois could say, "Where is the true recognition of a distinct society that shows the French are one of the two founding nations?" On all of these points I agree with Professor Noël.

Of course I have some disagreements – or, rather, qualifications – that I would add to these various theses. First, Professor Noël appears to characterize a No vote as a conservative vote, a vote for the status quo. This view is consistent with common sense. Here was a referendum on a large package of changes to the constitution. A No vote, rejecting the proposed changes, certainly appears to be a vote for the status quo and thus a conservative vote. In fact, I would suggest that just the opposite was true in these unusual circumstances, that the Yes vote – the overwhelming choice of all the political, economic, regional, and occupational elites – was really the conservative vote, the vote for the status quo. After all, when, in any country, have almost all elites supported significant constitutional change? Doesn't support for major political change always come from groups who are dissatisfied with the status quo? Of course, the Charlottetown Accord proposed changes, but I suggest that, its supporters saw these as the minimal changes necessary to preserve the status quo (along with their privileged positions in it).

Similarly, voting against the Charlottetown Accord may appear to be a vote against change and thus a vote for the status quo. In fact, for certain key elements of the No coalition, such as the nationalists in Quebec and the Reform party in the West, the status quo is unacceptable. They voted No because the accord did not offer enough change or because it offered change in the wrong directions. Of course the No vote was a coalition of different groups; for some members of the coalition – for example, the Trudeau federalists and perhaps many of the feminists – a No vote was a vote for the status quo and was conservative in this sense. But for the most dynamic and numerically significant members of the No coalition, a No vote was a vote for much more change (albeit in different directions) than was offered by the accord.

My second modification would be to Professor Noël's thesis that public opinion supported the accord at the beginning but changed as the referendum proceeded. In a certain sense this is undeniably correct. But I would propose an alternative scenario – that public opinion was fairly stable throughout this period and that public support for the Charlottetown Accord was in fact a short-lived abnormality of just several weeks. Professor Noël points out that there was sharp disagreement over how to reconcile the four equalities prior to the Charlottetown Accord and that this disagreement had reappeared by early October. Public opinion could just as persuasively be characterized as relatively stable throughout, with just a short blip of "consensus" that began around 28 August and was over by the end of September. This blip reflected the initial burst of enthusiasm of the political leaders, which was in turn amplified by the national media. This official enthusiasm had an anesthetizing effect on the minds of Canadians, particularly as it was cast in terms of good will and patriotism. But once this effect wore off, and as the details of the accord became better known, Canadians fell back on these very different visions of Canada's future, these competing concepts of justice. So although support for the accord appeared to fall off, it really just reverted to the same political stalemate that had existed before 28 August and that continues today.

A third comment concerns Professor Noël's paradigm of democratic deliberation over competing principles of justice and his suggestion that this is how we should try to understand the debate. While it is indeed one way to understand the debate, I think it would be a serious mistake, particularly for political scientists, to pretend that an alternative paradigm, a paradigm not of justice but of power, a paradigm of not just principles but of self-interest, was not also very much at work. These two paradigms are not mutually exclusive. Each of the four principles of equality, each of Professor Noël's four

principles of justice, is strongly grounded in the self-interest of identifiable groups in Canada. Implementing the equality of the two
founding nations is in the self-interest of Quebec nationalists. The
equality of the First Nations serves the self-interest of Aboriginals.
The idea of the equality of the provinces, which supports the creation
of this triple-E (American-style) Senate, is very much in the self-
interest of the less populated western and maritime provinces. So
each principle of justice has, if you like, its lower side. Each is
grounded in public opinion and perceptions of self-interest. In politics the two are almost inseparable. I am not saying that we should
pay attention simply to self-interest, but I do believe it is dangerous
and misleading to ignore this element.

This leads to my final comment. It is important to see the Charlottetown Accord not just as a deliberation over competing principles
of justice but also as a power struggle between competing groups
that have very different understandings of Canada and its future.
Professor Noël's paradigm is useful. It helps point a way towards
future dialogue, but it should not be permitted to obscure the problems that face Canada. In particular, it should not displace alternative
explanations of what happened, particularly the view voiced by Tom
Courchene (and shared by many others) that the defeat of the Charlottetown Accord was "a defeat of the old Canada. A defeat of the
two founding nations. The defeat of the elite accommodation model
of executive federalism, a system that was favourable to compromise
and national unity." And, I would add, a defeat of the status quo.
Courchene characterizes the new Canada somewhat pessimistically
as "more democratic but less generous and a threat to national unity."
I am not so interested here in saying whether this new Canada is
good or bad, although it is undeniably more democratic. One of the
most significant effects of the Charlottetown Accord is that it has
established the precedent of submitting proposals for major constitutional change to a national referendum. This is important because
it gives a potential veto power to various interest blocs, including
disaffected westerners and Quebec nationalists. There cannot be any
more elite accommodation in terms of constitution making, at least
on the grand scale that we saw in the Meech Lake Accord and the
Charlottetown Accord. This is a significant change in the way constitutional politics are conducted, and it may well block the kinds of
compromise that are necessary to keep Canada united.

I think Professor Noël is right when he says that we will now have
a respite from constitutional talks and proposals for change. But the
issues will not go away, because for at least two of the most important

groups that made up the No vote, the status quo remains unacceptable.

Thank you very much for agreeing with so much of what I have written and for saying it so clearly. I will not dwell on what we agree upon. I will just pick up a few of the other themes.

Let me start with Joe Clark. I have heard this anecdote before. I think I read it in *Deconfederation*. The anecdote is very meaningful to me, not for what it says about Joe Clark or about Canada's official bilingualism, but for what it reveals about commentators who think that important lessons can be drawn from such a story. In what country, outside English Canada, could a politician excuse his incompetence in a critical area by the necessity of learning a second language? The fact that such a lame excuse is considered not only legitimate but also revealing of a fundamental national problem tells us something about the type of arguments used against official bilingualism.

Regarding the meaning of the vote, I agree wholeheartedly that voting Yes was a conservative thing to do. Such a vote was conservative not only because it expressed, in a strange way, a support for the status quo but also because it approved an elite-driven process. In Quebec, most observers thought, as I mentioned earlier, that in the end the undecided would vote Yes, because this seemed to be the safe thing to do.

I disagree with the idea that, at the outset, the support for the Yes was abnormal, or just a blip. There was no sudden decline in this initial support. If you look at the polls taken throughout the campaign, you will find a gradual lowering of the support for the Yes side, which tends to confirm the idea that the initial support was more than a spurt of enthusiasm. At the outset, many seemed willing to say, "Well, if there is an agreement, why not?" For scholars, I suspect, the determining factor was their reading of the accord. Others were probably influenced by Trudeau. In Quebec, an important and unusual aspect of the campaign was the taped conversation of high civil servants discussing the bargaining over cellular telephones, and saying Bourassa had caved in. The expression was translated as "caved in," but the real term used was, I think, worse. It was something like "collapsed." The diffusion of this conversation proved very significant. In any case, the initial support does not appear to me as a mere blip, and the decline in support was gradual.

Regarding the question of power, here again I agree. One aspect that seems worth mentioning is that the debate took the form of a prisoner's dilemma where one can see what the other prisoner is doing. For a lot of people in Canada, voting No became easier once they learned that everybody else was also voting No. There is safety in numbers. This silent bargaining explains part of the decline of the Yes support. It also indicates that the campaign was a power game as well as a deliberation.

Notions of principles and conceptions of justice are not meant to replace notions of interests and power. They are meant to complement them when necessary. The basic case for which power explanations are not sufficient occurs when defining what is in one's interest is not obvious. In Quebec, as elsewhere, most people found it impossible to figure out whether the referendum proposals would be good or not for them in, say, the next ten years. When you cannot determine what is in your own self-interest, you refer to principles. This is the role principles play in politics. They do not replace interests and power games but, essentially, come into play when interests and power fail to offer adequate guidance.

PROFESSOR MORTON,
IN FURTHER RESPONSE

The next round of constitutional change must come out of Quebec. Quebec has to put up or shut up. The Parti Québécois and the Bloc Québécois have to make arrangements for a serious vote on sovereignty association. Since the defeat of the Meech Lake Accord, the working premise of constitutional reform has been that English Canada would make an offer to Quebec that would attempt to satisfy Quebec's constitutional aspirations. This offer has now been made. It was rejected both in Quebec and outside Quebec. So the next round must be a within-Quebec round. It is time for Quebec to tell the rest of Canada what it wants.

I also have a response to the question about whose side time is on. I know whose time side is against, and that's Brian Mulroney and his version of the Progressive Conservative party. Both risk completely disappearing in the next federal election, which is no more than eighteen months away. They have been unable to deliver on the constitution not once but twice. This is a government whose electoral base is primarily in the West and in Quebec. It seems a safe bet that they Conservatives will no longer be able to hold this improbable alliance together. If they try to sweeten the pot for Quebec – even through non-constitutional means such as administrative agreements – this will further fuel anti-Mulroney, pro-Reform party support outside Quebec. If they try to buy off Reform support in the West, this will further alienate and erode their Quebec base. They are being outflanked in both regions, and moves to shore up support in one will cause a backlash in the other.

I would also venture a brief comment on the Beaudoin-Dobbie process. Beaudoin-Dobbie was a series of roving constitutional commissions, through which politicians and "ordinary citizens" were brought together to discuss various aspects of the constitution and proposals for change. Personally, I think it was a cynical public-relations campaign from the very start. The government knew after Meech Lake that it could not again rely exclusively on a process of "closed-door" executive federalism. It also knew that this was the only way in practice that it could hammer out an agreement among government actors. So it orchestrated this elaborate and expensive process of moving these different commissions around the country to "consult the people." These conferences generated elaborate reports and plenty of media coverage; but once the whole business was over, the governments did go back behind closed doors to hammer out a deal – the Charlottetown Accord – only this time they had the cover provided by the Beaudoin-Dobbie Commission. Its cynicism aside, it was a clever strategy that looked as if it was going to work until the last three weeks of the referendum campaign.

3 Looking Eastward, Looking Backward: A Western Reading of the Never-Ending Story

BARRY COOPER

At the centre of Canada's current constitutional problems is the Quebec question. This question is multidimensional and complex. It has a long history. Moreover, it is not at all clear that the Quebec question can be solved within the existing constitutional regime. Indeed, so clouded have the issues become, so muddy the constitutional waters, that Canadians have grave difficulties providing cogent and coherent analyses of their own troubles.[1]

One reason, perhaps the chief reason, is that Canadians have been sheltered within a stable political world where serious political questions never were raised and where politics was conducted, over their heads, by political leaders whose legitimacy was as unquestioned as the conventions by which they ruled. Social scientists have spoken euphemistically (and perhaps now nostalgically) of a consociational and elite-accommodation model of political decision making.[2] In the past few years, the traditions and conventions that have governed the public affairs of Canada have been eroded, possibly beyond repair. At the same time, the self-interpretation of Canadians, their governing myths, have been severely challenged. These developments are perhaps to be regretted, but there is no question that the changes in Canada's public life provide a genuine opportunity for change for the better.

In this essay, I would like to provide an analysis of some of the more important dimensions of the current political disorder. In doing so, I shall be making some distinctions that may have been overlooked and I shall be stressing points that have, it seems to me, been insufficiently emphasized. The purpose of such an approach is less to criticize colleagues who have devoted their lives to the study of Canadian politics than to complement the work of "Canadianists" with perspectives drawn from the study of political philosophy. Topically, I would like to discuss, first, the distinction between state and society; second, the bearing of that distinction on what seems to me to be the most significant social event in recent Canadian history, the rapid secularization of the French and formerly Roman Catholic inhabitants of Quebec; third, I would like to stress the importance of regional mythologies within English-speaking Canada, particularly the difference between the self-understanding of citizens living in western Canada and that of citizens living in Ontario. Finally, I would like to indicate that the theory of liberal constitutionalism, which, it seems to me, has been systematically ignored during the great disruptions of recent years, can suggest the kind of principles that must be invoked if Canada is to retain its integrity as a regime. Accordingly, this essay has the simplest of all structures: analysis of a problem and the outline of a solution.

STATE AND SOCIETY

Section 1(2)(1)(c) of the *Consensus Report on the Constitution* (signed at Charlottetown on 28 August 1992 and known as the Charlottetown Accord) as well as the *Draft Legal Text* of the accord read: "Quebec constitutes within Canada a distinct society, which includes a French-speaking majority, a unique culture and a civil law tradition." Section 1(2)(2) reads: "The role of the legislature and Government of Quebec to preserve and promote the distinct society of Quebec is affirmed." These two provisions constitute what are often referred to loosely as "the distinct society clause" and are very close in wording and meaning to a set of similar provisions in the ill-fated Meech Lake Accord of 1987.

It is important to distinguish the two aspects of the distinct society clause because these two aspects point to, but do not resolve, a fundamental ambiguity. As a general interpretive principle, facts are relevant to problems and topics in the light of a context or a larger whole – and in connection with the distinct society clause, one would like to know what that larger context is. In antiquity, it was clear that the polis provided the context for the activities of *polites*, citizens, but it is clear that the polis does not do so today. Nor is it clear that the two chief alternatives, society and state, can provide a context equivalent to the context provided by the polis, notwithstanding the fact that much of our political vocabulary is derived from that ancient context. From the start, therefore, we are faced with ambiguous, conflicting, and overlapping sets of language symbols. Some critical clarification may be obtained, by reflecting not so much on the transformation of Greek political terminology as upon the later prominence of state and society both as realities and as terms invoked to make sense of reality.

The term "state" was first used in its modern sense by Machiavelli and was tightly bound to his sense of acquiring and his sense of necessity. I will mention only two points in this connection: first, for Machiavelli, what is fundamental is not the regime – or, as we might say, the constitution – but the orders that comprise it, namely the rulers and the ruled. Moreover, for Machiavelli, there is no difference between founding and acquiring. Either way, in order to establish or acquire a state, one must tear down what is already there in order to build or to build up one's own. Just as one is either ruler or ruled, there are no open spaces. Every place is occupied, which means that one must advance by removing others or by taking advantage of their misfortune. In short, one can never be secure enough. Another way of putting it is to say that, for Machiavelli, the distinction between friends and enemies disappears. This leads to a second Machiavellian insight: government is most effective when it is indirect, which is to say, when it manipulates and manages a population. Without going into great detail, I would simply observe that much of contemporary Canadian politics operates according to Machiavellian assumptions regarding the state.

It is conventional nowadays to distinguish state and society. Indeed, one may say that the ancient polis, which once provided the comprehensive context for politics, has split into the state (more or less in Machiavelli's sense) and society. Nowadays, moreover, we are likely to be of the opinion that society is more fundamental than the state. In both the Meech Lake Accord and the Charlottetown Accord, the invocation of the distinct society of Quebec preceded the role of the legislature and Government of Quebec, which is to say, the Quebec state. The fundamental character of society, according to modern opinions, has led to the conclusion that the true understanding of political things is found in sociology, the queen of the social sciences. The regal pretensions of sociology, however, are marred by a perhaps fatal ambiguity. When one asks "What is society?" the answer usually depends upon politics. Thus, one speaks of Canadian or American society, of Alberta society, and so on. The terms gain what precision they have because the realities to which they refer have distinct political boundaries. Matters are much more vague when one speaks of a world society or a class society; moreover, one must make suitable qualifications when speaking of the society constituted by Québécois – that is, the reality contemplated by section 1(2)(1)(c), and the social organism bounded by the borders of the Province of Quebec, which is multiethnic and multilingual, and in this sense no more distinct than Newfoundland, or Saskatchewan. The real problem, it seems, lies in the implications of section 1(2)(2), a provision that is usually identified as conferring "special status" on the Quebec legislature and government.

Some of the conceptual confusion and ambiguity regarding the state/society question can be removed if one considers the origin of society, as distinct from politics or the state. The social question arose "when it was observed or alleged that society, which is private (as we say today, 'the private sphere'), was not autonomous because it was not providing for the poor."[3] Thus, political intervention was thought to be required to establish or re-establish the social equilibrium. Properly speaking, however, the social question looks very much like the old question of the rich and the poor, familiar from Aristotle's *Politics*. The difference lies in its immediate predecessor, the religious question.

The religious question may be simplified as follows: Are human beings ruled by gods or God, and so by divine right, or are they ruled by themselves, and so on the basis of principles that, in the first instance, do not refer to the gods or God? In the history of Western Europe and Western political philosophy, the religious question was the occasion for ferocious religious war as well as for a profound response to it. To simplify greatly, Bodin, Hobbes, Spinoza, and Locke distinguished between politics and society in order to prevent political men from trying to save our souls at the point of a sword. Society and, more abstractly, the private sphere were set aside so that souls could flourish without political compulsion. This was not a solution to the religious question (a solution was proposed later by Hegel, but it turned out to be imaginary).[4] It was, however, a prudent compromise that made constitutional government possible.[5] The ambiguity between state and society, it seems to me, is reflected in the ambiguity between the distinct society clause, in the strict sense of section 1(2)(1)(c), and the granting of special constitutional status to one province, in the sense of section 1(2)(2). In the language of commonsense politics, the number of Canadians who would agree that Quebec is a distinct society is much greater than the number who would agree that the legislature and Government of Quebec should, in consequence, receive special constitutional powers and responsibilities. Among other things, such powers and responsibilities seem to conflict with the equality of provinces affirmed in section

1(2)(1)(h). The more substantial reason for this discrepancy, I believe, is that the purpose of the law of the constitution in Quebec is understood differently than its purpose in Canada, especially in western Canada. This is a question to which we shall return.

Perhaps more to the point, the distinct society clause, in the strict sense, is directly connected to the religious question. I refer not to the civil law tradition, enumerated in section 1(2)(1)(c), which was granted to Quebec by the British crown in order to safeguard the property of the Roman Catholic church, but rather to the transformation of the religious question, properly speaking, into the nationalist or ethnonationalist question, which occurred in consequence of the unprecedentedly rapid secularization of French-speaking Roman Catholics inhabiting the Province of Quebec.

SECULARIZATION IN QUEBEC

This transformation of the Québécois is, in my view, the most important single social factor responsible for precipitating the present disorder. Accordingly, it will perhaps be in order to recite a few details.[6] It seems to be obvious from the evidence of history that the actual existence of a French-speaking, culturally and even ethnically distinct population of Canadian citizens living chiefly in a single province is not *eo ipso* an occasion for constitutional turmoil. After all, the ancestors of the present population of Quebec lived there for several hundred years without such turmoil. The reason, rather, lies in the changes undergone by the French and Catholic population of Quebec during the past generation. At the end of the Second World War, for example, the health, education, and welfare services of the province were all in the hands of the Roman Catholic church. The abbé and the curé were respected figures, especially in rural areas. None of this is true today. It is, of course, a long and complex story, but the outlines are tolerably simple and clear: the emotions, sentiments, and attitudes that in the past were diffused through the church and associated institutions, such as the church-operated hospitals, charities, universities, and *collèges classiques*, have now been channelled into politics – specifically into political nationalism. Today, spiritual and intellectual life is guided not by the curé but by journalists, media stars, and university-based secularized intellectuals.

Consequently, we are faced with an unprecedented political problem. In the past, Canada was able to accommodate the divergent political expectations of French and non-French citizens. In Quebec, an alliance of the church and the provincial government was able to defend the culture, religion, and language of the distinct Québécois community in ways that made minimal demands on the non-Québécois Canadian citizens who were resident in the province. With the disappearance of the church as a significant social factor, the process of accommodation has been politicized and then constitutionalized. What used to be a matter of policy, of deal making and trade-offs, has become a matter of high principle, of political philosophy, and conflicting political realities. In Quebec, now, the state alone must protect the ethnic nation, the "distinct society."

Before the Quiet Revolution, the question of a politically significant distinct society did not arise. But it did arise when it was observed or alleged that the distinct society could no longer protect itself because the effective social authority of the church had disappeared and the traditional style of politics in Quebec was no longer legitimate.[7] Accordingly, the "social sphere" was understood to be dependent on politics and standing in need of political intervention – that is to say, state intervention – in order to restore or maintain a society that was no longer Catholic but was still French. According to this view, which is widely supported by Québécois regardless of whether they are federalist or sovereigntist, the law of the constitution is the appropriate instrument, in the words of section 1(2)(2), to preserve and promote the distinct society.[8]

REGIONAL MYTHOLOGIES

Neglect of a second distinction, between unity and identity, has added to the general confusion of Canadians regarding the nature of their current difficulties because it has blurred the cultural heterogeneity of English-speaking Canada. In the preface to his collection of writings on Canadian culture, *The Bush Garden*, Northrop Frye distinguished between national unity and regional identity. The question of Canadian identity, Frye argued, is badly posed. Identity, he said, is local, regional, cultural, and imaginative; unity is national and political. Frye was a skilful interpreter of cultural matters, especially of literature; his understanding of the tension between unity and identity illumines a central political issue. According to him, "the essential element in the national sense of unity is the east-west feeling ... expressed in the national motto, *a mari usque ad mare*." If the tension between unity and identity dissolves into either of its poles, the result is either "the empty gestures of cultural nationalism" or "the kind of provincial isolation which is now called separatism." The east-west feeling, he said, has developed historically along the axis of the St Lawrence drainage system. His phrase "provincial isolation called separatism" obviously refers to Quebec.

Later in the book, in a chapter which originally appeared as the conclusion to the first edition of the *Literary History of Canada*, Frye summarized his impression of the way that the Canadian imagination has developed in Canadian literature as being characterized by "what we may provisionally call a garrison mentality." The earliest maps of the country showed only forts. Governor Simcoe had read his Tacitus, and he established outposts along the Niagara frontier to keep the barbarians at bay until they swore allegiance and became *socii*. The cultural maps of a later time also showed only forts, according to Frye. A garrison is a closely knit society because it is a beleaguered society, held intact by unquestionable morals and authority. Motives count for nothing. One is either a fighter or a deserter. As Margaret Atwood, one of Frye's most gifted pupils, put it, "The central symbol for Canada – and this is based on numerous instances of its occurrence in both English and French Canadian literature – is undoubtedly Survival, *la Survivance*."[9] The point of garrison life, evidently, is to survive – a highly Machiavellian motif. Garrisons are also sites of military and administrative rule.

When the discourse of sensitive and intelligent minds contains elementary contradictions, these are not necessarily errors – accounts that are not adequate to reality. Assumptions may not have been sufficiently clarified, of course, but more to the point, Frye's account is interested. I do not mean by this that Frye did not intend to tell the truth or that he did not tell the truth, but I believe that the truth he told is limited and, as it were, deployed against another truth, and that it is thus at the service of a particular interest.

In the present example, Frye maintained that identity is regional, local, and imaginative (which is why the literature of one's own country can provide the cultivated reader with "an understanding of that country which nothing else can give him"),[10] and yet he also maintained that there is a Canadian mentality expressed imaginatively in a Canadian literature. If one holds to the first insight, by implication Frye becomes something of an emptily gesturing cultural nationalist; that is, the survival of the garrison, which is by all arguments the symbolization of an identity of some kind, has become an expression of a Canadian national identity. In the quotation given above, the "country" is identified with the abstract political unit and not with the concrete and etymological sense of land lying opposite an observer, which is to say, a local meaning. Now, Frye has said that the national sense of political unity is an east-west feeling centred upon the St Lawrence. This, let us say flatly, is nonsense. There is no Laurentian feeling in British Columbia, and the dim memories of such a feeling on the prairies are mostly hostile.

In sum, Frye made a useful distinction between unity and identity, which he then surrendered with his evocation of a national identity expressed in a national literature that makes articulate the garrison mentality. A plausible account of why this occurred – that is to say, an exposition of Frye's interestedness – is contained in the discourse of another literary critic, Dennis Duffy. In the concluding remarks to his fine study of Upper Canadian/Ontario literature, he declared that the book he had written was not what he had intended to produce. He had planned to write "another CanLit theme book" similar to Atwood's "thematic guide." The evidence, however, restricted his focus. In the works he considered, it was not Canada that was made imaginatively articulate; it was not even the contemporary political unit of Ontario; it was the heartland of Upper Canadian Loyalism, the wedge of land between the Ottawa River and Lake Huron. In that place the myth of exile (from the American colonies), covenant (loyalty to the crown), and return to a garden (the transformed wilderness) fully expressed the regional identity of "Canada." To be more precise, "Canada" as a symbol of identity is centred in the Loyalist heartland, is full of garrisons concerned with survival, and is indeed moved by feelings of a meaningful east-west axis. This "Canada," which is imaginatively real, is, however, imaginatively unconnected with even the Loyalists of Atlantic Canada, as Duffy pointed out.

It is even less connected with the West. Duffy sensed this. The "ampler Canada that Loyalism and its successors envisaged," the "noblest product Ontario had to offer to the rest of Canada" (namely, the east-west feeling centred on the St Lawrence and expressed in the national motto), was "sectionalized, misappropriated, its rhetoric employed to justify the smashing of the alternative Canada that had sprung from the Métis experience."[11] Duffy did not enlarge on what the Métis-inspired alternative might have been. He did, however, connect the alternative with the West, which showed that he sensed that an ampler Canada that did not betray itself was somehow linked to the export of the noblest product of Ontario. He did not dwell on what made that "vision of nationhood" noble, nor did he say what he meant by "nation".

Nevertheless, Duffy has clarified some of the unanalysed assumptions of Frye and Atwood: Canada the imaginative reality belongs to the experience of the Loyalist heartland. Like all such experiences, it is local. Canada the political reality, the noblest product of Ontario, was generated by the acts of sectionalization, misappropriation, and the use of rhetoric, "national" rhetoric, to smash an alternative that Duffy identified in an unclear way with the Métis. To put the matter bluntly, Canada the imaginative reality, centred in the Loyalist heartland, became Canada the political reality. By so doing, it betrayed its own regional identity and destroyed the possibility of an alternative political reality that might have grown from the Métis experience and in any event was located in the West. The contradictory statements of Frye, therefore, may be understood as reflecting the ambiguity of the term "Canada". In Frye's terminology, there is indeed a Canadian identity, but it is geographically restricted to the Loyalist heartland. There is a Canadian political unit as well, and it was created at the expense of what Duffy called Métis experience. It was also created at the expense of a genuine Canadian (that is, Ontario Loyalist) identity. Duffy described himself at the close of his book as standing at the corner where Mythology runs into Politics. His own activity in writing the book was likened to dashing into an intersection in the hope of slowing traffic long enough to glimpse its flow. So far, we have approached the intersection by way of the discourses of literary critics, along the street named Mythology; now let us consider the avenue of Politics.

Politically speaking, national unity is a matter of will. The greatest theorist of national unity was Rousseau; the greatest practitioner, Robespierre. "Il faut, une volonté UNE... Il faut qu'elle soit républicaine ou royaliste," said Robespierre the Incorruptible. National unity inspired by a single will does not mean stability. Like the will of an individual, it can change direction and preference without losing unity. Accordingly, in most circumstances, it is a formula for instability "puisqu'il est absurde que la volonté se donne des chaînes pour l'avenir."[12] There is, however, a significant and exceptional circumstance; the many become one when confronting an external and threatening other. Historically, this condition has arisen spontaneously in the circumstances of war, but never in post-Confederation Canada. One need only observe that the conscription crises were crises. Nor has the threat of United States economic control, which is a danger (if it is a danger) that falls far short of war, caused a unity of will in response. Nor, it hardly needs to be said, have unemployment, inflation, or any other elements of domestic incompetence. In short, only in the presence of an enemy can such a thing as *la nation, une et indivisible* exist. And Canada, the peaceable kingdom, has never experienced the requisite enemy.

Why, then, do we have the persistent calls for national unity? One explanation lies in the writings of Rousseau, specifically in his notion of the general will. It is not only opposition to a threat that can unify, he says, but also (in the same passage quoted above) "l'accord de tous les intérêts se forme par opposition à celui de chacun." That is,

Rousseau tacitly identified will and interest, with the assumption that will is a spontaneous or automatic interest. Thus, the *volonté générale* is, according to him, the interest of the people or nation: it is national unity. Accordingly, its generality must be opposed to each individual interest or will. The enemy of the *volonté générale* thus lies within the breast of each individual, each particularity. This has the convenient consequence that the doctrine of national unity can be broadcast in the absence of any threat, real or apprehended. The image of national unity is sentimental, and like all sentiments it is boundless. Thus, it can be enjoyed independent of any political realities. In Canada the sentiment is expressed, with nauseating regularity, by whining phrases such as "If only Canada were united, then ..." Then all things would be possible. The century would be ours. Furthermore, since will – and, by Rousseau's reasoning, interest too – must be made concrete and institutionally actual, it can be concentrated in a small body of men or women and even in the soul of one person, *uno solo*, as Machiavelli put it. The danger of tyranny in such a view has been explored by Rousseau's critics and is also apparent to the practical men who have understood and opposed those political events in modern history that bear the mark of Rousseau's reasoning.

These remarks on Rousseau's political thinking help clarify the matter of unity and identity. To summarize, Canadian identity, we say, is confined to the part of present-day Ontario which I called the Loyalist heartland. The Loyalist myth was forged by two crucial experiences. The first was the successful rebellion of the Thirteen Colonies and its consequences: the triumph of the Patriots, the foundation of the United States, and the defeat and expulsion of the Loyalists. The second was the War of 1812. In that conflict, the covenant made with the royal authority was confirmed, and Canada survived – a genuine garrison facing a genuine enemy – united until the Rebellions of 1837; and united still in the mythic aspirations of Ontario. I would draw from this the following conclusion. National unity is a symbol expressing "Canadian" identity, the identity of the Loyalist heartland. It was formed in the strenuous circumstances of exile, was maintained by strength of character and by a patient allegiance to the crown, and justified at last by military endurance. It is enough to observe, in this context, that neither the history nor the self-understanding of the Loyalist heartland applies to the West. For contemporary westerners "national unity" is an aspiration they have learned to distrust, because it appears as the manifestation of the garrison will, not simply of the Loyalist heartland but of the entire east-west axis extending from the St Lawrence Valley.[13] For the residents of Ontario, especially those who also reside in the Loyalist region of the mind, national unity, which includes the necessity of accommodating Quebec within the garrison, means something not merely different from the understanding of westerners but possibly something actually opposed to it.[14]

LIBERAL CONSTITUTIONALISM

Political things, as we know, are inherently subject to approval and disapproval, choice and rejection, praise and blame, because they raise a claim to our allegiance, obedience, and judgment. On occasion, as with the recent referendum, citizens are formally required to say yes or no. But on other occasions, too, we are called upon to judge an issue or policy in terms of justice. By and large, we equate justice with legality, which is not to say that there can be no laws that seem to us to be unjust. Such laws may be judged by reference to a larger context, namely, the constitution. Of course, the constitution, too, may be judged by reference to an even larger context, the context of political philosophy, but that would take us far beyond the current topic.[15] If it is agreed that, generally speaking, the justness of laws and policies can be decided by reference to the law of the constitution, we are invited or perhaps compelled to ask, What is the Canadian constitution?[16]

In his most recent in a series of essays on the constitution of Canada, Alan Cairns distinguished three aspects: (1) parliamentary government, or the mixed regime; (2) federalism, which he called the governments' constitution; and (3) the Canadian Charter of Rights and Freedoms, which he identified as the citizens' constitution.[17] Cairns noticed a certain tension or contradiction among and between these several elements of the constitution that have exacerbated the difficulties in reaching a democratically legitimate political agreement. I would like to address this same configuration of problems within a somewhat different context, provided most broadly by political philosophy. By referring to the context of political philosophy, I mean to suggest that we might profitably consider actual regimes in the light of the best regime. That is, one can consider constitutional democracy in Canada from the standpoint of what it might be if it were to do justice to the best motives of statesmen and citizens, instead of being bound by the ordinary, the banal, and the unavoidable. It goes almost without saying that by directing our attention to the best, we are able to assess the actual (and not confuse the actual with what is loosely called the ideal).

Canada is a regime. A regime is a formal and orderly system of rule (or government) that operates by means of conventions, practices, and traditions, as well as by explicit laws, rules, and regulations. The Canadian regime is a federal, parliamentary, liberal democracy. It is derived from the mixed regime (or mixed government or mixed constitution) celebrated by the great political philosophers of the early modern era.[18] Liberal constitutional governments – whether guiding unitary states or federal states, parliamentary democracies or presidential democracies – acknowledge a universal human dignity in the doctrine of natural or human rights, and they protect these rights by means of constitutional mechanisms and procedures.

Constitutional democracy is both safer and nobler for being formal. Its safety emerged from its adherence to forms and procedures, and its nobility is expressed in the demands that formalities exact in the act of observing them, as anyone who has ever seen the inside of a court or the House of Commons immediately senses. The underlying formal political principle in constitutional democracy, which sustains the assent by citizens to human dignity and their belief in the soundness of the doctrines of natural or human rights, is the principle of equality of citizens before the law. In a constitutional democracy, there is but one class of citizens.

The democratic notion that all men and women share in political nobility or political dignity is connected with the insight that all people have inherent virtue or excellence. That excellence or virtue cannot appear in politics, however, unless there is, first of all, equality. Put simply, equality is a necessary condition for excellence, for the appearance in politics and society of those men and women who excel or stand out and who thereby prove themselves to be unequal. Initial equality, it seems, is the condition for the development of eventual inequality.

More broadly, in any constitutional democracy, the condition for justice is the equality of citizens; if all citizens are not equal before the law, there cannot be justice. This does not mean that all citizens must live in the same conditions or in the same way. Equality of citizens before the law is formal equality – but formalities, as with courts and the House of Commons, are important in the Canadian regime. This is why the term "second-class citizen" is intolerable in a liberal democracy. Yet we have said that equality of citizens does not mean that everyone lives the same way. How is this possible?

In any regime, including a liberal democracy, there will, under a variety of circumstances, be superiors and inferiors, rulers and ruled, governors and governed. Sometimes the many are superior to the few, as with many customers in a restaurant and few waiters to serve them; sometimes the few are superior to the many, as with a few members of Parliament to govern many citizens. Even in a democracy there are menials and elites. But if a democracy is to remain true to its acknowledgment of universal human dignity, it must find a way to elevate menials and restrain the superior, at least as far as they are participants in the governmental system and are before the law.[19] Characteristically, this is done in two related and complementary ways, by offices and by institutions. Offices are formal positions that can shape the behaviour of office holders. It is widely claimed, for example, that many Canadians have been disappointed in the actions of Prime Minister Mulroney. But why were they disappointed? It was because they expected more of a person occupying the office of prime minister and because they thought he did not live up to the formal requirements of his office. Such formalities attract the best in men and women and so are connected to excellence and virtue, neither of which is common or expected. On the other side, in constitutional democracy, institutions come between citizens and their government. Governments maintain a limited independence of those who elect them so that they can also claim responsibility. To quote Harvey Mansfield: "As forms, institutions stand as obstacles to the immediate gratification of popular will, while at the same time facilitating and effecting the ultimate governance of the people."[20] Forms and the institutions provide a practical or pragmatic answer to the dangers of Rousseau's *volonté générale*, though hardly a theoretical analysis.

What Canadians have come to call the process of constitutional renewal bears a shadowy relationship to what classical political philosophy identified as the art of nomothetics, a comprehensive work of reflection that ended with the constitution of a regime that was, to be sure, not devoid of partisanship, but was beyond mere wilful partisan advantage. Indeed, the finished product must seem to be above partisan advantage in order to function. It seems safe to say that the recent process of constitutional renewal was seen by many Canadians as being directed precisely for partisan advantage, initially by the Liberal government of Pierre Trudeau and then by its successor, the Conservative government of Brian Mulroney. In addition, many westerners saw the process as continuing to serve the sectional advantage of central Canada. One consequence has been a decline in respect for the constitution. Instead of loyalty to the constitution, Canadians were asked either to provide ignorant enthusiasm for it or to regard it as a temporary investment, a means of getting what they wanted, and not as something above the citizens, something formal under which they were content to live.

Initially, constitutional regimes were liberal in the sense of liberty defined by what in the Enlightenment was called the rights of man or natural rights – rights that are loosely identified nowadays as human rights. Civil society, according to the great constitutionalists, is founded upon natural rights, rights that belong to human beings who have a nature deserving of certain specifiable rights. Constitutions were originally established for the sake of natural rights, but they did not in fact secure or legalize natural rights. No constitution can do this, for the simple reason that any constitution is a product of the art of nomothetics. It is an artifice, not a natural datum. Accordingly, constitutions actually establish and legalize civil rights.

Several implications follow. First, while it is true that one cannot be deprived of natural rights, it is also true that these rights are very easily violated. The mythic "state of nature" in constitutional theory is ended by an equally mythic consent to government. The truth expressed through this twofold myth is that limited civil rights are made more reliable by governments; though, because they already exist by nature, these rights are not created by governments or by anyone else. Moreover, the myth enjoins that the act of consent be individually undertaken: no one can consent for you, just as no one can vote in your place – voting being the exercise of an actual but limited consent within civil society. An alternative formulation maintains that liberty, understood in terms of natural rights, distinguishes sharply between rights and the exercise of rights in such a way that government has the task of protecting rights rather than either interfering with rights or guaranteeing their exercise. It seems fair to say that under the Canadian constitution today, particularly with respect to what Cairns called "Charter clientele groups," guaranteeing rights means ensuring that rights are exercised, not ensuring the possibility that citizens can exercise them.

That this change may prove if not fatal to liberal and constitutional democracy, then at least a serious threat, may be suggested by the following considerations. To begin with, group rights and group justice exist in some tension with the liberal doctrine of equality of citizens before the law. This is not to say that liberalism is hostile to groups per se. On the contrary, freedom of association is generally numbered among the freedoms that liberal constitutions are designed to secure. Moreover, the pursuit of profit by groups within liberal society has been recognized, at least since Montesquieu, as a substitute for glory and aristocratic military virtue, neither of which qualities is prominently associated with liberal citizens. One should recall, therefore, that the language of rights was initially developed as part of a strategic plan to dethrone the pretension that certain types of people or classes or groups had a natural or revealed right to rule. That is, the language of rights was developed to defend individuals against the actual or potential tyranny of groups and against the civil strife that contending group-based claims to rule invariably produce. By nature, liberals said, individuals have the right to be governed by their own consent and are justified in rebelling against governments that violate that consent.

Despite their basic decency and justness, not to say their internal coherence and prudence, Canadians, nevertheless, support liberal principles with variable enthusiasm. Members of groups targeted as beneficiaries of one or another legal or constitutional rule, whether MPs, Québécois, or disabled Aboriginal women, may find it relatively easy to make an exception for themselves. Nevertheless, it is indeed an exception, and thus it is of at least questionable legitimacy in a liberal regime.

That collective rights may prove a serious challenge to liberalism seems clear enough and has often been remarked upon. Collective rights also pose a threat to constitutionalism, insofar as the shift from securing rights to guaranteeing the rights of groups blurs the distinction noted earlier between state and society. The reason is clear and straightforward: any right whose exercise is guaranteed by the government is, to a greater or lesser extent, exercised by the government. Thus, when the right to look for a job is transformed into the right to receive the proceeds of a job – a right that is guaranteed, for example, by government payments of individuals or groups – the job is, in effect, undertaken by the government. In such a fashion does the state metastasize into society, acting on behalf of those whom it claims to benefit.

Studies in both Canada and the United States have succeeded in showing the highly questionable nature of such claims.[21] The chief consequence of government programs designed to guarantee alleged "social rights" is to transform the prospective beneficiaries of these programs into dependents of the state. More is involved than the failure of allegedly well-intentioned welfare policies: the intentions as well as the failure to realize them also have indirect constitutional implications.[22] By viewing citizen rights through the filter of guaranteed group rights, citizens find it increasingly difficult to understand themselves as constituting a body politic. Dependent groups can never form a majority capable of political action – though they can form various kinds of temporary "coalitions" – because they seek only their own interests and have no interest in exercising the moderation required of any particular group for the sake of the majority. As Mansfield observed, "A system of interests … is the very definition of a nation of dependents."[23] Such groups do not, one must repeat, seek out their economic interests, which is to say, profits, the economic manifestation of freedom. Rather, they seek out advantages that the government will secure for them, which is the opposite of the political manifestation of freedom. For their part, citizens are compelled to become generous and caring taxpayers.

The greatest victims of this kind of dependency in Canada are an identifiable group – namely, native people or Aboriginals. It is not clear whether, in constitutional terms, they are now or seek to be either overprivileged or underprivileged; but it is clear that they are not simply Canadian citizens and also that they are poor. Only the now discredited white paper of the Trudeau years has dared to make an argument connecting the ambiguous constitutional status of Aboriginals with their unambiguous poverty. The most egregious example of group rights is found in the distinct society provision, broadly understood. Unlike the "Charter clientele groups," this particular group right, if granted, would have at its disposal the entire apparatus of a provincial government. Should the alleged "inherent right to self-government" currently demanded by Aboriginals be acknowledged by the law of the constitution, they would be in a position similar to that of Québécois, with the difference that they would be faced with an even more stark option of choosing pride with poverty or continued dependency and resentment.

CONCLUSION

Let me conclude by summarizing the constituent elements of my argument and by justifying my title. "Constitutional politics," wrote Alan Cairns, "is never-ending."[24] Like the movie of the same name, this never-ending story is also a quest, a "constitutional odyssey," as Peter Russell said, in search of an answer to the question "Can Canadians be a sovereign people?"[25] If Homer's *Odyssey* is a reliable model, it should be remembered that Odysseus' homecoming and reclamation of his own sovereignty was accomplished with both great guile and great bloodshed. If it is true, in Cairns's words, that Canadians are called upon "to rethink what a constitution is,"[26] we should take this old cautionary tale to heart. Cairns's proposal is bold but not impossible. Moreover, it is a task that political scientists are perhaps better able to undertake than statesmen, politicians, or constitutional lawyers are.

To recapitulate briefly, I argued that the Quebec question – the demand by the Government of Quebec for constitutional recognition in the form of special status, powers, and responsibilities, to preserve and protect its claim to group distinctiveness – is at the centre of Canada's current political disorder. Quebec's demand, it seems to me, cannot be met within the current constitutional order or any modification of it that would preserve the integrity of the regime as a federal, liberal, and constitutional democracy. The conclusion is therefore clear, as Bercuson and I argued in *Deconfederation*. We would be better occupied, therefore, in discussing the procedures and terms of disengagement than in formulating additional plans for constitutional renewal that are as little likely to succeed as the previous ones.[27] In short, the dream of two founding peoples has been dreamed out. Quebec has changed fundamentally, and in a direction that points towards its political independence. Canada has changed as well, and in a direction that points to an incompatibility of its political principles with those of Quebec. We western Canadians are, in this respect, privileged because when we look to eastern Canada, we also look backwards in time. We, perhaps more easily than our fellow citizens in Ontario, can see the easterners' myths for what they are. We are not held in thrall by those myths, because they have never constituted our own local story.

Of course, the times are unpropitious. As Cairns pointed out, anyone contemplating the current political discussions in Canada "is advised to become comfortable with an almost operatic language of emotions, in which betrayal, treachery, dishonour, deception, distrust, and bad faith are liberally sprinkled through the accusing language of the losers."[28] The times are unpropitious, but they are always unpropitious. More to the point, they are a-changing:

We are a multicultural, multiracial, multihistorical, multireligious people, and we will be even more so in the future. The "leading edge" of this transformation, most evident in metropolitan centers, is the recently arrived immigrant population recruited largely from non-traditional source countries. These new arrivals are not guest workers. They must be treated and conduct themselves as full citizens of a society to whose evolving collective definition they make their own contributions.[29]

Accordingly, it seems to me necessary to cast our rethinking along lines that are sufficiently clear and sufficiently simple that the principles involved will be comprehensible to all Canadians. What is required, therefore, is a coherent account of the purpose of the regime in the light of a more or less adequate understanding of human nature.

This is obviously easier said than done. We can, however, identify the areas of difficulty and probable disagreement, and this at least is a start. As several scholars and commentators have pointed out, there is a fundamental ambivalence in the current constitution; this is neatly captured in Cairns's distinction, mentioned earlier, between the governments' constitution and the citizens' constitution. It seems clear, in the aftermath of the 1992 referendum, that pressure to change the governments' constitution (that is, parliamentary federalism, and the amending formula in particular) has increased in response to the new political reality of rights-bearing citizens taking an interest in "their" constitution. How that change will be accomplished in an institutional sense is anyone's guess, particularly in view of the requirements for changing the amending procedure. Nevertheless, something like the following principles, it seems to me, will have to be invoked.

First in number and in importance is the principle of the equality of citizens. To an extent, this principle is embodied in the Charter, but it is accompanied by non-egalitarian provisions that describe various ethnic, linguistic, cultural, territorial, and gender identities which, by nature, are attributes of groups qua groups, not of collections of citizens.[30] Now it is certainly true that as increasing numbers of "stake holders" claim a place at the constitutional negotiating table, agreement becomes more difficult because group interests are invariably understood as a zero-sum game; hence, the unusual rhetoric noted earlier by Cairns. The unsuccessful attempt by the Government of Canada to identify the Meech Lake process as the "Quebec round" and the post-Meech Lake process as the "Canada round" indicates this clearly. In the face of challenges from Aboriginal peoples as well as from "Charter clientele groups" to the Ontario-Quebec myth of founding peoples, it seems to me that resolution can come only by abandoning group rights entirely. In other words, by expanding the number of groups to whom constitutional recognition is extended, we are increasing the likelihood of short-term deadlock, as each group or its spokesperson seeks both to gain a group advantage and to avoid the stigma of second- or third- or n-class citizenship.

One of the most popular images used to describe Canadian politics has been borrowed from geology. Kent Weaver, for example, discussed the major "fault lines" of Canadian politics, namely, language and region, in his recent study for the Brookings Institution.[31] Like the major fault lines of the earth's crust, if the short-term pressures for movement are not relieved, they will build up to a major earthquake. It seems to me that if we rethink what a constitution is, we are drawn to conclude that the constitutionalization of group politics is not the direction to take, because it will increase pressure for change at the same time as it makes change more difficult to effect. Precisely because the demands of Aboriginals, multicultural groups, visible minorities, the disabled, and other allegedly disadvantaged groups, for constitutional recognition of their implicit but unacknowledgeable disabilities, promises to make constitutional change more difficult, Canadians might be persuaded to remove group characteristics from the constitution altogether. Again, let there be no misunderstanding: group activities are both important and legitimate in liberal democracies. For the same reason that affirmative action programs can never claim a single success, so constitutionalizing group rights will have the effect of removing all sense of pride from the achievements of members of designated groups. What possible reason could citizens in non-designated groups have to respect the achievements that did not belong to the persons who benefited by government action, rather than by their own efforts, but who conceivably might wish to claim the consequence of government action as their own doing? Group rights can, of course, be constitutionally defined – as in the Republic of South Africa until recently, or perhaps under the *sacrum imperium* of medieval Europe – but such regimes are not liberal democracies.

A second formal element of rethinking what the constitution is entails the equality not of citizens but of provinces. This is the underlying formal principle of federalism, just as equality of citizens is the underlying formal principle of liberal and constitutional democracy. This proposal has been supported by various provincial governments from time to time as well as by political scientists who are critical of executive federalism, federal-provincial diplomacy, or interstate federalism. In order to have effective regional or provincial representation in the central institution of the Government of Canada, namely, the Parliament of Canada, numerous proposals for Senate reform have been advanced in recent years. Something along the lines of what has been called a triple-E Senate, that is, a Senate that is elected, effective, and contains equal representation among all provinces (and is in this respect similar to the American and Australian senates) might provide the needed institutional embodiment of the second constitutional principle.

The objection that citizen equality and equality of provinces would never be accepted by the Québécois and their government has been analysed and perhaps answered in *Deconfederation*.[32] However, in that same objection is found the substance of Canada's constitutional dilemma and the chief obstacle to rethinking what a constitution is. A more fundamental obstacle may be found in discerning the limits of Machiavellian politics as currently practised in Canadian political life, and in particular in the limits of Machiavelli's teaching regarding the founding of regimes. Let me conclude by indicating the difficulty. Both Aristotle and Machiavelli agree that necessity is most visible at the beginnings of regimes because human beings are then most vulnerable and most in need of shelter. Both agree that political order is initiated and established for mutual protection. But thereafter they disagree. According to Aristotle, human beings continue their association in order to actualize what he called the good life; and whatever that life was, it was understood as an activity higher in dignity than mere security. For Machiavelli, as was mentioned earlier, we can never be secure enough to relax and pursue the good life in Aristotle's sense or any other sense.

Canadians have been taught, particularly through the myths of the garrison and *la survivance*, that they associated initially (and also thereafter) solely for reasons of life and its necessities, though we interpret these necessities mainly in terms of welfare, not war as did Machiavelli. We need not decide whether welfare is simply bloodless war and efficient population management to notice that Canadian political leaders have been assiduous if unschooled followers of Machiavelli's political teaching. They have learned well how not to be good and how to act on that knowledge; they have learned how to imitate the fox and the lion and how to rule indirectly. It is far from clear, however, whether Canadians find this bargain entirely to their liking. Accordingly, the more fundamental question Canadians must confront if they are to become a sovereign people is, as Peter Russell put it, whether they associate for the sake of safety or for some higher purpose.

COMMENTS ON
BARRY COOPER'S ESSAY
ALAIN NOËL

Halfway through the 1992 referendum campaign, *La Presse* columnist Pierre Foglia went to Windsor, Ontario, to find out the mood of the electorate in that part of Canada which was unknown to most of his readers. "Look at Erie Street," he was told by many, who thus summarized their understanding of Canada. Like all immigrants, Italians who lived around Erie Street had quietly assimilated, keeping only a few folksy traditions for episodic celebrations. Could not Quebeckers do the same? Foglia was asked repeatedly.[33]

Barry Cooper's contribution to this book is an academic version of the "Look at Erie Street" argument, an educated version of the call for an undifferentiated Canada. The Quebec question, argues Cooper, is "at the centre of Canada's current political disorder," and since it will not disappear, it must be solved through disengagement. Disengagement, however, does not mean self-determination for the nations involved; it implies instead the extirpation of the perceived problem through the departure of selected individuals, designated on the basis of ethnicity.

Cooper's conclusions derive from his definition of the problem. For him, Canada's constitutional difficulties stem from Quebec's demand for "group rights," a demand that he deems incompatible with the country's integrity as a federal, liberal, and constitutional democracy. Canada could acquiesce to Quebec's demand, Cooper notes, but it would then cease to be a liberal democracy and would join South Africa and medieval regimes in their constitutional recognition of group rights. The confusion here is twofold. First, Cooper wrongly assumes that group rights are incompatible with liberalism. Second, he confuses Quebec's demand for recognition with demands for group rights of a different type, and notably with demands coming from minority ethnic groups.

On the first idea, which portrays group rights as incompatible with liberal democracy, not much needs to be said, except that it stems from an unnecessarily narrow understanding of the liberal requirement for citizen equality. If group rights are defined as rights "ascribed to collections of individuals and ... exercised collectively ... through some mechanism of political representation," one must acknowledge, with political philosopher Allen Buchanan, that "many existing constitutions in what are generally recognized as liberal states include both individual and group rights, without any obvious evidence of incoherence or inconsistency."[34] The very triple-E Senate advocated by Cooper would constitutionalize group rights: "In *democratic* federal systems," notes Buchanan, "the rights ascribed to subunits (e.g., cantons or provinces) are to be understood, ultimately, as collective rights of the citizens of those subunits."[35] What matters for liberal democracies is not the presence or the absence of group rights, but rather the specific articulation between various types of rights and the justifications given for each type.

Barry Cooper's problem with group rights is by no means unique or distinctive. A central feature of the majoritarian impulse to deny Quebec's distinct status, Cooper's argument also reflects a procedural view of liberal democracy that has become predominant in English Canada.[36] As such, the argument is constitutive of one of Canada's main conceptions of justice. Barry Cooper, however, does not simply refuse the possibility of group rights. He defines these rights in a very particular way and, in so doing, prepares the ground for more pernicious arguments.

While he confuses liberal democracy with purely individual procedures, Barry Cooper also distorts the meaning of group rights by associating them loosely with social rights or with ethnic identities. Consider, for instance, Cooper's characterization of the welfare state. For him, "well-intentioned welfare policies" epitomize the "highly questionable nature" of group rights: as they create "guaranteed" rights, such policies transform groups of beneficiaries "into dependents of the state" and separate them from citizens, who "are compelled to become generous and caring taxpayers." The assumption here is that beneficiaries of welfare programs constitute a "group" supported by "rights." In fact, welfare programs benefit all of Cooper's "generous and caring taxpayers." Health and education alone account for more than half of Canada's welfare spending; assistance programs with income tests, on the other hand, represent less than 15 per cent of the total.[37] Moreover, recipients of public assistance do not constitute a stable group. Every year, more than 25 per cent of the poor move out of poverty and are replaced by others who were previously above poverty levels. Income security programs are also characterized by "a substantial turnover" and cannot be portrayed as the way of life of a given, well-defined group.[38] The confusion here is intended and interested: the invention of a group that can be castigated for its abuses of social benefits gives credence to the conservative view of welfare programs as major disincentives to work.

With respect to Quebec, which Barry Cooper sees as Canada's key constitutional problem, the procedure is similar. A group, "the French," is invented, to assimilate Quebec's demand for recognition with the particular claims of an ethnic interest group. In this case, the confusion is between Quebec as a society and French Canadians as an ethnic group. Cooper's entire argument flows from the definitions given in footnote 1. "For purposes of this argument," he explains, "*Canadians* refers to the multiethnic English-speaking citizens of Canada; *Québécois* refers to the French-speaking citizens of the Province of Quebec who identify with the ethnic descendants of the colonists of New France, whether or not they are *pure laine*, or 'old stock,' in any genealogical sense." Canadian society, Cooper posits, is multiethnic; Quebec society, on the other hand, is defined by ethnicity, regardless of genealogy. Thus, Pierre Foglia, whose parents were born in Italy, becomes, by self-identification with Quebec society, an "ethnic descendant of New France"; and so, I suppose, does James Tully. On the other hand, the Coopers, Bercusons, and Mannings all become part of a multiethnic, pluralist Canada. Clear implications follow from these definitions. First, Quebec's demands for recognition can be characterized as unliberal demands centred on ethnicity. Second, Canada's reluctance to recognize Quebec as a distinct society can be legitimated on liberal grounds. Third, harsh terms can be set for the eventuality of Quebec's independence.

In his chapter for this book, James Tully explains how Quebec constitutes not an ethnic entity but a global society, a pluralist and multiethnic nation just like English Canada. Since the Quebec Act of 1774, Tully argues, Quebec society has always been recognized, except in 1982 when long-respected conventions were broken. Hence, there is nothing new in Quebec's demand for recognition. There is nothing illiberal either; recognition and consent were constitutive of liberal societies.

The confusion between Quebec's demand for recognition and the claims of an ethnic group may be the result of a narrow understanding of liberalism. In Cooper's work, however, more seems at play. In *Deconfederation*, for instance, David Bercuson and Barry Cooper accept a breach in their procedural liberalism to recognize Aboriginal peoples, but they still define Quebec's demands as those of "the French." They then proceed to explain that since "the French" want to secede on ethnic grounds, others can do the same. On this basis, Bercuson and Cooper redraw the borders of an independent Quebec along perceived ethnic lines, leaving nothing to the new state but areas that they see as clearly "French."[39] Thus, an intellectual project claiming to reassert liberal values ends up dividing populations in the name of presumed ethnic identities. With these partition proposals, Cooper's confusion between national and ethnic demands fulfils its purpose. Reducing Quebec to an ethnic group allows the author to go well beyond the usual call for a purely procedural liberalism. With David Bercuson, Barry Cooper invents ethnic opponents, allocates them territories, and prepares and justifies a vindictive politics of ethnicity.

When he discusses Quebec's demand for recognition, Barry Cooper draws a comparison with South African apartheid. Facile comparisons between the rather civil disputes of Canadian politics and abhored practices abroad are always unfair to the Canadian proponents of legitimate views, and even more so to the victims of truly criminal practices. I must therefore refrain from associating Cooper's conclusion with a politics which, in the former Yugoslavia, has degenerated into "ethnic purification." It remains that, in the name of liberalism, Cooper proposes to draw what amounts to ethnic battle lines. It is sad for a liberal to end up defending such a position.

4 Constitution Making and the Myth of the People

JANET AJZENSTAT

Unhappy is that country which is obliged to reform her constitution.
Machiavelli

A number of dubious assumptions about the role of citizens in liberal democracies plague Canada's ongoing constitutional debate. The crucial one – to my knowledge, never explored or challenged – is that liberal democracies require public involvement in the constitutional process. Canadians have simply taken it for granted that because liberal democracies facilitate popular participation in day-to-day politics, they must as a matter of course promote popular participation in constitution making.

The argument of this paper is, first, that liberal democratic theory warns against popular participation in the process of drawing up a new constitution and, secondly, that the participation of political groups, interests, and individual Canadians in the negotiations is heightening contestation in the constitutional arena and hastening the country's breakup.[1]

I do not argue that liberal democratic theory objects to citizen participation in the drafting and ratifying of ordinary constitutional amendments. What is frowned on is citizen participation in the process of founding. Canadians today are not involved in debate on

The author acknowledges the assistance of the Social Sciences and Humanities Research Council of Canada (Strategic Grant 806-90-1002) and thanks the following for their helpful comments: Howard Adelman, Leah Bradshaw, Joseph Carens, and Reg Whitaker, as well as the participants in the Conference on the Canadian Constitution held at Colorado College in the fall of 1992.

limited constitutional reforms. What we are doing bears no resemblance, for example, to the kind of constitutional debate the Americans engaged in over the equal rights amendment. We are refounding the country. We have convinced ourselves that if we are to survive as Canadians, we must have an entirely new constitution.[2]

In the textbook definition, constitutions (1) define the form of government; (2) in a federal system, determine relations between the levels of government; (3) protect individual and political rights; and (4) provide for the amendment of the constitution.[3] Canadians are contemplating changes in all four dimensions, and some observers are of the opinion that we will only resolve the constitutional dilemma by making the constitutional reform agenda as inclusive as possible.[4]

Let me give a brief preliminary outline of the liberal democratic position. It is true that liberal democracy welcomes popular participation in day-to-day politics. Why, then, does it discourage participation at the constitutional level? The argument is that the constitution is superior law, defining the limits of government power and the conditions of participation in the political process; if the citizen's individual and political rights are to be secure, that superior law must not be open to political manipulation. To put it simply, liberal theory regards the constitution as the rule book for the political game. A good rule book should not be changed too abruptly or too often and – most important – not by the players while they are on the ice.

It is widely acknowledged that the Canadian political scene has never been more divisive and that there has been a staggering loss of public confidence in the political system.[5] What is usually said is that the divisiveness and loss of confidence stem from Canadians' exasperation at the limited opportunities for participation in politics, especially the politics of the constitutional process.[6] The suggestion here is that the divisiveness and loss of confidence may well be the consequence of subjecting the constitution to the push and pull of political interests as groups and individuals exercise what they have come to regard as their democratic right to participate in constitution making.

PARTICIPATION IN CONSTITUTIONAL REFORM

The debate on the Meech Lake Accord dealt as much with the process of constitutional reform as with the substance. Virtually all participants – academics, political leaders, the media, individual Canadians – regardless of their views on the package as a whole, argued that the amending procedures were seriously flawed because they denied the Canadian public a significant role.[7] Deborah Coyne's denunciation of the Meech process is typical: "Eleven men sat around a table trading legislative, judicial, and executive power as if engaged in a gentlemanly game of poker, with little regard for the concerns of individual Canadians."[8]

In the period after the failure of Meech, proposals to enhance participation proliferated. The one favoured by most people would have given constitution-making powers to a constituent assembly, elected or nominated according to a formula that would guarantee its representative and popular character.[9] Amendments drafted by this body would be ratified in a national referendum.[10] The appeal of the constituent assembly lay in the idea that Canadians would speak directly on constitutional issues, circumventing the cabal of politicians that had been responsible for the Meech debacle. Former Supreme Court Justice Willard Estey argued that "the people must have a direct voice, undistorted by brokerage politics between the Prime Minister and the premiers."[11] Premier Gary Filmon proposed an assembly composed of "people from ordinary walks of life, opinion leaders, [and a] various cross-section of people from every region of this country." It was important, he said, to "take away from the perception that the Constitution is only the product of the thinking of elected people."[12]

Although the Conservative government rejected the idea of a constituent assembly, arguing that Canada's elected representatives in Parliament and the provincial legislatures had the authority to speak for the country on constitutional issues, it was obliged to make concessions to the demand for a participatory process. Launching the post-Meech round of negotiations in the spring of 1991, Prime Minister Brian Mulroney and Constitutional Affairs Minister Joe Clark promised to encourage participation through public forums. The Spicer forum was the model. The idea was to allow individual Canadians to have their say on constitutional issues early in the process, before reform proposals were put in final form by the first ministers.[13] The decision to hold a national referendum after the Charlottetown Accord had been drafted followed naturally.

It hardly needs to be said that the Conservatives' measures did not gratify everyone. Anne Bayefsky wrote early in 1992: "There is a massive effort by the federal government to create the illusion of public consultation. Exhaust the country with the Constitution and then spring the solution on the populace three months from now."[14] A month before the referendum, another observer complained that the government was unwilling to give Canadians "real power" in the constitutional arena; the Conservatives, he said, were not "really serious about involving people in constitutional change."[15] It is impossible to tell to what degree dissatisfaction with the constitutional process contributed to the No vote; it was surely a factor. Even the fact that ardent advocates of popular constitution making such as Clyde Wells were in favour of the Charlottetown Accord could not erase the idea that the process leading to Charlottetown had been as offensively elitist as the process that had led to Meech. Two very different arguments for enhanced participation surfaced during this period. The first, implicit in the government's proposals for consultative forums, suggested that it was crucial that a wide variety of political groups and interests – especially those that had been slighted in past debates – be welcomed at the bargaining table. The second, contained in the argument for a constituent assembly, rejected the idea that participation in the constitutional process should involve groups, parties, and interests. The great merit of a constituent assembly, according to this second line of thought, was that it would represent the people and the country, rather than interests and regions, and so be better able to forge a national consensus.

In the heat of political debate a speaker sometimes drew on both lines of thought, but it is important to distinguish them: the one suggests that a constitution should reflect contributions from the country's organized political groups, regions, sectors, and so on. The other abhors the idea of a constitution as an aggregation of particular demands. It suggests indeed that constitution making by organized political interests contributes to the likelihood of failure in the constitutional arena. Underlying the two positions are different visions of good government. The argument for the inclusion of groups rests – shakily – on the idea I have already described as problematic: that liberal democracy demands popular participation in constitution making as well as in day-to-day politics. The second draws on a doctrine that is in many ways opposed to liberal democracy. I am not suggesting that everyone who argued for a constituent assembly favoured the overthrow of liberal democracy. It is the case, however, that the effort to marry an analysis of the problems inherent in constitution making by lobbies to the demand for a participatory constitutional process led some Canadians to flirt with a definition of democracy that is first cousin to the totalitarian form of "people's government" so recently rejected by the states of Eastern Europe. In this paper I endorse the criticisms of the Meech process that are implicit in arguments for a constituent assembly, but I reject the assembly alternative.

As other essays in this volume argue, Canada's constitutional saga is not over. The demands of Aboriginals and the people of Quebec for recognition in the Canadian constitution are still alive. It is entirely possible that with the election of new governments at the federal level and in Quebec, still another round of constitution making will begin. At the same time, it is very clear that future amendments will not be regarded as legitimate unless they are drafted and ratified by procedures that are at least as participatory as those that contributed to the making (and unmaking) of Charlottetown. If the argument of this paper is correct – that encouraging participation heightens contestation in the constitutional arena, eroding confidence in the impartiality of constitutional law – then the attempt to legitimate future constitutional amendments will, paradoxically, undermine their legitimacy, involving the country in still further demands for reform of process and substance.

Canadians are caught between a rock and a hard place. We must have constitutional reform if we are to hold the country together. But we can only obtain reforms by means of procedures which themselves threaten to destroy the federation. Readers will ask what remedy I propose for the gloomy situation I describe. Can anything be done to increase the likelihood of achieving a constitutional settlement that Canadians will tolerate? As a theorist, I feel no compulsion to offer remedies. As a citizen, I am desperate for one. What weak comfort I have to offer is suggested in the conclusion.

PARTICIPATION AND CONTESTATION

The conviction that the people of Canada are being shut out of constitutional negotiations has grown as opportunities for participation have increased. The Meech Lake Accord is usually depicted as the prime example of elitist constitution making. In reality, it was the most widely and publicly debated constitutional proposal to that point in our history. The fact that there were few opportunities for groups to influence the wording of the accord before it was presented to the public is undoubtedly what people have in mind when they argue that the Meech process was not participatory. The fact remains that Meech was rejected, and that before it was rejected it was the subject of passionate debate among all sectors and regions of the country. Complaints that Meech shut people out are not convincing unless they focus solely on the drafting process. I have already suggested that complaints about the lack of opportunities for participation in the Charlottetown process are even less well founded. There is indeed something profoundly perplexing about the fact that Canadians continue to entertain the idea that the process of drafting and ratifying amendments to the constitution is elitist while they are involving themselves in that process to an unprecedented degree.

What explains the anxiety attached to constitutional politics, the perception of being left out, unrepresented and unrecognized? Popular constitution making began in earnest with the making of the Constitution Act, 1982. Alan Cairns describes the 1982 Act as the "precarious result of a byzantine process in which accidents, personality, skill and sheer will power were central to the final outcome."[16] The signal feature of the process was the participation of organized political interests representing a broad spectrum of popular opinion. Human rights commissions, civil liberties groups, bar associations, research institutes, and groups supporting the rights of women, the handicapped, the gay community, and ethnic minorities reviewed the various drafts of the 1982 Act emanating from meetings of the federal and provincial governments, seeking to influence the wording of clauses in the Charter of Rights and Freedoms, and fighting attempts by the provincial premiers to dilute the Charter's effects.[17] Observers at the time welcomed the participation of the public in Charter making as a salutary check on the high-handedness of Canada's governing elites.[18] It is not as clear today that group involvement has been without troublesome consequences.

The insertion of section 28 in the Charter is regarded as a victory for the feminist movement.[19] Sections 25 and 35 were a victory (if an uncertain one) for native peoples.[20] Multicultural groups take credit for section 27, and minority language groups for sections 16 to 23.[21] Feminists, ethnic associations, and groups representing the handicapped and aged were successful in their struggle to secure mention of their clients and members in 15(1) and (2). In contrast, right-to-life groups, homosexual rights organizations, and advocates of property rights did not secure recognition.[22]

The assumption, not usually stated, was that those whose characteristics were specifically mentioned in the Charter would be entitled to political benefits of a kind that the "unlisted" would not enjoy.[23] "Since 1985, women have achieved remarkable advances," argues Kathleen Mahoney, "largely due to Charter guarantees of equality before and under the law and the right to equal protection and equal benefit of the law without discrimination."[24] Her claim is that feminist organizations have been able to obtain political objectives that would have been impossible if they had lost the battle over sections 28 and 15. The unstated corollary is that the groups that were not successful are unlikely to enjoy similar advances.

That constitutional recognition confers advantages in the legislative and judicial arenas has been argued by a number of political scientists.[25] We do not have to suggest that Charter groups always have the advantage.[26] The perception that some groups may be privileged is enough to spur contestation. Groups are involved in a constant struggle to gain and maintain constitutional status. Among the interests most vociferously protesting the Meech Lake Accord were aboriginal and multicultural organizations, feminists, and minority language associations; in other words, the groups that had been successful in securing recognition in the 1982 Act.[27] Having their rights enshrined in the 1982 Act proved a source of anxiety rather than assurance for these groups. The same groups again were involved in the scramble be included and to be ranked well in the Canada clause of the Charlottetown Accord.

If the Charter was intended as a unifying force in this country, it has surely failed. It was meant to counter the divisive forces of regionalism; individuals would know that their rights were theirs as Canadians rather than as citizens of a province or region. Perhaps the notion of a bill of rights as unifying was doomed from the first; most of Canada's national symbols (the CBC, the railways, medicare) express satisfaction with law and government rather than a desire for individual liberty. In any event, it is not clear that the Charter has countered regionalism, and it is very clear that it has introduced a new and dangerously intolerant kind of divisiveness – the quarrel among sectors of the polity for constitutional ascendancy.[28]

This is not the place to embark on a debate about the degree of national feeling and sense of citizenship that obtained in this country before 1982. (Was there ever a sense of Canadianness of the kind George Grant describes?) What I am convinced of is that a sense of national community cannot survive constitutional politicking. Canadians have been able to think of only one response to Canadian divisiveness – more public participation in constitution making. Our favoured remedy is killing the patient.

CONSTITUTIONAL POLITICS

As the constitutional reform agenda lengthened, more opportunities opened for group contestation. Reporting a speech by Constitutional Affairs Minister Joe Clark on the national unity issue in June 1991, Graham Fraser said, "There are fundamental disagreements about the future shape of the country that make it hard to see how a constitutional agreement can be reached that does not simply replace the existing deadlock with another one." He went on: "For despite the repeated suggestions by Mr Clark and Prime Minister Brian Mulroney that the national unity debate should be non-partisan, it is clear that every constitutional proposal inevitably reflects ideological and political assumptions."[29]

To illustrate his point, Fraser noted that while the New Democratic Party was calling for the enshrinement of social and economic rights in the Charter, the Ontario wing of the Liberal Party of Canada was demanding reform of the division of legislative powers and other constitutional measures to strengthen Canada's "economic integration." At the same time, the organization known as the Group of 22 was arguing for constitutional recognition of "four economic freedoms – the free movement of labour, capital, goods and services." As Fraser argued, the demands were ideologically incompatible. If the NDP had its way, Canada's constitution would reflect socialist principles. If the Liberal proposal or the Group of 22 was successful, the constitution would enshrine the principles of the economic market.[30] These groups were demanding that particular modes of distributive justice, that is, particular political ideologies, be given an advantage through clauses inserted in the constitution.[31]

Constitutional politicking is a new phenomenon in this country. I have implied that it began with the making of the 1982 Constitution Act. Donald Smiley argues that the intrusion of political demands into the constitutional debate began with pressures emanating from Quebec in the years after the Quiet Revolution: "Up until the 1960s all but a few of the Canadians seriously concerned with public affairs were constitutional conservatives in the sense that they did not believe that the values and interests they respectively espoused required explicit constitutional reforms."[32] It is certainly the case that what was novel in the 1960s is now commonplace. David Milne contends that Canadian political leaders now routinely look to constitutional change as a remedy for grievances whose causes lie in the complexities of a modern political economy.[33]

Let me suggest the following scenario. Quarrels among governments in the 1960s and early 1970s taught the lesson that there are political gains to be made in the constitutional arena. Once this perception was abroad, political interest groups were bound to demand a place at the constitutional table and bound to resent attempts by the old club of eleven to slam the door on them.[34] To legitimate their demand for inclusion, groups portrayed participation in the constitutional arena as a democratic right, like the democratic right to petition in electoral politics and in the legislature. And as the argument for popular involvement in constitution making gained ground, the demand for participation escalated. Groups that hung back from the fray soon realized how much there was to lose if they did not formulate demands in the new political arena.

It is time for a closer look at the distinction, briefly sketched in the introductory section of this paper, between statute law and constitutional law, and between participation in the ordinary business of politics and participation in constitution making. Smiley's comments about "constitutional conservatives" are instructive. What grounded the conservatives' assumption that their political values and interests did not require explicit constitutional expression was the supposition that constitutional law is neutral with respect to political argument and ideology. For the constitutional conservative, ideology is the stuff of day-to-day politics; the constitution, as superior law, is above it. For the purposes of this paper, we do not have to ask whether the liberal constitution is in fact always neutral, or strives for neutrality. It will be enough if readers accept Smiley's suggestion that until sometime in the 1960s when the search for a new constitution began in earnest, Canadians conducted their political life in the belief that the rules of the political game were not irredeemably biased.[35]

Where the constitution is regarded as neutral, politicking in the political arena will be a relatively benign affair. The competition among parties, and the jockeying of organized groups and interests – during elections, in the media, and in the legislature and representative bodies – furthers the aggregation of diverse interests to produce legislation for the common good and confers legitimacy on the outcome. Open debate confers legitimacy because, under a neutral constitution, laws are always open to challenge. It is the boast of the liberal state that it does nothing to limit complaint and debate, and nothing to prevent opposition groups and parties from organizing to plot the overthrow of particular laws and policies. As decrees of the executive branch of government, laws must be obeyed; as measures emanating from the legislative branch, they may be endlessly contested.[36] The fact of debate and popular participation does not undermine the requirement to obey; and the fact that obedience is required does not limit continuing debate. The result (we must imagine our constitutional conservative arguing) is that no political loss is entirely without remedy. If interests remain unaggregated and if the players retain their energy, the game can be endless. Those who fall rise to fight again.

The important point for this paper is the suggestion that the contestation inherent in day-to-day politics is manageable because (or if) the political actors assume that no class or interest is constitutionally privileged. It is manageable because the actors believe that the constitution is neutral. Now we must ask, What happens when the struggle for political advantage is carried on in an arena where the assumption of constitutional neutrality is one of the issues in the debate?

In 1984 Alan Cairns described what he saw as the task before Canadians then: "We need to find a ... resting place, with meanings we can all share, which contains and accommodates our rampaging differences within a framework of tolerance and civility."[37] For the constitutional conservative the framework that best accommodates rampaging differences, ensuring tolerance and at least a degree of civility, is the neutral constitution. I suggest that if we are still searching today for the Canadian resting place that Cairns describes, it is because, for a variety of reasons – not least the fact of constitutional politicking – Canadians are no longer sure that the neutral framework, indeed any framework, is possible.

Graham Fraser argued that recent constitutional proposals reflect ideological assumptions. It is not clear that he would go so far as to say that such proposals are inevitably ideological and that it is absurd to posit the idea of a neutral "framework" or constitution to mediate the battle of ideological groups. But the idea that the neutrality assumption of liberal democracy is merely one more ideological position has long been mooted by political philosophers.[38] Marxists argue that the liberal constitution is the invention of the wealthy, benefiting the few at the expense of the many. Feminists maintain that it is the product of male thinking, upholding the patriarchy and oppressing women.[39] Within liberalism itself there is a continuing debate about whether the liberal constitution entails welfarism. Rawls's liberal democratic constitution demands one ideological posture; Nozick's requires quite another.

The damaging – or liberating – idea that the liberal democratic constitution is an ideology, or that it privileges some ideological measures, was bound to escape from the political theory classroom sooner or later. The great problem for Canadians is that the moment has come sooner. In the next round of constitution making the challenge will be not merely to meet the demands of Quebec and the Aboriginal peoples, to redraw the country's boundaries, to incorporate the interests of the provinces, territories, and federal government, and to pacify the Charter groups; the constitution makers will also have to cope with the suggestion that all rules by which the demands made by those participating in the process might be mediated are contestable – because all constitutional rules are ideologically biased. Canadians are attempting to remake a liberal democratic constitution at a time when the virtue has gone out of ideas such as universality, neutrality, and objectivity, which are the enabling ideas of liberal democracy.

Had constitutional reform proceeded at a modest pace, we might have escaped some of the consequences of the recent revolution in political thought. Not all constitutional change with an ideological bent provokes deep rancour – if introduced gradually. The growth of the positive state made radical changes in the Canadian political system and constitution without rousing the kind of devastating contestation that is now threatening the country. As I suggested in my introduction, it is the scale of the proposed constitutional changes that is making the difference. There is today scarcely an aspect of the constitution that is not described as flawed, elitist, discriminatory, or unjust.

Demands for constitutional reform have the form of pleas for justice on the part of groups that have been deprived. A few claims of this kind do not necessarily imply that the constitution was thoroughly and inescapably unjust in the past; but as the constitutional agenda lengthens, it becomes harder not to draw that lesson. The more it is argued that particular demands will benefit the groups in question, the more obvious it becomes that although the proposals may well benefit groups or regions or governments, it will be at the expense of other groups and national interests – and the easier it becomes to regard the constitution as the product of battling ideologies in an arena where strength wins the day. The idea of the liberal democratic constitution as a framework that enables and contains the jockeying of parties, interests, and ideologies, while guaranteeing citizens an area of freedom from government intrusion, grows ever more distant.

Readers must not conclude that I would recommend a return to the happy ignorance of previous days, before assumptions about the neutral constitution became a matter of debate. Return is impossible. Pandora's constitutional box is open. But more than this, arguments for a return to the neutral constitution will only stoke the anxiety of today's constitutional contestants, increasing divisiveness. The attempt to resurrect notions of neutrality, constitutional law as superior law, and rights as inalienable – those ideas so dear to the constitutional conservative – would inevitably be interpreted as an attempt by dominant groups to entrench their gains. It would be taken as a bid to define out of the game groups whose constitutional agenda is not yet complete – an attack on the underdogs, the final proof that the system is undemocratic, elitist, and ideologically biased.

CONSENSUS AND CONSENSUS BUILDING

What has been said so far in this paper argues that past participation in constitution making and demands for a still more participatory process are exacerbating political contestation to the point where it can barely be accommodated. We must now consider the claims of those who argued that a measure such as a constituent assembly would secure the consensus on which a new constitution could be erected. This is the argument that distrusts the participation of organized political interests in constitution making for many of the reasons that I myself have given. It is bound to be resurrected if there is another round of constitution making, and after the picture I have just sketched, it may seem like the voice of sweet reason.

In the post-Meech period the Canada West Foundation argued that "constitutional reform is too important to leave to the regular partisan-dominated political process."[40] Keith Spicer called for a "manifestly non-partisan" constitutional constituent assembly.[41] We can imagine our constitutional conservative nodding with approval at this aspect of the argument for a constituent assembly. He or she is as convinced as any proponent of the constituent assembly that the constitution should not be subject to contestation by particular political interests.

The problematic aspect of the argument for a constituent assembly lies in the idea that it will transcend particular demands by requiring consensus. The constituent assembly is to rise above ideology by expressing the will of all. The minority report of the Beaudoin-Edwards committee argued that a constituent assembly would yield a "truly national consensus to point the way out of the maze in which we are lost."[42] Participants in an academic forum held in April 1991 argued that the constitutional process should be guided by a new "rule of consensus." Spicer contended that in any constitution-making procedure "the rule would be extremely high consensus."[43]

The suggestion was that only the ill will or incompetence of politicians and interests wedded to the established institutions was preventing us from realizing a Canada in which we can say yes to everyone's projects and ambitions.[44] When "special" and "partisan" interests are eliminated from the political process, the pure, single-minded will of "the people" will float to the surface. In this argument, "representation" and "participation" take on a meaning foreign to Canadian experience and traditions to date. A representative body is to speak for all citizens, for the people as a whole, and not for a majority or for an aggregation of interests. Participation in the new definition demands more than that everyone be guaranteed an opportunity to engage in debate. The requirement is that all must find their contribution mirrored in the final consensus.

The argument for consensus began as an element in proposals for a constituent assembly but is now applied to day-to-day politics. What is commonly said now is not merely that consensus is required for the pre-political constitutional process; it is that a consensual process is preferable to parliamentary democracy. By the new definitions of representation and participation, Canada's legislatures are not and never have been representative and the parliamentary system is not democratic.[45] In the words of one theorist, the "parliamentary process is adversarial and majoritarian, the antithesis of a process that not only hears all voices but takes all experiences and aspirations into account."[46] The Spicer commissioners noted their agreement with the forum's participants who suggested that the parliamentary system is "too partisan and far too adversarial."[47]

The phrases "active politicians" and "elected people" have become terms of abuse.[48] The minority report of the Beaudoin-Edwards committee maintained that "parliamentarians have no monopoly on creativity, intelligence, or concern for the fate of the nation." It continued, "Government suggestions that they are the only proper representatives of the people's will, when the people themselves are telling us that they are not, are unacceptable manifestations of political ego."[49]

That "dialogue" among "non-politicians" on constitutional issues would be more productive than meetings of elected representatives was argued at length in *Maclean's* magazine in July 1991.[50] With the help of Decima Research, *Maclean's* chose twelve Canadians to represent the dominant lines of thinking on the constitutional crisis. Conflict management experts from Harvard University presided over a weekend meeting of these representative citizens, described by *Maclean's* as a model for resolving Canada's crisis. The fact that no one participating knew about the framing of constitutions or the procedural details of politics was suggested as reason to have confidence in their conclusions. The proposals endorsed by the twelve were meant to "diminish dramatically" the power of political parties.[51]

Is this sudden Canadian enthusiasm for consensus and the general will merely a romantic indulgence? Do its proponents realize how far from the traditions of liberal democracy their proposals would lead us? Bernard Crick tells us that the alternative to a political regime is a regime of slavery; although politics is often unsavoury, government without politics is intolerable.[52] The idea of living in a "people's democracy" where the government speaks for all is now anathema to the inhabitants of Eastern Europe and the former Soviet Union. They are struggling to establish political parties that can compete for office, and political interest groups that can articulate the views of sectors of the society. Canadians speak as if they hope to abolish parties and interest groups. We are indulging in the language of political tyranny.

Despite our apparent enthusiasm for the consensual, apolitical regime, I do not think that Canada will be given over to democratic tyranny.[53] The prospect is utterly incompatible with anything in the Canadian experience. The danger associated with the demand for consensus is, rather, that it heightens the contestation and divisiveness of constitutional debate. In fact, I suggest, the argument for consensus is being put forward by political leaders who hope to legitimate particular claims by defining the consensus. The idea of "the people" and the popular will has different meanings, depending on the speaker.

To see the ramifications of what I am saying here, we must take another look at the constitutional interest groups. Lack of confidence in the political system, distrust of politicians, dissatisfaction with opportunities for effective citizen participation, impatience with political forms and formalities: such signs of political unrest are found not only in Canada but in most of the Western nations today. Many of the complaints articulated by the Canadians who appeared before the Spicer Commission could have been duplicated in the United States, Britain, Australia, and Western Europe. The phenomenon is commonly referred to as "new politics."[54] Canada's Charter groups exhibit all the signs of the "new politics." Their political objectives cannot easily be subsumed under the categories of the old right-left spectrum. They are "postmaterialist," that is, concerned not so much with material benefits for their clients and members as with "recognition" and with opportunities for the expression of political demands.[55] They espouse "individual expression and quality of life," as one observer put it.[56]

This is not the place to discuss the effects of the shift to new politics in the ordinary political process of the legislative arena. Here I want to say only that the shift has had special consequences for Canada because Canadian political debates are now so closely linked to demands for constitutional reform. The demands of "new politics" groups are less amenable to conciliation through the bargaining and trade-offs that are a feature of quantitative who-gets-what-when-and-how politics. Postmaterialist arguments wear the mantle of principle; to compromise is to compromise principle. What this means in Canada is that groups seized with a vision of the good operate in an arena where the terms of political mediation and the rules of political debate are not a given, but are one more item on an ever-changing reform agenda. New politics adds a further dimension of intolerance to the contestation in the arena of constitutional debate.

Our problem in Canada is not that we have suddenly conceived a passion for democratic tyranny. It is that at some point in our recent history we opened the door to popular participation in constitution making. There are no certain rules of political debate in the constitutional arena, because the rules of political debate are what is at issue. There are no limits on the kinds of demand that can be advanced, because the redefinition of limits is the task in hand. Canadians now conduct much of their political debate in an arena where the prizes go to the strongest.

CONCLUSION

Participatory constitution making is promoting the kind of profound discontent with the constitutional order that erodes the sense of nationhood and threatens liberal democracy. But a non participatory constitutional process can now have no legitimacy. Is there a way to resolve this dilemma?

After Meech Lake, Roger Gibbins suggested that we find hope in the simple fact that constitutional reform is becoming more difficult to achieve. If constitutional politics proves unprofitable, political interests may be forced, in sheer desperation, to abandon the dangerous battle for constitutional advantage and return to the relatively benign jockeying of day-to-day politics.[57] Canadians would be left to live with the damage that has been done. We could hope that the settled habits of 125 years would pull us through. It might be added that even "new politics" presupposes a certain level of prosperity, a secure and ordered social life, freedom of speech, and political debate.[58] In other words, it takes for granted many of the benefits of the old liberal democratic constitution.

It is also important that although Canadians appear to be convinced that enhanced participation in the constitutional process is necessary, they are not convinced that reform of the constitution is the most important issue facing the country.[59] If reviving feelings of nationhood, if common sense about the conditions necessary for life in a free and prosperous country do not save us, perhaps sheer apathy will.

COMMENTS ON
JANET AJZENSTAT'S ESSAY
ROBERT J. JACKSON

With the indulgence of our chairman, I shall repeat what I said yesterday at the World Affairs Council – that there is a joke that must always be told in the United States about this topic of the Canadian constitution. It goes like this. In a prison where an American and a Canadian were on death row, the warden came by the day before they were going to die and said, "We always give prisoners one last wish. What would you like yours to be?" The Canadian said, "I'd just like to discuss the constitution one more time," to which the American said, "Then shoot me dead right now."

Now, I agree with almost everything in the Ajzenstat paper and found it to be an intelligent and provocative assessment. But I am in the difficult position of having to comment after hearing this morning some exciting commentaries on the referendum process, especially the discussion of principles. So, in effect, I do not intend to discuss principles at all.

When I was a young student at Oxford, we had two types of speaker. There were analysts and specimens. The specimens were the politicians, who were analysed like insects – put under a microscope. These are the people who were on the Yes and No sides of the referendum campaign. The analysts were the professors who came to study the politicians or activists. On this topic I am a specimen, and I regard most Canadian political scientists as being specimens as well. In fact, I was quite surprised to hear at this conference that there are a few people in Canada commenting on the question of the constitution who do not seem to be specimens. If you examine which political scientists were commenting during the referendum campaign, you will find that almost all, in one way or another, were in the pockets of either the Yes or No campaign – being paid as much as $80,000 by the Federal-Provincial Relations Office or some other government agency for discussing aspects of the constitution. There were a few political scientists who were not paid by one party or the other. I, a specimen, was totally on the No side. I was not, however, paid and I am sure that now that I've taken such a strong No position, I probably won't be being paid in the future either.

Regarding referendums in general, Professor Ajzenstat has told us that there are always problems with them, and I think Canadians may have learned that lesson by now. No matter how many times some of us wrote and told the Canadian public that referendums would divide the country – that they would inevitably separate the people into corrosive Yes and No forces, and that there would not be a consensus – they went ahead and had one anyway. If we examine referendums around the world, we find that almost all of them ended up dividing people, and in the countries that are most similar to Canada, they ended up dividing people in such a way that the majority usually voted No. We should remember that in the two earlier Canadian national referendums, in 1898 and 1942, the people divided into two camps, English and French, and in both cases there was a lot of corrosive fallout from what happened.[60] But I think a better example might be to look at Australia. That country has had forty-two referendums on the constitution, and almost all have failed. Only eight passed, and they were on fairly detailed, administrative questions. As soon as some emotion or corrosive ideas were added to them, the referendums died. I think Canadians now have learned the lesson that we shouldn't be having referendums at all. So although I was totally on the No side, which I supported in every way possible, in fact I thought that we should not be holding a referendum.

Having discussed the specimens, I shall now say a few words about the politics of the referendum campaign. In my opinion, most of the rhetoric could be dichotomized into two kinds of argument. One was "If you're not on the Yes side, you're making the country fall apart." This was well illustrated this morning. During the campaign there was a huge propaganda effort backed by an amazing amount of money. When you add the cost of the referendum itself and all the publicity, the total amount is staggering – especially for a country going through difficult financial times. Then there was the No side, which I think has not been discussed at all. Those of us on the No side did not make much attempt to discuss the content of the proposals either. I agree that we did push the content as much as we could, but basically we did so in order to make people concerned about the changes, to make them think there might be hidden things in the accord, things that could frighten them. I think, in fact, that we did this fairly well. In referendum politics, each side attempts to exploit a simple, easy principle that can be driven into the body politic. For example, in the American election campaign, the debate came down to "Are we going to have change or are we not going to have change?" Bill Clinton exploited this to the maximum. Parties do the same type of thing in referendums.

Let me go back to the free trade deal that some of you have mentioned. I was the senior policy adviser to the Liberal party during the period before the last general election, and I would like to give you some background on how the Liberals decided to oppose the free trade deal, since this has not been written down. More than a year before the general election, the first day I went to work on Parliament Hill, Mr John Turner asked me to go for a walk behind the hill. This was not a walk in the snow. This was a walk behind Parliament Hill in the night. And when we went behind Parliament Hill, Turner said to me, "Bob, you have one major responsibility. Get me to the free trade deal, and I will win the general election." When it came to the final argument in the Liberal party about what we were going to do – whether we would rip up the deal or support it – there were only three people present. One was the senior hatchet man from the political side, and he was afraid to say anything for fear he would be in trouble afterwards, so he took neither a Yes nor a No position. I took the position that we should not rip up the deal; we should simply say that we were opposed to it, for it would be a mistake to appear so emotive as to be ripping up deals. The legislative adviser said that we must rip it up or the New Democratic Party would outflank us on the left and would will win the election. It was a straightforward as that. The Liberal party then moved straight to rip up the deal, and Mr Turner announced the policy in the afternoon. On this prime question, caucus was not consulted; the party was not consulted. The leader made up his mind that the principle could help to win a general election.

Why do I say this? I think much of the stuff about the constitutional debates in Canada is a kind of side show. In *Stand Up for Canada: Leadership and the Canadian Crisis*,[61] I show what is happening in Canada. Today, there is far too much of a growth of "ideology of difference" in the country. There are too many hyphenated Canadians around. Secondly, the institutions are seriously flawed. Thirdly, we have weak leadership. The last data on leadership in the country indicate clearly that Canadians do not trust any of the politicians; and these data also show us that only 8 per cent of Canadians have confidence in federal political institutions themselves. This is incredibly low even by comparison with the United States, where the results are quite low as well. When you move to Prime Minister Brian Mulroney, the polls are an indictment of him. But it's not just criticism of Mulroney that concerns me; it's criticism of leadership in general. Fourthly, I believe that we are headed towards a five-party pizza parliament. An "Italianization" of the Canadian parliament is coming. Fifthly, Canada has a major fiscal crisis. The federal-provincial combined debt is now over $550 billion, and the interest on it consumes more than one-third of every tax dollar collected. Canadians are not facing up to this crisis and they will have to do so.

What should you do, then, if you are on the No side because you believe that with all these problems haunting Canada, the federal government must be prevented from getting weaker? Those of us who were on the "strong federal government" side believed that we had to have a strategy, and the best strategy was to show how weak the Charlottetown Accord was, how many vagaries it contained, how many gaps there were in it.

I do not have time to go through all the criticisms, but let me give you the political message in one simple argument. The Canadian governments wanted to change, in one referendum, on one day, sixty or so clauses of the constitution. That is almost one-third of the total way that Canada governs itself. By contrast, the United States has not been able to get through an equal rights amendment, passed after many years of preparation, let alone saying that it could change one-third of its whole constitution in a referendum. The Charlottetown constitutional proposal was shown to be full of vagaries and gaps. There was a hierarchy of rights within it. Indeed, the proposal was completely incoherent – an intellectual mess – and it was extremely easy to convey this fact to the public. Moreover, the process was very poorly constructed. A leader of the Yes campaign told the Canadian people they did not need to see the final text. "Why do you need to see the final text?" she asked. "Canadians cannot even read their own VCR manuals." How do you think that remark struck the Canadian public?

The truth is that the constitutional proposals had changed many times during the previous year. Remember that one year before these constitutional proposals we had the Meech Lake Accord. It failed. After Meech Lake we had the Beaudoin-Dobbie inquiry. In the earlier discussion today we heard about that. But it was not mentioned that after Meech Lake and Beaudoin-Dobbie we had another set of proposals, a status report, then another set of proposals, a consensus report. We had six different sets of constitutional proposals within one year – and then, with the last one, we were supposed to change one-third of the constitution, in one day, in one referendum. It was very easy to explain to the public that this was a ridiculous proposal and that the politicians could not even produce a legal text. While I agree with the Yes supporters who said the public would not read the legal text anyway, this does not alter the fact that they wouldn't give us the legal text until two weeks before the vote and that they changed the text massively six times during the year. When we attacked the proposals during the campaign, pointing out that disadvantaged people, mentally disabled people, and older people were not included in the deal, Joe Clark said, "Well, if it's not in the deal, we'll put it in next time." This kind of "we can change it" could be mocked very easily. It was easy to stand up as a No person and say, "Will they make Brian Mulroney Emperor of Canada the next time they decide to change things?" It was extremely easy to attack this whole process.

The Yes side had all the money, all the leaders, all the organization; and it had the backing of the three major parties. But it had a stupid messed-up deal called the Charlottetown Accord, which had been changed six times in twelve months.

The real problem with Canada is that we have incredibly weak leadership. All seventeen prime ministers until Brian Mulroney believed in three arguments. Number one, they believed that there should be a strong federal government – and I would remind all Conservatives that it was the first prime minister, a Conservative prime minister, who said that the provinces should be "local" governments. Sir John A. Macdonald wanted a strong federal government, and all his successors until Mulroney have to a large extent been in favour of a strong federal government. Number two, every prime minister until Brian Mulroney has believed that the federal government should be able to interfere in the economy when necessary. Number three, every prime minister until Brian Mulroney has believed in building a strong social policy for the country so that all Canadians, from coast to coast, are equal. Mr Mulroney let us down. He may well go down in history as Canada's worst prime minister. The point is that this constitutional deal was a series of deals brought to us by Brian Mulroney. It was a compromise. It was full of politics and deals, and was finally exposed as precisely that. The Charlottetown Accord was not based on a vision or a coherent philosophy of how to govern the country. The people were right to turn it down.

5 Judicial Politics Canadian-Style: The Supreme Court's Contribution to the Constitutional Crisis of 1992

F.L. MORTON

Foreign observers are justified in their astonishment at the sweep of constitutional amendments proposed by the (now defeated) Charlottetown Accord. The accord would have affected sixty-four clauses of the Canadian constitution, increasing its actual length by one-third. Almost no aspect of the constitution was left untouched: the Senate, the House of Commons, formulas for representation and election to both chambers, the federal division of powers, First Ministers' Conferences, Aboriginal self-government, all were affected. Perhaps most baffling was the Canada clause. The Canada clause was to serve as a preamble to the "new" constitution. Symbolically, it delineated the constitution's "essential values." On an operational level, it directed the courts to adjudicate future constitutional disputes in a manner that accorded with these values.

If this array of "essential constitutional values" bewilders foreign observers, it also sparked controversy among Canadians. Some attacked it as a sinister attempt to undermine the Charter of Rights and Freedoms (see Jackson in this volume). Others worried that it was a dangerous symptom of Canada's recent infatuation with

I would like to acknowledge the helpful suggestions of Peter Russell and Louis Massicote, and the research assistance of Stéphane Bernatchez and the Centre de recherche et documentation of the political science department at the Université de Montréal. The research for this paper was supported by grant no. 410–92–0320 from the Social Sciences and Humanities Research Council.

constitutionalizing the partisan claims of special interests (see Cooper in this volume). There were, of course, its defenders (see Tully in this volume). This paper aims not to defend or criticize the Canada clause as much as to explain its genesis.

The Charlottetown Accord can only be fully understood in light of the new forms of judicialized politics made possible by the 1982 Charter of Rights and Freedoms. The explosion of interest group demands for constitutional recognition and status – as exemplified in the Canada clause – was a response to the Supreme Court's activist Charter jurisprudence. The success of certain interest groups in using Charter litigation to advance their policy agendas encouraged others to try to gain a constitutional toe-hold from which to mount similar campaigns of systematic litigation. Quebec, by contrast, sought the addition of a constitutional principle (the distinct society clause) that would insulate its public policies from such counter-attacks in the courts. To make the same point differently, if the Supreme Court had continued to exercise the self-restrained, deferential style of judicial review that characterized its pre-Charter jurisprudence, there would have been no great rush to climb aboard the constitutional bandwagon of 1992.

ANTECEDENTS TO THE CANADA CLAUSE

Various predecessors of the Canada clause can be found in pre-Charter constitutional proposals and recommendations. In 1972 the final report of the Parliamentary Committee on the Constitution recommended a preamble that "would proclaim the basic objectives of Canadian federal democracy." These seven objectives included such now familiar principles as federalism, the protection of human rights, bilingualism, multiculturalism, the recognition of Canada's native peoples, the promotion of economic, social, and cultural equality, the reduction of regional disparities, and the seeking of world peace and security.[1] Bill c-60, the Constitutional Amendment Bill introduced by the Trudeau government in June 1978, contained a similar preamble with essentially the same declarations.[2] The report released by the Canadian Bar Association later that year also recommended a preamble "setting forth the essential attributes of Canadian federalism."[3] Following the defeat of the "sovereignty association" option in the Quebec referendum, the federal government issued a similar "statement of principles," as part of its proposals for constitutional renewal in June 1980.[4]

The existence of such prototypes prior to 1982 challenges the thesis that the Supreme Court's activist interpretation of the Charter is a major factor in explaining the 1992 Canada clause. This problem is more apparent than real. A review of the early prototypes reveals a fundamental and relevant difference from the 1992 Canada clause: they were all intended as constitutional preambles and were intended to guide future *political* development of the constitution, *not judicial* development. The 1972 report stressed that a preamble is "not legally binding ... [while] the rest of the constitution ... will be subject to judicial interpretation." The purpose of the preamble was to serve as "a source of inspiration to [the] country."[5] The proposed Constitutional Amendment Act of 1978 similarly stressed that "the provisions of the preamble ... are not legally binding in the sense of being enforceable in a court."[6] In a similar vein, the Canadian Bar Association's proposal stated that the preamble "can serve to set forth the basic values sought to be fostered by Canadians through *government*"[7] (emphasis added). Perhaps even more significant, the detailed contents of these proposed preambles were almost never an issue.[8] The lofty and poetic "statement of principles" proposed by the federal government in June 1980 was clearly inspirational in purpose and was not intended to be parsed by judges.

The polite discussion of preambles during these pre-Charter years rested on the assumption that governments, not courts, were the primary engine of constitutional development and adaptation. This assumption was wholly consistent with Canada's tradition of parliamentary supremacy and with the courts' self-denial of any active role in the development of rights policy during the 1960s and 1970s.[9]

A related criticism might be based on section 27 of the 1982 Charter of Rights and Freedoms. Section 27 is text (not preamble) and declares that the Charter "shall be interpreted in a manner consistent with the preservation and enhancement of the multicultural heritage of Canadians." Here is a directive for constitutional interpretation aimed at the courts, and it precedes the Supreme Court's subsequent Charter activism. As explained below, section 27 did later serve as a model for the distinct society clause. But this is the extent of its significance. At the time of its adoption, section 27 was perceived as being mainly symbolic, a tactical political concession by the Trudeau government, and not a significant part of the Charter. In his 1982 annotation of the Charter, Peter Hogg characterized it as "more of a rhetorical flourish than an operative provision,"[10] and he did not even discuss it in the 1985 edition of his authoritative treatise, *Constitutional Law of Canada*.

The lack of significance attributed to section 27 may be seen in the half-hearted (and unsuccessful) attempt by Quebec Premier

Lévesque to have an early prototype of a distinct society clause inserted in a *preamble* to the Constitution Act, 1982.[11] If the leader of the separatist Parti Québécois and his advisers had seen any advantage to be gained by having it included in the *text* of the Charter, they obviously would have insisted that it go there. Indeed, the Quebec government even lost interest in having it included in the preamble, as it dawned on Lévesque's principal negotiator, Minister of Intergovernmental Affairs Claude Morin, that the other governments viewed the preamble as "strictly interpretive and without any concrete impact on the division of powers."[12] Yet five years later, the newly elected Liberal government of Robert Bourassa demanded that a distinct society clause be inserted into the main body of the Charter. What had been a matter of indifference during 1980–81 had become a matter of the utmost importance by 1986. The difference, I suggest, was Quebec's newly acquired fear of the Supreme Court's activist Charter jurisprudence and the threat this posed to the autonomy of Quebec cultural and language policy.

SUPREME COURT'S ACTIVIST CHARTER JURISPRUDENCE

The Supreme Court of Canada's Charter jurisprudence has marked a sharp break with the Anglo-Canadian legal tradition of parliamentary primacy and judicial self-restraint. Prior to 1982, the interest-group use of litigation to pursue public policy change was as unsuccessful as it was rare. It was generally viewed as illegitimate, an American idiosyncrasy, a derogation from the Canadian tradition of responsible government. This view was shared not just by political elites but also by the judiciary, which had bluntly rejected several opportunities to engage in greater judicial activism during the 1960s. A brief comparison of the Supreme Court's non-use of the 1960 Bill of Rights with its interpretation of the 1982 Charter of Rights and Freedoms suggests the magnitude of this change.[13]

Under the 1960 Bill of Rights, the Supreme Court ruled in favour of the rights claimant in only five of thirty-five decisions between 1960 and 1982. In only one instance did it actually declare a federal statute invalid.[14] In the area of criminal procedure, it refused to read in a "Miranda-style" right-to-counsel warning[15] and explicitly rejected appeals asking for a Canadian version of the "exclusionary rule" that would prohibit the use of evidence that had been obtained in a manner that violated the rights of the accused.[16] In the field of abortion rights, the court flatly rejected requests to find a "right to privacy" in the Canadian constitution and sent abortion-rights crusader Henry Morgentaler to prison for ten months.[17] With respect to issues of racial and sexual discrimination, the court said that the right to "equality before the law" required only equal application and administration of laws, not equal laws, and upheld a law that clearly discriminated against women.[18] Against this background, constitutional experts soothingly observed that "the Canadian judiciary has historically been quite different from its counterpart in the United States [in that] Canada's judges do not have an activist tradition."[19] They confidently predicted that Canadian courts "will be fairly circumspect in using the Charter to nullify the acts of governments and legislatures."[20] How wrong they were!

In its first one hundred Charter decisions (1982–87), the Supreme Court ruled in favour of the rights claimants in thirty-five cases and struck down nineteen statutes.[21] Within five years, Charter cases came to constitute one-quarter of the court's annual docket.[22] The court also reversed its earlier positions on most of the above-mentioned issues. Its legal rights rulings have transformed Canadian criminal procedure. The court has adopted an exclusionary rule that is at least as rigorous as the American practice.[23] The right to counsel has been interpreted to discourage almost any police questioning of suspects in the absence of counsel[24] and to preclude judicial use of almost any form of self-incrimination at any stage in investigative process.[25] A recent comparative study concluded that the accused in Canadian courts now enjoy more "due process" rights than their American counterparts.[26]

On abortion, the same man returned to challenge the same law, only this time the court struck down the abortion provisions of the Criminal Code.[27] On equality rights, the Supreme Court has interpreted the Charter to prohibit not just unequal laws but laws that have an unequal ("disparate") impact on historically underprivileged groups, an interpretation whose breadth again surpasses its American counterpart.[28] Despite the framers' rejection of petitions in 1981 to include sexual preference as a prohibited ground of discrimination in the Charter, in 1992 there were two rulings from Ontario declaring homosexuals to be protected by section 15 of the Charter.[29] At the remedial level, the court recently gave its approval to judicially ordered "affirmative remedies," such as the expansion of social benefit programs that unfairly exclude (that is, discriminate against) a disadvantaged group.[30] While the court stressed that such remedies could be used only in special and rare circumstances, within a month lower courts had ordered a costly extension of spousal benefit plans in the two homosexual rights cases referred to above.

CHARTER WINNERS

The Charter has served as a field day for single-issue groups, a power trip for judges, and a gold mine for lawyers.[31] For present purposes, we need concern ourselves only with the opportunity the Charter has provided many single-issue interest groups to successfully pursue their respective policy objectives in the courts rather than in the electoral-legislative arenas of politics. Civil libertarians have succeeded in persuading the courts to revise the criminal law process to provide significantly greater procedural protections for the accused. Feminists successfully launched the Women's Legal Education and Action Fund (LEAF), which has pursued an active and successful agenda of systematic litigation, including judicial nullification of the abortion law.[32] Feminists and other "equality seeking" groups persuaded the Supreme Court to lay out the jurisprudential basis for future challenges to "systemic discrimination" – policies that have an unequal effect on historically underprivileged groups.[33] Homosexuals have persuaded lower courts to extend to them the protection of the section 15 equality provisions.[34] Canada's official language minority communities – anglophones within Quebec and francophones outside Quebec – have successfully enlisted the aid of the courts to extract more educational services from provincial governments.[35] Finally, Aboriginal groups won a major victory in a Supreme Court decision that restored Aboriginal fishing rights and set a precedent for generous judicial interpretations of similar claims in the future.[36]

These groups are not always allies, and sometimes their objectives conflict.[37] Such differences notwithstanding, these groups constitute the primary beneficiaries of the Supreme Court's new Charter activism, and they share several characteristics. They are all self-described "outsiders" who believe that the traditional institutions of parliamentary democracy and federalism have failed them. As beneficiaries of the Charter, they have become strong partisans of the Supreme Court and its new political activism. With the exception of the civil libertarians, they have both encouraged and applauded the group orientation of the Supreme Court's Charter jurisprudence. Their support for a group-oriented jurisprudence is a corollary to their self-identification as "equality seekers." The equality they seek is not equal (that is, the same) treatment with other Canadians, but preferential governmental treatment that either "compensates" them for past wrongs or "promotes" equality in the future. They support a policy regime of equality of results rather than the traditional liberal regime of equality of opportunity. Indeed, they insist that the liberal principle of nondiscrimination against individuals must be temporarily suspended until the goal of equality of results is achieved. In its 1989 *Andrews* decision, the Supreme Court accepted this view of the Charter's equality rights provisions.

Despite their differences, these groups have achieved common ground in their identification with the Charter and their enthusiasm for the courts. Alan Cairns has dubbed them "Charter Canadians."[38] For obvious reasons, they have also been described as the "Section 15 Club"[39] and the "Court Party."[40] They have become as much a part of Canada's unwritten constitution as the Charter is part of the written constitution. They view the sections of the Charter that relate to their interests in a proprietary manner as "their sections" and are quick to defend their constitutional turf against the inroads of either governments or each other. Cairns (and also Cooper in this volume) confuses the Supreme Court's interpretation of the Charter with the Charter itself and identifies the latter as the cause of the new constitutional expectations of Charter groups.[41] This is a mistake. The recognition of various groups and equality rights in the text of the Charter was a necessary but not sufficient condition. If the Supreme Court had continued to interpret the 1982 Charter in the same self-restrained and deferential manner as it had approached the 1960 Canadian Bill of Rights, there would have been little incentive for groups to fight over degrees of constitutional recognition.

This "Charter-claiming" activity takes place as easily outside the courtroom as inside.[42] The leaders of the constituent groups expect to be consulted about, if not actually participate in, any formal constitutional changes. When they were not consulted in the process leading to Meech Lake, they coalesced to form a potent opposition. Their success in defeating the Meech Lake Accord reinforced their determination to protect their constitutional turf and status in any future round of constitutional negotiations.

QUEBEC AS A CHARTER LOSER

The Supreme Court's new embrace of judicial activism has contributed directly to Quebec's growing alienation from post-Charter Canada. Indeed, the Supreme Court itself facilitated the adoption of the Charter and the Constitution Act, 1982, over Quebec's protests, by its 1981 decision in the *Patriation Reference*.[43] In a decision unprecedented in the common law world, the Supreme Court accepted jurisdiction to determine the content of what all parties conceded was a constitutional convention – a practice not part of the formal written constitution, and thus hitherto considered nonjusticiable.

At issue was the alleged convention of unanimous provincial consent to constitutional amendments affecting provincial powers. The Supreme Court rejected this position, ruling that all that was required was a "substantial degree of provincial consent." A majority went on to rule that the opposition of eight provinces meant that the Trudeau constitutional package failed to meet this requirement and that it was thus "unconstitutional." But the court then distinguished constitutional law from convention, holding that only the former was legally enforceable by the courts.

This decision of "legal but unconstitutional" forced the Trudeau government and the eight opposing provinces back to the bargaining table. The moral legitimacy of the federal position had been undermined, while the eight opposing provinces had to face the reality that there was no longer any legal barrier to Trudeau's threat of unilateral amendment. As Michael Mandel has argued, by reducing the required threshold of constitutional legitimacy to "a substantial degree of provincial consent," the court had set the stage for the isolation of one or two provinces from the rest of the "Gang of Eight."[44] Given the political agenda of the Parti Québécois government, it was all but inevitable that it was Quebec that would be isolated. This happened one month later, when all the provinces except Quebec accepted an amended version of the Constitution Act, 1982. When the Lévesque government returned to the Supreme Court a year later to argue that the 1982 amendments had violated Quebec's historical right to a constitutional veto, a unanimous court flatly turned it down. Quebec nationalists did not forget the role of the Supreme Court in this whole affair, and it was not by accident that one of the powers demanded and received by Quebec in the subsequent Meech Lake Accord (1987) was the power to nominate the three Supreme Court judges from Quebec.[45]

The Supreme Court further contributed to the alienation of Quebec by its subsequent Charter decisions in the 1984 *Quebec Protestant School Boards* case and and the 1988 *Public Signs* case. Both involved language rights and both struck down Quebec legislation. The first struck down the education provisions in Bill 101, the "Charter of the French Language," which restricted access to English-language education in Quebec. This loss of control over the field of public education – a power Quebeckers had long considered a sacred provincial monopoly – alarmed leaders of both parties and started the push for new constitutional negotiations which culminated in the Meech Lake Accord of May 1987.

THE MEECH LAKE AFFAIR (1987–90)

The Meech Lake Accord was the culmination of what was appropriately dubbed "the Quebec round" of Canada's constitutional odyssey. It followed logically from the judicial decisions recounted above. The Meech Lake process, at least at the outset, simply reflected Quebec's attempt to get back some of the constitutional powers and status it had lost in the preceding five years. One of the most important elements in this counterattack was the distinct society clause – a novel interpretive section aimed directly at the new power of the Supreme Court. The distinct society clause and the debate it engendered provides the most recent and relevant background for our understanding of the Canada clause.

After Quebec's exclusion from the 1982 constitutional accord (which it blamed in part on the Supreme Court), the Quebec National Assembly enacted a retrospective "blanket" exercise of the section 33 notwithstanding clause, effectively insulating all existing Quebec statutes from legal challenges under the new Charter. In addition, the Lévesque government routinely began to insert a notwithstanding clause in every new piece of legislation. Notwithstanding so many "notwithstandings," the Quebec government still suffered a major constitutional and political defeat in 1984, when the Supreme Court ruled that Bill 101's restrictions on access to English-speaking education were an unconstitutional violation of section 23 of the Charter.[46] Section 23, which established a constitutional right to minority language education, was a key part of Trudeau's policy of expanding bilingualism as a vehicle for national unity, and he successfully insisted that it be exempted from the section 33 legislative override. The Lévesque government thus watched helplessly as the Supreme Court struck down one of its most important language policies.

This experience drove home the realization for Quebec elites that the constitutional status quo was no longer acceptable. They could not make the Charter go away by ignoring it or by relying upon the section 33 override. This realization coincided with the election of the new Conservative government of Brian Mulroney, who had signalled a more conciliatory constitutional position towards Quebec than his Liberal predecessors. In 1985, both the Parti Québécois (PQ) and the Quebec Liberal Party responded by publishing documents setting forth the conditions that would have to be met for Quebec to "rejoin" the constitutional family. Not by coincidence, both documents contained proposals for special constitutional recognition of Quebec. The PQ document called for recognition of "le peuple

Québécois,"[47] while the Liberals used the less expansive concept of "distinct society."[48] Neither document specified whether this new clause was to form part of a new preamble or to be inserted into the text of the constitution. The Quebec Liberals went on to defeat the PQ in December, and in April 1986 the new Liberal minister of justice, Gil Rémillard, repeated the demand for a "distinct society clause" to ensure that Quebec's "unique identity would not in any way be jeopardized."[49]

The ambiguity of how this would be achieved (and the source of the threat) was clarified when Rémillard unveiled Quebec's new five-point program to other provincial governments in the fall. Until then, it had generally been assumed that the proposed distinct society clause was intended for a new constitutional preamble and was not seen as problematic.[50] Now, Rémillard explained, it was necessary that the clause go into the main body of the constitution to give it "greater legal weight."[51] When Ontario questioned the appropriateness of this change, Rémillard explained that his government was being pressured by the Parti Québécois on this issue. The PQ had pointed to sections 25 and 27 of the Charter, the sections providing interpretive guidance with respect to Aboriginal rights and multiculturalism. Since these were both within the body of the constitution, the PQ demanded to know why the Liberals had agreed to relegate Quebec "to the second-class status of the preamble."[52] His government now considered it absolutely necessary, Rémillard warned, that the distinct society clause be included in the body of the constitution.

While the issue of placement continued to bother other provinces, the federal government accepted the insertion of the distinct society clause within the body of the Charter, explaining that it "would guide the courts in their interpretation of the constitution."[53] Ontario and Manitoba were not happy about the clause, however, and proposed amendments declaring that the Charter and Aboriginal rights would not be affected by the distinct society clause.[54] The Quebec response was as revealing as it was blunt: "These amendments would effectively strip the clause of all meaning."[55]

To understand Quebec's response requires some knowledge of "the Charter two-step," the distinctive method of legal reasoning adopted by the Supreme Court to handle Charter claims.[56] Section 1 of the Charter declares that the rights it proclaims are "subject to such reasonable limitations as can be demonstrably justified in a free and democratic society." The Supreme Court chose to interpret section 1 as requiring two separate stages of Charter analysis: (1) Has a right been restricted? (2) Is the restriction a reasonable one? Only if a statute fails both these tests is it declared invalid. The court also recommended a "large and liberal" interpretation to the right in question, which usually entailed a subsequent finding that the impugned statute did indeed restrict the right. The court then transferred the burden of proof to the government to justify the restriction by demonstrating that it was "reasonable." Since most government statutes "limit" individual freedom in some respect, the question of the reasonableness of the limitation – the second step in Charter analysis – has become the crucial determination in most Charter cases. To meet this burden of proof, a government must persuade the court of the "pressing and substantial" purpose of its policy and the proportionality of the means used to achieve this purpose.[57]

If Quebec had succeeded in having the distinct society clause added to the constitution, it could have then used this directive to help persuade judges of the reasonableness of its restrictive language and education policies. An analogy to cards may be instructive. The distinct society clause would have given the Quebec government a constitutional trump card that it could throw on the judicial table when courts reached the "reasonable limitation" stage of section 1 analysis. The "distinct society card" would presumably tilt the balance in favour of a finding of "reasonableness." This strategic advantage would be nullified, however, if the Charter or Aboriginal rights were given a similar constitutional status. It would be trump versus trump, and Quebec's advantage would be dissipated.

While most provincial governments eventually accepted Quebec's insistence that the distinct society remain in the text of the constitution, it became a principal rallying point for opposition to the accord. As Pierre Trudeau, the most influential spokesman for the opposition, declared, the distinct society clause constituted "a victory for those who never wanted a Charter of Rights entrenched in the constitution." When it was combined with the other Meech Lake proposals guaranteeing that three of the nine Supreme Court judges come from Quebec and that all Supreme Court appointments be restricted to candidates nominated by their respective provincial governments, Trudeau charged that this would "transfer supreme judicial power to the provinces."[58]

Trudeau's critique became the rallying point for the Charter Canadians opposition to the accord. The point here is not who was right or wrong, but rather that the focal point of conflict had become the Supreme Court's interpretation of the constitution. Both sides wanted the insertion of language that would "guarantee" the judicial interpretations they wanted, or would at least prevent those they feared most. An unlikely alliance of Charter Canadians, supporters of Senate reform, and Aboriginal groups began to coalesce to try to block the Meech Lake Accord, but they would probably have failed had the Supreme Court itself not intervened.

The speculative debate over the distinct society clause suddenly became disastrously concrete in December 1988 when the Supreme Court struck down the "French only on public signs" provisions of Bill 101.[59] Quebec's prohibition of English-language signs violated the Charter right to freedom of speech, ruled the court. At this point, as Peter Russell observed, "all hell broke loose."[60] Despite Robert Bourassa's 1985 campaign promises to amend this policy, his government now gave in to strong public pressure from Quebec nationalists. Not only did Bourassa reinstate a revised prohibition of English-language signs, but he insulated it from further Charter challenges by appending the section 33 notwithstanding clause. This inflamed public opinion outside Quebec, which saw Quebec's use of the section 33 override as an attack on the Charter and a betrayal of national bilingualism.

Within French Quebec, this experience confirmed the "threat" of the Supreme Court's exercise of judicial review under the Charter and the necessity for a distinct society clause. Matters went from bad to worse when Bourassa suggested that Quebec would not have had to use the override if there had already been a distinct society clause to "guide" the court's decision to a different result. Outside Quebec, this view reinforced the suspicion of the distinct society clause as a clever ruse that would allow Quebec to achieve indirectly what it was now perceived as doing directly: denying equality to its English-speaking minority. The distinct society clause, its critics now crowed, would allow the courts to play Quebec's trump card, thus shielding the Quebec government from the stigma and political criticism provoked by using the section 33 override power. This linkage of the override power to the distinct society clause may not have been justified,[61] but it proved to be a fatal blow to the besieged Meech Lake Accord.[62]

The process of constitutional renewal had now come full circle. The Supreme Court's 1984 *Protestant School Boards* decision had helped to launched the Quebec round. Now its *Public Signs* decision set in motion the ill-fated conclusion of the Quebec round. Judicial politics thus shaped the tempo of the Meech Lake process as well as the contents of the accord.

THE CANADA CLAUSE AS A REFLECTION OF CHARTER POLITICS

The defeat of the Meech Lake Accord cast the Canadian polity into a constitutional crisis. Quebec now felt twice rejected and withdrew from further constitutional discussions. The Quebec government set October 1992 as a date for a referendum for Quebeckers to vote on their future relationship with English Canada. This date served as a challenge and a de facto deadline for Ottawa and the nine other provinces to come up with a better – and final – offer to Quebec. The result was the Charlottetown Accord and the Canada clause.

The seeds of the Canada clause were planted in the dying days of the Meech Lake Accord. In a desperate attempt to win approval before the three-year deadline expired, the pro-Meech governments had cobbled together a "son-of-Meech" proposal designed to gain the consent of the three holdout provinces. If the holdouts would accept the accord, the other first ministers would agree to embark on a whole new set of constitutional initiatives that addressed criticisms of Meech.[63] These initiatives included Senate reform, Aboriginal self-government, sexual equality, minority language rights, and the promise of a "Canada clause giving constitutional expression to the defining features of the Canadian community."[64] While this "son-of-Meech" plan failed to rescue its dying parent, it became the blueprint for the next round of constitutional negotiations.

The criticism of Noël and others that the Charlottetown Accord was a hodgepodge of contradictory principles and provisions applied with special force to the Canada clause. Quebec, of course, was allowed to retain the distinct society clause along with a separate recognition of its power "to preserve and promote" this distinctness. But this recognition was now countered by a second "fundamental characteristic" – the commitment of all governments to "the vitality and development of official language minority communities *throughout Canada*" (emphasis added). Aboriginal rights and self-government received prominent (indeed, triple) recognition, but this was hedged by respect for human rights and especially the "equality of male and female persons." The balancing act was thorough indeed. Individual rights were paired with collective rights; parliamentary democracy with respect for rights; the "diversity" of the provinces with the "equality" of the provinces. The only principle to stand alone and unqualified was multiculturalism, a testimony to its perception as non-threatening.

Amongst elites, the Canada clause sparked a legalistic but lively debate that turned on competing conceptions of equality. Small-c conservatives, led by Preston Manning and the Reform party, attacked the clause (and the accord generally) for granting "special status" to Quebec and Aboriginals. According to Manning, this abandoning of the constitutional principle of the "equality of all citizens" was a recipe for political disaster: "The constitutional granting of special status to more and more groups based on factors such as race, language, culture and gender can only lead to a house divided against itself."[65]

Similar criticisms were voiced by Pierre Trudeau and by one wing of the Court Party. Trudeau condemned the accord as creating a society "where collective rights take precedence over individual liberties." Deborah Coyne, a founder of the "Canada for All Canadians Committee," criticized the Accord for creating a "hierarchy of group rights that threatens to undermine equality." She also pounded away at such provisions as the distinct society clause for "weakening the Charter." Coyne and Trudeau conveniently omitted to say that what the distinct society clause weakened most were minority language rights, the first and most pre-eminent group right of Trudeau's 1982 Charter. Predictably, Manning and most of his supporters did not see the weakening of the Charter or the courts as a problem.

A different wing of Charter Canadians, led primarily by professional feminists from the National Action Committee on the Status of Women (NAC), shared Trudeau's and Coyne's concern that the Canada clause would weaken the Charter, but did not share their blanket condemnation of group rights. NAC's legal experts parsed and dissected the Canada clause and found that despite its affirmation of both individual rights and the "equality of male and female persons," it "reduce[s] the content of Charter rights and expand[s] the basis on which Charter guarantees can be limited."[66] A corollary criticism was that the Canada clause created "a hierarchy of values," of which the Quebec and Aboriginal governments would be the primary beneficiaries. Feminists objected not to the principle of collective rights but to the fact that the Canada clause would reshuffle the deck, with women's rights losing its former pre-eminence.

The only point on which these three groups of English-Canadian critics agreed was that the accord generally, and the Canada clause specifically, gave too much to Quebec. In Quebec, however, nationalist opponents of the accord successfully argued just the opposite. From their perspective, the Charlottetown Accord was a weak reflection of Meech Lake, especially the transformation of the distinct society clause into the Canada clause.[67] The distinct society clause was now hedged in with so many qualifying and competing values as too render it "virtually without any value for Quebec ... an actual setback."[68] According to one commentator, the distinct society clause had been transformed from a "Trojan horse" into "a sword of Damocles ... hanging over the head of the Quebec people."[69]

The different critiques of the Canada clause reflected a deeper difference within the No vote about the acceptability of the constitutional status quo. The Trudeau federalists and the Charter Canadians were against the accord because it changed the status quo. As one prominent feminist put it, the Canada clause "takes back rights won by women and minorities in 1982."[70] This failure "to maintain the 1982 balance" was to be resisted.[71] To small-c conservatives and the Reform party, however, the accord was flawed because it extended the dangers of "special treatment" for groups that had begun with the Charter. From this perspective, the accord was bad because it entrenched the status quo.[72] Quebec nationalists also condemned the Canada clause because it would not affect the status quo, but they wanted it changed in the opposite direction – to provide stronger group rights for the Québécois. Dislike of the Charter in Quebec, at least among elites, has long been recognized. The October referendum suggested that contrary to the accepted wisdom, there might now be growing disillusionment with Charter politics in English Canada as well.

The Canada clause thus pleased almost no one. The problem with it may be captured by returning to the analogy of cards. The Mulroney government had tried to solve the objection to Quebec's receiving a constitutional trump by giving everyone trump. But if everyone holds a trump, no one does. Publicly, the defenders of the Canada clause continued to maintain that it would assist judges in interpreting competing constitutional powers and rights. The truth was closer to Peter Russell's retrospective assessment: "No one in their right mind could seriously believe this list would provide useful guidance to the judiciary in interpreting the constitution."[73] The Canada clause had become a constitutional *bouillabaisse*, and the voters decided it smelled fishy.

CONCLUSION

Traditional legal theory sharply distinguishes the process of formal constitutional amendment carried out by governments from the judicial function of interpreting and applying constitutional powers and rights. Legal realists effectively challenged this distinction by showing that judicial review constitutes a de facto form of ongoing constitutional amendment. The preceding analysis adds a new dimension to our understanding of constitutional politics by showing how "micro-level" constitutional politics – the informal process of judicial amendment – can influence "macro-level" constitutional politics – the formal process of constitutional amendment.[74]

The Supreme Court of Canada's activist interpretation of the Charter since 1982 has conferred quasi-official constitutional status on a variety of nongovernmental groups. The success of these groups at micro-level (judicial) constitutional politics has given them incentives and expectations to participate at the macro-level. These nongovernmental groups want a seat (or at least an official voice) at the first ministers' constitutional bargaining table. They view participation in macro-level constitutional politics as necessary to protect their constitutional turf from encroachment by governments or by other nongovernmental interest groups. Conversely, governments and nongovernmental groups that have lost at the micro-level seek amendments that provide a legal toe-hold from which to recoup their losses and enhance their status in future litigation. The Canada clause may be seen as an artifact of this process.

The Supreme Court may have influenced the Canada clause controversy in a more subtle fashion. If the court had not opted for the "two-step" approach to resolving Charter claims, Canadians' preoccupation with interpretive clauses might not have developed. The court could have read section 1 as simply a commonsense caveat that "no right is absolute," and then proceeded to interpret the rights according to traditional canons of legal reasoning: text, framers' intent, past practice, and reasoning by analogy.[75] This approach would have focused judicial scrutiny on "whether the present case resembles the plain case [that is, precedents] sufficiently and in the relevant aspects."[76] This perspective, which seeks to sculpt the scope of a right by identifying internal limitations, does not lend itself to constitutional directives such as the distinct society clause. Perhaps the converse is more obvious. A judicial method that finds almost everything violates a right, broadly construed, and then seeks to determine if the limitation is "reasonable" (external limitations) invites the addition of constitutional clauses that "cue" judges about what is reasonable. Suffice it to say that while the adoption of a traditional approach to reasoning about the meaning of rights would not have prevented the distinct society and Canada clause controversies, the court's choice of the "two-step" has encouraged this new preoccupation with interpretive clauses.

Judicial politics Canadian-style differs in another important respect from its American counterpart in that it does not focus on judicial appointments. There is no Canadian equivalent to the Judge Bork or Clarence Thomas hearings before the Senate Judiciary Committee or the ideologically charged judicial recall elections in California. It is intriguing to speculate what would have happened if Quebec had chosen to pursue its policy of Charter damage control by focusing exclusively on acquiring the new power to nominate three of the nine Supreme Court justices – and if it had never even mentioned a distinct society clause. Perhaps this initiative could have opened up the whole issue of a reformed judicial appointment process appropriate to the new power exercised by the Supreme Court. With a new, more open and accessible appointment process, perhaps political actors would have focused their competition on the appointment of judges rather than on the texts the judges interpret.

In reality, Quebec's initiative to acquire the judicial nominating power was accepted but diluted by extending analogous nominating powers to all the provinces. There was no interest in, or debate over, further reform of the judicial appointments process. Instead, the idea of interpretive clauses modelled after the distinct society clause took root in Canada's constitutional *zeitgeist*. As a result, partisan competition over constitutional status has expressed itself in conflict over the actual wording of proposed amendments to the constitution. Since no political actors, governmental or nongovernmental, can be confident about influencing judicial interpretations through the appointment process, they have tried to accomplish the same end by placing interpretive clauses within the body of the constitution. Or, to put it in Christopher Manfredi's more formal concepts, the rules of micro-constitutional politics have become the focus of macro-constitutional politics.[77]

The problem with this tactic is that it is so obvious. Political rivals are quick to spot such attempts to gain a constitutional trump and will demand either its withdrawal or the addition of a countervailing declaration of their own status. This process, as Peter Russell has observed, is "a mug's game."[78] It leads to cumbersome and arcane provisions such as the Canada clause and the obscure, legalistic public debate they encourage. Perhaps it also explains why growing numbers of Canadians have become fatigued and even angry over the constitutional fare served up by their leaders.

But while the Canadian political elites may have deserved the popular rebuke they received on 26 October 1992, the Supreme Court of Canada also shoulders some of the responsibility for the Charlottetown Accord. The Canada clause may have been a "mug's game," but a more subtle version of the game was already being played with gusto in courts across the country. Despite Pierre Trudeau's liberal vision of the Charter as an instrument that would promote individual rights, the Supreme Court developed a more group-oriented jurisprudence, which in turn encouraged the kind of group claims that are found in the Charlottetown Accord.[79]

6 Diversity's Gambit Declined

JAMES TULLY

After the Charlottetown Accord was voted down in the referendum, Alain Dubuc, editor of *La Presse*, wrote:

Ce que la victoire du NON illustre, c'est d'abord l'incapacité des citoyens d'en arriver à un consensus. Il s'agit là d'une impasse structurelle, qui s'inscrit dans l'histoire et dans les mouvements sociaux et qui est beaucoup plus significative que les maladresses d'un texte juridique ou les errements des politiciens.

What the victory of the "No" shows is the inability of the citizens to reach an agreement. This is a structural impasse, which is inscribed in history and in social movements, and which is more significant than the awkwardness of a legal text or the mistakes of politicians.[1]

I would like to follow Dubuc's suggestion to approach Canada's constitutional difficulty as an impasse, rather than as a crisis, and see where it leads. This is not a new suggestion. For over fifteen years the term "impasse" has been widely used in official documents and

I would like to thank all the participants in the conference for their papers and helpful comments. I owe a special debt to Alan Cairns and Alain Noël whose excellent papers and constructive criticism made me realize I had to rework my paper from the ground up. My gratitude goes to Curtis Cook, who chaired the conference with serenity and gave me patient and thoughtful encouragement as I struggled to rewrite my paper.

among participants, both Aboriginal and non-Aboriginal, to characterize the constitutional state of affairs. Thus, in approaching from this perspective, one will not stray too far from the language that has been customarily used to describe – and so partly constitute – the character of the constitutional situation itself. Of course, "impasse" has always been contested. The reality is richly ambiguous and needs to be seen in a variety of ways to learn one's way around. As the other contributors show, it can be seen as a "crisis," a "never-ending story," "three nationalisms," "postmodern condition," and so on. Each of these enlightens the complexity we are trying to understand. Nonetheless, I want to approach it across this customary and more familiar face once more, in the gathering darkness of our time, to see if there are not some aspects that have been overlooked (perhaps because of our customary way of looking at the impasse) and which, seen retrospectively, might point to passages through the impasse.

Dubuc describes the impasse as the "inability of the citizens to reach agreement" on constitutional reform. This formulation is broad enough to describe the Canada round (the negotiations leading up to the Charlottetown Accord and the referendum campaign) and the entire series of failures to reach agreement ever since citizens, in addition to first ministers, governments, and legislatures, have had a decisive say, in one way or another, in the process. The series of constitutional negotiations in which citizens have a decisive say began, according to its most acute chronicler, Peter Russell, with Premier Lesage's withdrawal of support for the Fulton-Favreau amending formula in 1965 and Premier Bourassa's withdrawal of support for the Victoria Charter in 1971, both in response to the perceived wishes of the citizens of Quebec. According to Russell, the second feature of the series is that the constitutional reforms are of such a fundamental nature that they call into question the constitutional identity of Canada. The series consists of five rounds: Fulton-Favreau to Victoria Charter (1964–71), the new constitutionalism of Quebec nationalism (1976–79), the patriation of the constitution (1979–83), Aboriginal self-government and the Meech Lake Accord (1983–90), and the Canada round (1990–92).[2]

Expanding Dubuc's formulation to describe the complex conditions of reaching agreement in the Charlottetown Accord and the referendum, the impasse is characterized by: (1) the inability of seventeen representatives to reach an agreement on constitutional reform by means of multilateral negotiations and a variety of popular consultations; (2) in turn, the inability of citizens to come to agree by means of public deliberation and a referendum; and (3) the inability of provincial and territorial legislatures, as well as band councils and traditional Aboriginal governments, to ratify the deal. "Citizen agreement" was understood in the referendum to be as close as possible to a consensus among Aboriginal chiefs and citizens on reserves, and to be a majority of non-Aboriginal and Aboriginal citizens in each province and territory. These demanding conditions are not stipulated in the amending formulas of the Constitution Act, 1982, nor in the *Report of the Special Joint Committee on a Renewed Canada* (Beaudoin-Dobbie Report) of 28 February 1992, nor in the Charlottetown Accord. Rather, in the typically Canadian common law manner, a majority of the seventeen representatives came to see them as *conventions* of constitutional reform by virtue of a set of precedents in the course of the five rounds of the series.

Why have representatives, citizens, and legislatures been unable to come to an agreement? What is the nature of the impasse they are unable to traverse? Is it impassable – a permanent *arrêt* or *cul de sac*, as separatists in Quebec and western Canada insist, which Canadians have come across after their long travels together and which they can now overcome simply by going their separate ways cross-country? Or is the impasse of a different kind – a little more closely attached to citizens' tangled identities as Canadians than this first interpretation implies? Is it, rather, that Canadians, Canadien(ne)s, and Kanataians (Aboriginal peoples) have become in part who they are, both in their similarities and differences, by virtue of their participation in centuries of intercultural interaction and negotiations; and, *eo ipso*, that they have become so entangled in their ways of negotiation and interaction that they can no longer find a path to agreement in this *nastawgan* (the Teme-augama Anishnabi word for the network of trails and waterways that define a people and their ways)? Our interpretation will be satisfactory if it can account not only for the inclination to drift towards three (or more) "solitudes," as Alan Cairns does so well in his chapter, but also if it can account for the countervailing disposition of "Canada *dans la peau*" – the attachment to the federation and the inclination to try negotiations once again.[3] (The expression *dans la peau* is a playful allusion to Cole Porter's love song, "I've Got You Under My Skin.") If this interpretation of the impasse is more satisfactory than the first one, is there a way of looking at the self-entanglement – a change in vision – which enables Canadians to see their way to agreement?

FIRST REASON FOR THE IMPASSE

"Surely the impasse is obvious," one might say. "The reform of a constitution by agreement rather than force is the most difficult task in politics. Anyone familiar with practices of 'reaching agreement' knows it is impossible under the complex conditions of the Charlotte-town Accord. Failure to come to agreement in this maze is not due to 'inability' but 'incapacity.' The process is impassable."

Is there a level of complexity at which one can say in principle that humans are incapable of reaching agreement – a theoretical meta-game that fixes the limits of constitutional games of reaching agreement at, say, executive federalism? (And how would we reach agreement on this proof?) I think not. Defenders of absolute mon-archy in the seventeenth century used to say with certainty that kings, lords, commoners, and citizens could never acquire the abilities to reach the agreements necessary to sustain parliamentary democracy.

Of course, the first reason for the "inability" of representatives, citizens, and legislators to arrive at an agreement is the sheer diffi-culty of acquiring, mastering, and exercising the requisite abilities. The representatives consult their constituents, advance and defend proposals for reform, listen to the proposals of others, consult advi-sers, negotiate multilaterally through various rolling drafts to a com-posite accord that renders to each his just due, all the while checking with their constituents through polls, talk shows, and so on. Citizens observe this process, listen critically to their representatives, to a variety of intermediary groups in civil society, and to court challenges and high-profile attacks on the negotiations; they convey their pro-visional judgments on the rolling drafts to their representatives, they deliberate among themselves on the merits of the final agreement with respect to their special and regional concerns, as well as to the good of the federation as a whole, and then they cast their vote. Finally, if it gets this far, legislators go through the process of delib-eration again and then ratification. (The Charlottetown Accord stopped at the second stage; the Meech Lake Accord made it to the third by skipping the second; and patriation disregarded Quebec in the first, and skipped the second and third.) This mixture of dem-ocratic, representative, and federal procedures comprises a daunting repertoire of what I will call "federal abilities" to negotiate and delib-erate to an agreement. The mix will be even more complex if there is another round, for the Supreme Court ruled that the Native Wom-en's Association of Canada should have a representative at future multilateral negotiations.

Moreover, like all practical skills and virtues, these federal abilities ought to be acquired through practice and exercise over time within established practices of constitutional reform, just as citizens acquire the democratic abilities to deliberate and vote by engaging in estab-lished practices of elections. Yet Canadian citizens do not have established practices in which these federal skills are taught and transmitted, nor do they have much experience in exercising them. In the years before 1990, only Quebeckers (in 1980) had the experience of a constitutional referendum. Consequently, defying Aristotle's insistence on the priority of practices to abilities, Canadians have tried to establish practices in which the federal abilities could be acquired and mastered in the course of trying to exercise them. It is as if they were being asked to bring the game of hockey into being and learn how to play it as they careened around on the ice.

Accordingly, since 1980, in the course of the rounds, colourful suburbs of new practices of constitutional negotiation have sprung up around the drab old central practices of executive federalism. These include federal, provincial, and territorial institutions of popular consultation and discussion; an array of commissions, from the Commission on the Political and Constitutional Future of Québec (the Bélanger-Campeau Commission) and the Citizens' Forum on Canada's Future (the Spicer Commission) to the Beaudoin-Dobbie inquiry; polls, assemblies, reports such as the *Report of the Constitutional Committee of the Québec Liberal Party* (the Allaire Report); court challenges; Aboriginal commissions, circles, and consensus negotiations; lobbying by civil society organizations representing a wide variety of groups such as women, visible minorities, linguistic minorities and environmental movements; television debates, local coffee parties, demonstrations, civil disobedience; and so on. Citizens in these nascent practices struggled to master the federal abilities to participate in diverse ways in the process of trying to reach an agreement.[4] The remarkable capacity of Canadians to learn these multifaceted abilities in practice, even in these interregnum (or Arendtian) circumstances, can be measured by contrasting the haphazard and unfocused judgments of the early Citizens' Forum with the increasingly better focused and well-reasoned judgments during the referendum campaign.

Whereas the representatives who participated in the old practices of executive federalism, and the so-called ordinary citizens who participated in the Beaudoin-Dobbie deliberative forums, were able to reach agreement among themselves on the Charlottetown Accord, as well as on the earlier Meech Lake Accord, the Charlottetown Accord was not one that the majority of citizens in the inchoate practices would agree to.

Given the short time span and the fragile relations between the two types of practice, which deteriorated further as the campaign unfolded, the surprise is perhaps that the gap between representatives and citizens was not greater. For example, the Yes vote in Quebec of 43 per cent was 7 per cent higher than the polls predicted. Four provinces and one territory voted Yes. Nova Scotia was within 1.5 per cent of Yes. The overall Yes was 45 per cent, even though the prime minister was extraordinarily unpopular and Canadians were in a devastating recession. If the Charlottetown Accord had been treated as a rolling draft rather than a final accord, and if the referendum period had been lengthened and treated as a constitutional deliberation rather than an election campaign and if it had been treated as a learning process to sample citizen opinion and receive suggestions for further adjustments rather than being presented as the last word – in such circumstances, who is to say that the gap might not have been narrowed in another round of multilateral negotiations and referendum, until an agreement was provisionally reached?

This is not an idle question. The Charlottetown Accord will be treated in this provisional, stepping-stone manner in any future negotiation, just as the Beaudoin-Dobbie Report was a guideline for the Charlottetown Accord, the Meech Lake Accord for the Beaudoin-Dobbie Report, the court challenges to the patriation package for the Meech Lake Accord, the 1980 referendum for the patriation package, and so on, right back to the Quebec Act of 1774, and even earlier.

SECOND REASON FOR THE IMPASSE

The second reason for the impasse is the complexity of the Charlottetown Accord's amendments, which representatives negotiated and which citizens were assumed to be able to deliberate and reach agreement on. These amendments included all the demands that had accumulated in the previous four rounds: Senate reform, primarily to address the grievances of the western provinces; distinct society status for Quebec and provincial say in appointments to the Supreme Court; a limit on the expansion of federal spending powers in provincial jurisdictions; changes in the amending formula for the territories; a social and economic proposal; recognition of the need to protect the environment; and, towering above all these in terms of change, the recognition of Aboriginal governments as one of three coordinate orders of government in Canada after a century of suppression, the rebuilding of Métis governments and settlement of Métis land claims, and the establishment of a partial framework for the negotiated redress of the unjust taking of Aboriginal lands.

In addition, each of these amendments, designed to respond to legitimate demands of specific members of the federation, had within it, as a direct result of the multilateral negotiations, safeguards for the other members. For example, Senate reform, in approximation to the West's demands for the equality of provinces, contained a double-majority rule for legislation affecting French language and culture, and Aboriginal and territorial representation. Similarly, the distinct society clause was limited by a clause protecting the anglophone minority in Quebec; and so on through each amendment. These two-sided amendments were in turn to be spliced into the constitutional fabric in a way that did not "derogate" from other sections of the constitution and the Charter of Rights and Freedoms: the federal and provincial powers in sections 91 and 92; gender equality in sections 15 and 28; multiculturalism in section 27; linguistic minorities in sections 16–23, 59, 93, and 133; affirmative action groups in section 15(2); Aboriginal and treaty rights in section 25; and the rights and freedoms of sections 1–15(1). Furthermore, nearly one-half of the amendments set out processes for future negotiations, rather than being definitive amendments, and the accord itself was a provisional "best-efforts draft," thereby ensuring that there would be further negotiations.

Finally (though it came first in the accord), an interpretive Canada clause, setting out eight rows of "fundamental characteristics" and three clarifications, was to be prefixed to the constitution. The Canada clause had three crucial roles. First, from now on, the entire constitution was to be interpreted by the courts in the light of these fundamental characteristics. Second, the amendments mentioned above were seen by the seventeen representatives as changes to the central institutions of Canada which brought them in accord with, and so gave recognition to, the fundamental characteristics of Canada; for if these are the fundamental characteristics of Canada, then the character of the fundamental institutions of Canada ought to embody them in a just arrangement. Third, citizens were thus asked two neatly focused questions during the public deliberations: Are these the fundamental characteristics of Canada? If so, are the amendments to the central institutions in accord with the fundamental characteristics? Consequently, the Canada clause provided an invaluable form of organization of an otherwise diffuse collection of amendments and helped to focus public deliberation around the two questions.

Although the Canada clause provides a perspicuous representation of the complexities of the accord, it does not resolve disagreement. Even if everyone said yes to the first question, there are innumerable ways of responding to the second, for any arrangement of Canada's political institutions can be shown to be, on some interpretation, either in accord or in discord with these (or any other) fundamental characteristics. So, on this line of argument, the impasse might be simply an instance of the general indeterminacy of interpretation. Even if citizens were to master the federal abilities in practice, an infinite series of constitutional rounds would never reach agreement. The impasse is in interpretation: "anything goes" (to allude to another Cole Porter classic).

But this trendy antidemocratic line of argument cannot be correct, for it does not account for the degrees of convergence that were achieved in practice. The representatives converged on agreement over the fundamental characteristics and on a set of amendments in accord with them. The citizens converged over time on a limited number of reasons, or what Alain Noël calls "conceptions of justice," for answering Yes or No to the two questions. Therefore, if we wish to understand the impasse, we require a survey of the negotiations and deliberations which will clarify these two paths of convergence on the fundamental characteristics and on their application as norms in amending the central institutions: the one path leading to agreement, which the representatives took, and the other leading to a limited number of reasons for voting Yes or No, which the citizens took.

Let us begin the survey with the fundamental characteristics. Like the negotiations for the Declaration of Man and Citizen in the summer of 1789, the "best-efforts" version of the Canada clause was arrived at after months of struggle over every word. The fundamental characteristics are arranged in eight irregular rows of discordant characteristics. The four overlapping ways Canadians govern themselves sit in the first row. Canada is a "democracy" with a "parliamentary" but also "federal" system of government and with the "rule of law." Next, the first people to govern this land, the Aboriginal peoples, are self-governing yet are one of three orders of government "in" Canada. Quebec's "distinct society," protected and promoted by the government and legislature of Quebec, is then juxtaposed to "the vitality and development of official language minorities," to which Canadians and their governments are "committed." "Racial and ethnic equality" is paired with "cultural and racial diversity," and "individual and collective human rights" sit hand in hand on their own row. The equality of male and female persons follows, and the principle of the "equality of provinces" stands shoulder to shoulder with the provinces' "diverse characteristics" in row (h). (A concordance of discordant characteristics.)

"What a mess!" the Reform party, English-Canadian nationalists, former Prime Minister Trudeau, and Parti Québécois leader Jacques Parizeau responded in unison.[5] "How could agreement ever be reached in this maze, let alone by using it as a guide to constitutional reform and future interpretation? The Canada clause is its own impasse."

Although the Canada clause can be seen in this way, is there not another way of looking at it? Could it not be that these are some, or even many, of the fundamental characteristics of Canada, giving it its distinctive character among the countries of the world? Maybe the characteristics are heterogeneous because Canada is heterogeneous. Perhaps it strikes us as a mess because we are not accustomed to looking on Canada as the (negotiated) arrangement of all these diverse characteristics but, rather, we are used to viewing Canada from the perspective of some subset of these characteristics, as if our customary subset constitutes the fundamental, or predominant, character of Canada. I will call this customary, unilateral way of looking on Canada "diversity blindness."

For example, one person might be accustomed to seeing Canada as characterized by parliamentary government, linguistic minorities, individual rights, and provincial equality. The other fundamental characteristics go unnoticed, are not seen as fundamental at all, or, when noticed, are seen as subordinate, etched in the faintest of hues behind the captivating colours of the core subset. Another Canadian – perhaps used to seeing Canada as constituted by the fundamental characteristics of a federal form of government, distinct society, collective rights, and provincial diversity, with the other characteristics pencilled in lightly behind these bold characters – tries to bring these characteristics to the attention of the first person, and vice versa. As the other, unnoticed or subordinated characteristics come to the attention of each person, their response will be, as a matter of course, to say that these less important characteristics make a mess of the character of Canada as a whole, disrupting the purity and unity it has under their familiar subsets of characteristics. They will attempt either to efface the disruptive characteristics, assimilating them to their fundamental characteristics, or to subordinate them to the supremacy of their characteristics; or, failing these two strategies, they will vote against the accord. So the fact that it strikes us as a mess cannot be a reason for concluding that agreement is impossible or unreasonable, for we may be blinded by a unilateral vision of Canada.

THE COMPETING VISIONS OF CANADA

Now the fundamental characteristics of the Canada clause are in fact many of the fundamental characteristics of Canada. They were not plucked out of thin air. Most of them were gathered from the constitution and its surrounding documents. Others were collected from the considerations that justices take into account in constitutional decisions and from the public discourse on the constitution over the centuries. They are the commonplaces or touchstones that Canadians refer to in talking about the constitution and in giving reasons for their views on it. Some are older than others. Aboriginal government is the oldest. Quebec's distinct society dates from the seventeenth century and linguistic minorities from 1791. Cultural diversity is the most recent arrival. If this exercise had been attempted a century ago, or if it were to be attempted a century from now, no doubt some different fundamental characteristics would appear and some of them would fade in prominence or even pass away. Yet there would probably be enough of a family resemblance to this temporal character sketch to recognize it still as Canada. The Canada clause is a sketch of our fundamental characteristics, just as a sketch of all the Haida totem poles at Skidegate is of the Haida characteristics.

The phenomenon of diversity blindness – of taking a subset of the fundamental characteristics as the fundamental character of Canada – is a common feature of Canadian constitutional politics. An organized subset of fundamental characteristics is standardly called a vision. In the above example, the first person is said to have a "one-nation," "central," or "Charter" vision of Canada, whereas the second person has a "two-nations" vision. By bringing into prominence other subsets of fundamental characteristics, and disregarding or subordinating the remaining characteristics in each case, it is possible to generate the diverse visions of Canada: – "three nations" (the five hundred Aboriginal nations, Quebec, and the Rest of Canada), "three orders" (Aboriginal, provincial, and federal), "multicultural" (many cultures all of a kind), "two cultures" (of French and English linguistic minorities), "gender equality" (applying over all the other differences), and so on. Although the visions are different, they overlap because they share a limited set of fundamental characteristics. Some visions have several characteristics in common, varying perhaps in emphases; others have fewer. Thus, together, the visions form a complicated network of overlapping and criss-crossing relations among the fundamental characteristics. Hence, representatives and citizens converged in their two different ways because they negotiated and deliberated from within the light (and shadow) cast by their different visions. Richard Simeon succinctly summarizes: "There is no single vision of Canada: rather, there are multiple, often complex, visions which interact with each other in complex ways."[6]

"Vision" is an accurate term for the phenomenon we are trying to understand. Since a vision based on an organized subset of fundamental characteristics discloses only a limited aspect of the character of Canada and thus overlooks other aspects, it should be called a "point of view" or. "perspective," because "vision" implies a comprehensive view of the whole. However, if "point of view" was substituted for "vision," it would obscure the way the various visions of Canada function. Although they disclose Canada only from one point of view, they are taken as comprehensive views of the whole. They are perspectives on Canada parading as visions of Canada. So when proponents of the competing views meet, as in the above example, and disregard some characteristics of the others or subordinate them to their frames of reference, their ways of looking at Canada remain unshakable. One's own vision is not seen as one point of view among many. It is the immovable form of representation against which the confrontation takes place. The "others" are assimilated within it.

It is as if a person thought that "My Canada *includes* Quebec" and "Aboriginal government *within* Canada" were perspectiveless phrases that did not dispose us to one view rather than another – when in fact the subordination has already been accomplished. Canada appears as a thing over and above the members that fit into it. This thing is associated in one's mind with the federal government, as if it were not only a fundamental characteristic in which all Canadians share but also a super characteristic, not coordinate with the others, but all-encompassing. The seating at First Ministers' Conferences seems to confirm this.

These two examples illustrate that a vision is held in place by the uses of common forms of expression of the fundamental characteristics – and their related terms – in the multiplicity of activities of talking and thinking about the constitution of Canada and its reform. The common forms of expression are not as often the terms discussed and questioned as they are the taken-for-granted linguistic uses in which discussion and questioning take place, providing an undoubted background understanding of the character of Canada against which proposals are evaluated. They form the axis around which our constitutional thought turns. Let us call language games with such habitual forms of expression "federation stories."

Since such a background understanding is based on customary ways of expressing a subset of fundamental characteristics, it is often thought of as an interpretation or opinion, because it looks like one interpretation or opinion of the character of Canada, among many

(just as the vision it grounds should be called a "perspective"). However, it does not function in negotiation and deliberation as an
opinion or interpretation among many. Rather, a federation story is
the matter-of-course language of description and evaluation in which
proposals and other competing stories are evaluated and interpreted
– the motionless system of judgments in which opinions and interpretations are taken up. (Kanienkehaka [Mohawk], for example, are
not of the *opinion* that they form a nation, are members of a confederation, and are in treaty relations with the Government of Canada.
This is not an *interpretation* they happen to be entertaining these
days. Similarly, Franco-Manitobans are not of the *opinion* that they
are a linguistic minority ... and so on.)

A federation story is one understanding customarily taken as *the*
comprehensive understanding, as the ground of all others. When a
person is confronted with a story that competes with the fundamental
characteristics, she or he treats it as a (mis)interpretation or opinion,
and translates and discusses it in the familiar and customary terms
of his or her own. The common expressions of one's own story remain
hegemonic and are reinforced by everything one says and does.
Competitors return the compliment. When theories of the constitution are constructed, they are (unavoidably) built on the sturdy and
unquestioned linguistic usages of the federation story in terms of
which a particular theorist thinks and acts.

These competing customary ways of acting with the words of our
fundamental characteristics – and the thousands of stories of the
history and workings of Canada in which they are spoken and
written, time out of mind – hold the competing visions in place and
are the ground of diversity blindness. They are an instance of what
Tim Fuller, the gracious host of this conference, calls (following
Michael Oakeshott), a "mode of experience":

A mode of experience is an emergent line of thought or practice within
experience as a whole, a line which attempts to get a grip on the whole, to
make experience wholly coherent or manageable from its own point of view.
It is an inference from, and potentially an assertion about, what the whole
of experience might be like in the absence of seeing the whole as such. Yet
being abstract, all modes of experience necessarily misrepresent the whole.
Most people most of the time are content to understand the world within
the orderly framework of a particular mode's construction of the world.[7]

When Canadians come to discuss the constitution, they negotiate and
deliberate in the light of the diverse visions and in terms of the
diverse stories with which they have learned to think and talk about

the character of Canada since childhood and schooling. These different yet overlapping ways of thinking about the character of Canada are deeply inscribed in the diverse cultures, political struggles, and ways of life that make up Canadian history and social movements. They are modes or ways of experiencing Canada, of being Canadian. Since each understanding articulates the way political power should be organized from its perspective, when it is brought forward as the comprehensive understanding, each necessarily posits its arrangement of political power as normative. This is the basic impasse – not inexperience, complexity, the shortcomings of a text, or the mistakes of politicians, but, as Dubuc writes, a "structural impasse" inscribed in Canadian "history" and "social movements."

THE MIDDLE GROUND

If Canadians were to agree that they were members of a single political society coming together to reach agreement on constitutional reform, there would be no deep historical or social impasse on the trail to agreement, even if there were superficial ideological differences. They would deliberate in accordance with, or in the articulation of, a shared understanding of either the common good, as in communitarian interpretations of popular sovereignty, or the procedural principles of justice, as in liberal interpretations of popular sovereignty. However, there has been no such shared understanding of Canadian society to provide the common ground of negotiations. Instead, Canadians come to negotiations with their diverse visions of the federation, grounded in their multiple histories and social movements, and these are actually reinforced, as we have seen, by the way the discussion proceeds.

Canadian federalism consists of the continual negotiation, in terms of these competing federation stories, on an intercultural middle ground that has been slowly woven together and worn smooth over centuries of criss-crossing and overlapping negotiations and interactions, from the first Haudenosaunee (Iroquois)-Canadien federal treaty at Trois-Rivières in 1645 to the Charlottetown Accord of 1992.[8] The impasse is the difficulty to negotiate "multilaterally" (as the Canada round was described); that is, in a federation of different understandings held together neither by the imperial conquest of one vision (although this is often attempted) nor by the transcendence or supersession of our resplendent multiple lifeworlds and assimilation to an artificial meta-vision (this strategy too has its supporters), but by nothing more (or less) than the tangled relations of negotiations, interactions, agreements, and disagreements on the middle ground over time. What lies at the bottom of the Canadian federation is neither a unifying constitution nor a common vision, but the multiplicity of activities of multilateral negotiation itself. (Once you grasp this, the rest follows.)

To see both the difficulty of bringing the middle ground of fundamental characteristics into being (because the competing stories are so different) and the possibility of a middle ground (because the stories criss-cross and overlap here and there), one need only recall the three interwoven aspects of Canadian constitutional history and social movements in which the competing visions have their place. These three aspects compose what Alan Cairns, their perceptive cartographer, calls "Charter federalism."[9]

The first aspect is that Canada is not founded in the sovereign people's giving rise to a unifying constitution. It is founded in a gathering of pre-existing constitutional associations federating together through negotiations over an immense expanse of time and space. The ancient federations of the five hundred Aboriginal First Nations were added to by the great treaty federations formed between the crown and the First Nations in the early modern period. Then came the constitutional acts of colonial federation of 1763, 1774, 1791, 1840, 1867, and 1870; the Indian Act dictatorship of 1876, which suppressed but did not extinguish Aboriginal governments; the addition of the new provinces and territories in this century, with Newfoundland finally joining Confederation in 1949; the treaty federation of Cree, Inuit, and Naskapi governments in 1975; the new provinces of Nunavut and Denedeh today; the ongoing decolonization of the territories; the refederation of Métis governments; the dismantling of the Indian Act and the negotiation of new federal relations with the First Nations; and so on. Canada is a historical "gathering" or "federation" of already constituted peoples of diverse kinds, whose former legal and political cultures continue through and into the federation. No great founding revolution or constituent assembly clear-cut the dense old forms and imposed a unifying constitution on the members in an original act of state building, as in liberal and communitarian theories of popular sovereignty, or in France after 1789. Canadien(ne)s, and later Canadians, appear to have followed, not often faithfully, the footsteps of the First Nations they encountered in their well-worn practices of "treaty federalism" (see the section "First Nations and Federalism," below).

Of course the people are sovereign – first in their provinces, territories and First Nations; then in the Canadian federation and the

Assembly of First Nations as a whole. This was acknowledged in the way the referendum was counted and in studies of citizens' relative allegiances to their provincial, territorial, and federal governments.[10] The second aspect of the federation creates one crucial condition for a middle ground. Canada is more than a confederation, or mere alliance, of these various pre-existing members sharing coordinate sovereignty. The federal parliament democratically represents the citizens of Canada and governs them, with respect to its section 91 jurisdictions, as a single people or nation. This is a fundamental characteristic which every vision shares and highlights (see the section "Equality and Asymmetry," below). Although federal and provincial jurisdictions are laid out separately in the Constitution Act, 1867, they overlap in a variety of ways and rest on continual negotiations. This aspect has given rise to the centralist vision of Canada, which regards itself as the comprehensive vision rather than one legitimate vision among many. This view of the federation from Ottawa, so to speak, sees it as a single unified society with the provinces subordinate rather than coordinate. Seen from any other point of view, it is "domineering federalism."[11]

The Charter of Rights and Freedoms evinces the same duality of national and federal forms. It asserts jurisdiction across an apparently undifferentiated "society" in section 1, while it recognizes the coordinate sovereignty of the provincial legislatures in section 33, and Quebec specifically in section 23; and justices interpret the Charter in accord with the juristic cultures of the different provinces.[12] Section 33 was extended to Aboriginal legislatures in the Charlottetown Accord.

The third aspect, cross-cutting this already complex picture, is an assortment of constitutionally recognized "minorities" and "individuals" that are not subordinate to federal and provincial governments but are sovereign in their own spheres. These include the rights and freedoms of individual citizens in sections 1–15(1); official language minorities spread across the country and recognized in sections 16–23, 93, and 133; multicultural groups in section 27; disadvantaged groups in section 15(2); gender equality in sections 15 and 28; and more. Commentators were surprised that the Charter could generate minority and individual constituencies who were just as attached to their Charter-visions of Canada as the older constituencies were to their visions, inscribed in the two earlier aspects of Canadian constitutional history. But the Charter recognized, rather than created, rights and freedoms which social movements have organized, struggled for, and envisioned as fundamental characteristics over the last one hundred years.

As a consequence of these three aspects of Canada's history and social movements, Canadians have multiple and overlapping constitutional identities and allegiances. The often-tense relations among these various constituents of the federation are constantly negotiated, contested, and reconceptualized over time.

Let us imagine that a problem arises concerning relations among some of the members of the federation. Negotiators meet right after spring thaw at Johnson Hall. Previous forms are observed but are modified to fit the occasion. Condolences are given; hatchets buried. The negotiators exchange the stories of their clans, nations, federations, then colonies, provinces, federal government, territories, Assembly, linguistic minorities, multicultural groups, and social movements; each explains the situation in the light of the fundamental characteristics of the federation as he or she sees it, and then listens to the others. There is a similarity among, say, these four stories, another between two of them and three others, and so on. Overlapping agreement seems possible. The sun goes down. The negotiators consult their constituents and return at daybreak. They recall the spirit of Deganawida for inspiration. An agreement is reached or not, a new link added to the chain of agreements stretching back in time. Some powers are shared, others not.

Next decade there is another meeting. Some of the negotiators are the same, others are new to the game. Perhaps there is a new problem – the former agreement did not work as planned, they misinterpreted one anothers' understanding of the agreement, or the agreement was broken. The chain of previous agreements is the constitution of the federation and the guideline for the negotiations (there are always various ways of being guided). The chain is polished and new links added; others fall out of use, are removed and blue-boxed. A middle ground of practices of negotiations, with their changing rules, conventions, and rituals, evolves. So it goes on – endlessly.

As an unintended result of this form of federation, the shape of the federation as a whole lacks unity. It is a historical *nastawgan* – nothing over and above the negotiated relations of the members through time. It is more than an aggregation yet less than a unity – a "gathering" or recollection (*nous nous souvenons*), like an old-growth forest with its federation of old and new lifeforms. It cannot be taken in at a single glance. It is too complex and ragged to fit any one theory, whether liberal, nationalist, or economic. Despite what Joe Clark may say, the multiplicity of individuals and intersecting communities of various kinds is not itself a "community," any more than the set of all provinces is a province. There is no one conception that can do justice to all the fundamental characteristics. The conceptions clash in unheard-of ways.

This motley federation appears incomplete and offends against the requirement of a pure and unified identity held by centralists and separatists, and by any person bound to a single vision. The much-sought-after unified identity cannot be found at the level of the whole federation, nor in any of the parts, nor even in the individual, as a result of the three tangled aspects of Canada given above. The requirement of unity is an illusion given by the visions and their linguistic expressions, for, as we saw, they enframe without acknowledgement (as opposed to a point of view). Is this incompleteness a flaw requiring radical reform in accordance with some vision or other?

As I think about this paragraph, I look up at the fireplace, then my gaze moves to the window and out to the snow-covered lawn with its cross-country ski tracks. Beyond the lawn, the ice-covered Ottawa River and people ice-fishing in their huts come into focus as the foreground fades. These scenes in turn become indistinct as my field of vision moves across the Ottawa to the church steeple at Oka, and then, after a spell, to the two mountains against the blue sky. My perspective is displaced yet again as it moves to the left and I see the Mohawk village of Kanesatake and the sacred Pines Forest. Now I imagine myself in the Pines looking in this direction. How would these scenes be painted by Cornelius Krieghoff, or Ellen Gabriel? A hundred thoughts rush to mind.

Do I experience the inability to capture the scene in a single identifying depiction that does justice to each of its fundamental characteristics as a flaw to be reformed or as an occasion for wonder and celebration? Is the fact that the various parts of the scene are equally multifaceted troubling? Need this craving even arise?

"But surely you want to say Kanesatake is a 'nation', a fixed identity, like Quebec and Haida Gwaii?" Yes, as a Canadian I recognize, affirm, and celebrate Kanesatake as a nation, a living identity. Yet also as a Canadian I want you to see that Kanesatake is a member of the larger Kanienkehaka Nation and the Haudenosaunee Confederation, and is related to the Algonquin Nation and to Oka, Quebec, and Canada. Québécois(es) live in Kanesatake, and Kanienkehaka live in Oka and Montreal. I am trying to draw your attention to this *nastawgan* (or labyrinth) of aspects, of modes of experience, while rendering each its due, without belittling any.

CONVENTIONS OF JUSTIFICATION

As Alain Noël elucidates in his chapter, the citizens from each region and social movement viewed the Charlottetown Accord in the light of their respective and overlapping visions and measured it against their immanent standards. Citizens in the old colonial provinces –

the Atlantic provinces, Quebec, and Ontario – deliberated in the light of a two- and/or three-nations view; citizens of the western provinces in the light of one nation, provincial equality, and individual rights; the Aboriginal chiefs in the light of two nations (the equality of First Nations and the federal government); the linguistic minorities from the two-cultures vision; feminists from the perspective of gender equality; multicultural groups from the perspective of Canada as one nation of many cultures; and so on. For 45 per cent, the accord gave satisfactory recognition to their fundamental characteristics in the Canada clause and the corresponding amendments. For 55 per cent it did not.

For the No voters who deliberated unilaterally, entirely within the immanent standards of their vision, it looked a mess. The Canada clause was an object of ridicule, and the corresponding amendments were beyond the pale of reason. Other No voters deliberated comparatively, measuring the accord first against the standards of their vision and then measuring how poorly their vision had done relative to others. For them, the Canada clause was an unjust "hierarchy." The formulation of the fundamental characteristics did not give full recognition to their characteristics, but whittled them down; secondly, the characteristics were arranged so that theirs were subordinate to those of others. As a result, the amendments institutionalized this unjust hierarchy. The first, immanent, form of deliberation was successful because the standards of appraisal were well known beforehand and often had a shared exemplar. The provincial equality vision had the concept of a triple-E Senate; the distinct society vision had the impeccably federalist precedent of the distinct society clause in the Meech Lake Accord; and the division of powers had the Allaire Report. The straightforward comparison that the accord was "less than Meech," for example, may well have decided the Quebec vote.[13]

The second or comparative advantage form of deliberation rapidly developed, and it was fuelled by the campaign strategy of the Yes forces. They incited voters to look in the accord for gains for their vision in relation to the gains of others. The citizens wasted no time in embracing and reversing this national sport. The gains for Quebec were compared unfavourably with the gains for Aboriginal peoples or for the West, the distinct society against linguistic minorities, the Charter and gender equality relative to Aboriginal governments, and so on. This way of thinking about the accord inclined citizens to interpret the multilateral negotiations as a sport of this comparative-advantage type and to ask how relatively strong or weak their representatives were in upholding their respective understandings of the character of federation. The Aboriginal leaders were said to have given away too much; Premier Bourassa was said to have "collapsed" or "blinked" in the face of the others; and so on. When spokespersons for the No side asked what the gains were for the country as a whole, they standardly meant the country as given in their centralist vision.

If this survey accounts for the convergence on a small set of reasons for voting Yes or No, given by the fundamental characteristics in each vision, it does not explain how the negotiators, who held a fair range of competing visions, reached unanimity in both the Charlottetown Accord and the Meech Lake Accord (other than, say, by blinking). Nor does it explain how the No voters could move from a seemingly impassable convergence on allegedly irreconcilable visions, held fast by their cultural and historical outlooks, to agreement on some future accord. For this, a closer investigation of negotiation on the middle ground in this type of multilateral federalism is required.

Could this strange kind of negotiated federalism, which Canada has engaged in for so long, with so many diverse members and arrangements, possess within its practice a form of justice that is appropriate to it and perhaps worthy of some attention? As we have seen, it appears to be nothing but endless struggles to impose unilaterally one or other of these visions on the whole, coupled with the attempts by the others to resist such assimilation, to seek recognition, coexistence, and redress, perhaps with a view to gaining hegemony themselves eventually. Since the Canadian constitution and institutions have been formed by these long and arduous contests, they can always be interpreted as supporting any of the visions to some extent. None has ever been completely victorious. Is there anything more in the games of negotiations than the will to power and the reign of interest, of racism and domination, of strategies of assimilation, marginalization, genocide, and resistance, of threats of secession and good riddance, of horse trading and arm twisting, of comparative advantage and blinking, of dice rolling, pork barrelling, and log rolling?

When a claim for reform is advanced in multilateral negotiations on the basis of one ordering of the fundamental characteristics, it is not justified by an appeal to a shared vision, since none exists. Nor can it be justified by an appeal to the proposer's understanding of the federation, for this is not shared by the others. Rather, it is justified by an appeal to some grounds or reasons that the others also accept as binding. Conversely, when other negotiators resist the reform as unjust, as undermining or subordinating their conception of the fundamental characteristics, they too must appeal to similar intersubjective reasons to warrant their objection. These middle grounds are of two types. The first is an appeal to a fundamental characteristic that is shared by some, or sometimes all, of the negotiators (for example, parliamentary democracy, rule of law, and individual rights) but usually construed slightly differently in each case. Call these reasons "overlapping consensus" and set them aside for now.

The second type of intersubjective middle ground or reason consists of the "conventions of justification" appealed to by negotiators, which are shared by all. A just agreement is one that each and every negotiator agrees satisfies the prevailing conventions of justification. If there are such conventions standardly used to justify an appeal for or against reform, each member is bound (on pain of self-contradiction) to recognize the appeals of others insofar as they can be justified by reference to the same conventions. They would be the conventions of justice for multilateral negotiations, providing the criteria by which the justice of the multilateral claims and counterclaims could be mutually accepted or rejected serially until accommodation and agreement were reached. They would thus be the normative foundations of Canadian federalism.

Although conventions of justification vary over time, just as the fundamental characteristics do, there are three that have stood the test of time and become relatively stable touchstones of constitutional negotiations:

1   The members of the federation should be recognized in their own terms through the negotiations and in the constitution (the convention of mutual recognition and continuity, or self-identification).

2   Constitutional agreements should be based on negotiations that are fair by the customs of each member involved (the convention of multilateral negotiations).

3   Negotiated constitutional agreements should require the consent of those affected and/or their representatives (the convention of consent, or *Quod omnes tangit*, "What touches all must be approved by all").

If any federal relation among any number of members satisfies all three conventions, it is a just relation. If all federal relations among members were to satisfy the conventions, Canada would be a just federation.

To have mastered the federal abilities to negotiate and deliberate in accordance with these three conventions is to have acquired a federal attitude. The conventions are not always respected in any given negotiation. Canadian constitutional history is littered with examples of such injustices. Nevertheless, the fact that the three conventions are employed both to call a reform just and to decry it as unjust is pragmatic proof that they are *in deed* conventions of justification. I shall illustrate this first with a few examples from the recent negotiations and from older precedents.[14]

CONVENTIONS OF JUSTIFICATION IN PRACTICE

The Canada round and the Charlottetown Accord were responses to the accumulated objections to the previous rounds, especially to patriation, the First Ministers' Conference on Aboriginal Rights, and Meech Lake. The objection to patriation and the Charter of Rights and Freedoms by Quebec and, initially, by the other provinces was not an objection to the content of the Charter. Rather, their first, combined objection was that the Charter could not be introduced without their consent because it affects provincial jurisdiction as recognized in section 92 of the Constitution Act, 1867.

This appeal to the "convention of consent" was taken to the courts by three of the provinces.[15] They asked, Does patriation affect provincial powers in section 92? Is there a convention requiring provincial consent? And is provincial consent a constitutional requirement? The Supreme Court replied that the patriation package affects provincial powers, that a "substantial degree" of consent is required, and that observance of the convention by the federal government is a political, not legal, matter. To determine if a convention exists, the majority of the court reviewed the five previous amendments that affected provincial powers. Four of these had the unanimous consent of the provinces. The fifth, which affected only Alberta, had the consent of Alberta. One would think this would be unequivocal evidence for unanimous consent, but the court ruled that the evidence supported a requirement of a "substantial degree" of provincial consent without specifying what that meant. Accordingly, Prime Minister Trudeau gained the consent of all the provinces except Quebec, in exchange for the notwithstanding clause, by means of negotiations which included all the provincial premiers except Quebec's in their crucial phase, and he proceeded to patriate the constitution and add the Charter to it.

Second, the provinces' claim that they were "affected" by the Charter was based on the recognition of their jurisdiction over property and civil rights in section 92 of the Constitution Act, 1867. Since the Charter transferred at least some jurisdiction over civil rights to the federal courts, it altered the constitutionally recognized identity of the provinces and thus required negotiation and consent. Underpinning this appeal was the "convention of recognition and continuity." When a member, such as a province, joins a federation, its pre-existing juristic culture (its laws, customs, religion, and form of government) is recognized and continues into the federation unless the member agrees to its alteration. This convention of recognition and continuity developed in the early modern period, in imperial common law and the law of nations, in opposition to the feudal (or "Norman") convention of discontinuity; that is, the right of a conqueror or a federation to discontinue and destroy the juristic culture of a conquered or federated member without its consent. The convention is based on the widely shared assumption (which we saw above, in the section "The Competing Visions of Canada") that people live and act in a culture of conventions and to destroy this is to destroy their forms of life.[16]

Section 92 is based on this convention. It recognizes and continues the jurisdiction which the federating colonies had over, among other things, property and civil rights prior to 1867, and it extends this jurisdiction to the prairie provinces as if they were colonies that already possessed it. In the patriation round, the three conventions were thus satisfied for all the provinces except Quebec. The Quebec legislature condemned the patriation procedure for violating criteria of fair negotiations, for proceeding without its consent, and for affecting its provincial jurisdiction.

Quebec then returned to the courts to ask if it possessed a veto.[17] Quebec argued that its consent was required, not only by virtue of its status as a province under section 92, but also because it was a distinct society, one of two non-Aboriginal founding nations of the federation, and because this fundamental characteristic was affected by the Charter. The constitutional evidence for Quebec's status as a distinct society is the Quebec Act of 1774, the imperial statute on which Quebec's consent to obey the crown rests. The Quebec Act, in turn, is based on the convention of recognition and continuity. After 1760, when the French crown ceded external sovereignty over Quebec (Canada) to the British crown, Quebeckers successfully negotiated the recognition and continuity of their century-old autonomous nation, or juristic culture – their civil law, language, system of property and international trade, and their customs and religion.[18] This was confirmed in the Quebec Act, and as a result of *Campbell v. Hall* (1774), it cannot be altered without Quebec's consent. When the colony of Upper Canada was formed by the Constitutional Act, 1791, it was understood by Canadians and Canadien(ne)s to be equal in juristic status to Lower Canada (Quebec), thereby giving constitutional recognition to the reality of the "two non-Aboriginal nations" vision. This then became the precedent for section 92 in 1867.

The Supreme Court dismissed Quebec's appeal on the ground that it could find no convention recognizing Quebec as one of two founding nations in earlier amending negotiations. The court presumed that a convention can be said to exist if and only if the participants explicitly refer to it in the course of the negotiations. Since they could find no explicit formulation of the convention, they concluded that it did not exist. This has struck many commentators, especially anyone familiar with the common law tradition of conventions, as a misunderstanding that is typical of legal positivism, of the difference between a legal rule, which is explicit, and a convention, which by definition is a norm implicit in, or presupposed by, conventional practice.

This formulation of the distinct society clause provided the prototype for the clause in the Meech Lake Accord, the Beaudoin-Dobbie Report, and the Charlottetown Accord. The force of the clause is to show that the Charter "affects" the continuity of Quebec's juristic culture in a manner distinct from the way it affects the common law provinces who agreed to it. The Charter affects the provincial jurisdictions of civil rights, language and education that are part of Quebec's unique civil law and linguistic traditions guaranteed by the Quebec Act. If, therefore, Quebec's unique civil law and language are to be recognized and are to continue, the Charter and its traditions of interpretation must be brought into accord with the civil and linguistic traditions of Quebec – not vice versa (or it would be a case of discontinuity). Accordingly, the distinct society clause is designed as an interpretive guideline, ensuring that the Charter, when applied to Quebec, will be interpreted in recognition of and continuity with, rather than in violation of, Quebec's civil law and linguistic traditions.

Constitutional negotiations before and after patriation have tended, without exception, to confirm the provinces and Quebec in their defence of the three conventions and their interpretation. All the proposals for an amending formula from 1927 to the Charlottetown Accord have included a veto for Quebec in one form or another. If the formula proposed is less than provincial unanimity, such as regional vetoes or the current seven-and-fifty rule, it has always been understood that the provinces affected would have to agree to this formula in fair negotiations. Even the amending formula in the patriation package itself requires unanimity for fundamental amendments, and it allows provinces to opt out of amendments they disagree with; section 38(3). The original draft of the patriation proposal also contained another traditional federal device of dissent and reconsideration – an opting-out provision that allows a province to let the emotional dust of constitutional negotiations settle and to give the amendment sober second thought before agreeing to it.

Moreover, the decisive precedent is the 1867 constitution. It was based on three years of multilateral negotiations, and the consent of all parties was explicitly required. Those who could not agree, Prince Edward Island and Newfoundland, simply stayed out until they decided to opt in. Although the Constitution Act, 1867, does not contain an explicit amending formula, it takes the unanimity convention for granted. The only section dealing with amendments, section 94, stipulates that unanimous consent of the provinces affected is required if the common law provinces wish to harmonize their diverse legal systems. Finally, the federal government, all the federal political parties, and all the provinces have acted since 1982 on the understanding that the Constitution Act, 1982, involved an exceptional breach of conventions that can be redressed only by gaining Quebec's consent through further negotiations and the insertion of a distinct society clause. Indeed, Canada has witnessed a broadening of the convention of consent, from provincial "governments" to "legislatures" (1982), to provincial "citizens" (1992).

These three conventions are also embodied in a vast literature on the constitution, which the provinces drew on in presenting their cases. Statements of earlier prime ministers, such as Diefenbaker in 1960, the decisions of the Privy Council under Lords Watson and Haldane, the exemplary interpretation of the 1867 constitution from Quebec's perspective by T.J.J. Loranger in 1884, the understanding of the colonies as coordinate bodies – first to the crown, from 1791 to 1867; then, as provinces, to the federal government in the "compact theories" from 1829 on – all reiterate these conventions. Lord Watson set out the classic synopsis of Canadian federalism constituted by the three conventions:

The object of the Act [of Confederation] was neither to weld the provinces into one, nor to subordinate provincial governments to a central authority, but to create a federal government in which they should all be represented, entrusted with the exclusive administration of affairs in which they had a common interest, each province retaining its independence and autonomy.[19]

This way of thinking about federalism is derived in part from the earlier view that the Thirteen Colonies were autonomous bodies, coordinate to the crown, and legislation that affected their jurisdictions required the consent of the colonial assemblies. In turn, this understanding is derived from the early modern conventions of the recognition and continuity of local forms of government, law, and property in the "multiple kingdom" of Britain. These were given an influential theoretical formulation by the Irish theorist William Molyneux in 1698 in his interpretation of John Locke's *Two Treatises of Government*.[20]

The three conventions of justification comprise the Canadian tradition of federalism, which is complementary to the liberal tradition of citizenship. In liberal theories of citizenship, whether individualist or communitarian, each individual member brings to the political association his or her pre-existing culture of rights, duties, and freedoms, whether they be natural, traditional, or birthrights. If this individual juristic culture is altered in any way by the political association, it requires the consent of each member at least once. The same is true for each federal member, by the first and third conventions of justification, in the analogous federal tradition. Second, the individual citizens unanimously agree that all future amendments to their juristic status, by which they conditionally "entrust" individual powers to the political association, can be made without unanimity – by the majority principle and representative government, free speech, access to the courts, etc. – as long as these laws are beneficial and respect the conditions under which the powers were entrusted. This entire tradition is expressed in sections 1–15(1) and 28 of the Charter. The same is true with regard to the second and third conventions of the federal tradition, as Lord Watson succinctly stated in his careful formulation. The federal members are free to introduce any sort of amending formula short of unanimity, as long as this rests on the negotiation and agreement of all members affected; and conditionally they are free to entrust as many powers to the federal government as they agree to, as long as this is understood as conditional entrustment, not alienation, and always renegotiable in the future, thus preserving the recognition and continuity convention. In a free federation the two traditions of federalism and citizenship work in tandem (*foederis aequas dicamus leges*). As a consequence, the entire federation is woven together by relations of trust.[21]

The remarkable manner in which the practice of constitutional negotiations conformed to these three immanent conventions after 1982 shows the extent to which they are the well-worn customs and usages of Canadian federalism, *dans la peau*. This is especially true with respect to the convention of fair negotiations as the means of redressing earlier breaches of convention. In Quebec, the Constitution Act, 1982, was widely perceived as unjust, having violated all three conventions and thus having breached the trust between

Quebec and the rest of Canada on which Quebec's allegiance ultimately rests. It was then argued by some that Quebec thus had the
right to separate from Canada, just as the Thirteen Colonies, when
the imperial parliament by-passed the consent of the colonial assemblies, had the right to separate in 1776.[22] Instead of following this
line of argument (based explicitly on the radical interpretation of
Locke's *Two Treatises*), which Quebeckers were "free to choose" (as the
Allaire Report correctly phrased it), Quebeckers freely chose the
classically Canadian path instead. The majority voted out the government of separation (the Parti Québécois) and elected a Liberal
government provincially and a Conservative government federally
with the express mandate to redress the injustice with "honour and
enthusiasm" by means of further negotiations. The majority of Quebeckers again followed this conventional path after 1990, demanding
further negotiations when the Meech Lake Accord was blocked. This
fidelity to the normative conventions of Canadian federalism is all
the more remarkable because the accord was blocked by the non-
ratification of the legislatures of Manitoba and Newfoundland, who
were not affected by the distinct society clause yet whose consent was
said to be required; whereas the Constitution Act, 1982, directly
affected Quebec, yet Quebec's consent was said at the time not to be
required.

Conformity to the very same conventions is evinced in the behaviour of the majority in the rest of Canada. Even though they accepted
the Constitution Act, 1982, since all three conventions had been
honoured in their case, they nonetheless immediately entered into
negotiations with Quebec. Furthermore, the majority of citizens
polled in the rest of Canada did not reject the Meech Lake Accord
because they objected to the distinct society clause, but, rather,
because the demands of the rest of Canada were not taken up in the
negotiations, because the negotiations were unilateral and were
unfairly held in private, and because an appropriate form of consent
had not been gained.[23] These objections conform exactly to the three
conventions, and they were immediately acted on in setting up the
procedures for the Canada round.

FIRST NATIONS AND FEDERALISM

The objections of the Aboriginal peoples to patriation and the Meech
Lake Accord, as well as their demands in the Canada round, are based
on three remarkably similar Aboriginal conventions of justification.
During the four First Ministers' Conferences on the Aboriginal right

of self-government (1983–86), during the Meech Lake round, and throughout the Canada round, their objection was that these constitutional changes were imposed on them without their consent. This violates the first convention of Aboriginal federalism – the convention of the unanimous consent of member nations to a federation. The convention is embodied in the practice of the Assembly of First Nations, in the 5,000 to 12,000 years of Aboriginal federalism, in the treaty making between the First Nations and the crown over 400 years, and in the exemplary constitution of the Haudenosaunee (Iroquois, or Six Nations) confederation, the Great Law of Peace (*Kaianereko:wa*) (c. 1450).[24]

The second objection of the First Nations is that the Charter of Rights and Freedoms is unacceptable as it stands, because it encroaches on the jurisdiction of Aboriginal laws and traditions. Aboriginal scholars such as Aki-kwe (Mary Ellen Turpel) and Patricia A. Monture-Okanee argue that the Charter is written in terms of Euro-Canadian traditions of jurisprudence, which conflict with Aboriginal traditions.[25] If Charter imperialism and discontinuity are to be avoided, it must be altered to recognize and conform to their juristic culture, and it must have their consent, just as in the case of the provinces and Quebec (see the section "Aboriginal Peoples and the Accord," below). The convention of justification for this requirement is the Aboriginal convention of recognition and continuity, embodied in centuries of Aboriginal federalism. Section 84 of the Great Law of Peace enshrines the convention in the same way the Quebec Act and section 94 enshrine the non-Aboriginal analogue: "Whenever a foreign nation is either conquered or has by its own will accepted the Great Peace [that is, joined the confederation], their own system of internal government may continue."[26]

How, then, are these objections to be met? They are to be met by fair multilateral negotiations in which the Aboriginal peoples, through their assembly and their national associations or separate nations, are recognized as nations on equal footing with the federal government, with their traditions of negotiation respected and their status as sovereign nations continued through the negotiations, irrespective of the degrees of political power they agree to entrust to, or share with, the federal government. This third convention is based on the inherent right of self-government which the Aboriginal peoples possess by virtue of being, as the Charlottetown Accord puts it, the first peoples to govern this land. The right of self-government, grounded in the long use, occupation and governance of a recognized territory, is expressed in the Great Law of Peace, and it is

independently corroborated by the similar (Bartolian) justification of
every European nation and by the criteria for sovereignty in international law.[27]

For the First Nations, the three Aboriginal conventions constitute
their background understanding of the practice of treaty negotiations
with the French, Dutch, and British crowns and, since 1867, with the
federal government. Since 1664, the conventions have been encoded
in the belts of two rows of wampum exchanged at the treaty negotiations to record the agreement. The Haudenosaunee confederation
explained to the Canadian House of Commons Committee on Indian
Self-Government in 1983 that the background white wampum beads
symbolize the purity of the agreement, the two rows of purple symbolize the Aboriginal and newcomer nations involved, and the three
beads separating the two rows symbolize peace, friendship and
respect. The two parallel rows "symbolize two paths or two vessels,
travelling down the same rivers together. One, a birch bark canoe,
will be for the Indian people, their laws, their customs and their
ways. The other, a ship, will be for the white people and their laws,
their customs and their ways. We shall each travel the river together,
side by side, but in our own boat. Neither of us will try to steer the
other's vessel."[28]

On the basis of the Two-Row, or *Gus-Wen-Teh*, vision of the mutual
recognition of coordinate sovereignty, the Aboriginal peoples have
entered into over five hundred treaties with the crowns and the
Canadian government. These have given rise to a parallel constitutional history in Canada, based on the same three conventions as the
non-Aboriginal constitutional history, and thus to a complex set of
relations of treaty federalism between the First Nations and the federal government.[29] The crucial point for the First Nations is that
their status as sovereign, self-governing nations has continued
through the federation, even where they have agreed to put themselves under federal "fiduciary trust" to some extent or other or have
ceded the use of land to the crown (*kitipanimissinow* – "we rule
ourselves," in Cree). Where no treaties have been made, they remain
self-governing nations with jurisdiction over their lands. As Lord
Watson, Lord Loranger, and Upper Canadians were formulating
their three conventions of federalism at the turn of the century, the
Haudenosaunee were doing the same for the three parallel Aboriginal conventions in *The Redman's Appeal for Justice* (1924), which they
presented to the League of Nations.[30]

Finally, the Aboriginal peoples trust the crown to have recognized
and confirmed *Gus-Wen-Teh* in the Royal Proclamation of October
1763, in response to their united negotiations and their resistance to

invasion, 1760–63. Here, as the documents and correspondence show, the crown recognized the "Indian nations" as being equal in status to European sovereign nations (just as it had done since 1696) and proclaimed that no land could be ceded by them except through negotiations between the crown and the chiefs of the Indian nations involved, in a public place and not under duress. Lands not ceded to the crown in such negotiations were to remain "Indian lands" under Aboriginal governance. Applying Emeric Vattel's concept of "guardianship" in international law (1758), Aboriginal sovereignty had continued intact through the various treaty relations of interdependency. The Royal Proclamation thus provides the crown with a complementary vision of treaty federalism, in which the treaties were negotiated from 1791 in Upper Canada, through the great numbered treaties of the late nineteenth and early twentieth centuries, to the Charlottetown Accord itself, and on to the process laid out in it for further negotiations. The specific land claims against treaty violations, the comprehensive land claims for untreatied lands, the court challenges, the demands for self-government, the resistance to invasion at Oka, and the dismantling of the Indian Act have all been justified in accord with the conventions of *Gus-Wen-Teh* and the Royal Proclamation.[31]

Hence, the Aboriginal peoples saw the Charter as a violation of the middle ground of Aboriginal and non-Aboriginal conventions that underlay the entire history of Aboriginal-Canadian treaty federalism. Since the Royal Proclamation is constitutionalized in section 25 of the Charter, and Aboriginal rights in section 35, it follows that the sovereignty of Aboriginal peoples is now recognized in the constitution. Because their status was disregarded in practice, patriation constituted a violation of the Charter itself. They tried unsuccessfully to have their conventional status as self-governing nations acknowledged in the conferences of 1983–87. Since the Meech Lake Accord proceeded without their agreement, Elijah Harper could not consent to it in the Manitoba legislature.[32]

Since 1990, the conventions of the Aboriginal peoples have been conventionally recognized by the citizens and governments of Canada. Their inherent right of self-government was recognized immediately in the Beaudoin-Dobbie Report, their representatives were brought into the constitutional negotiations, their Aboriginal forms of negotiation were respected, except in the referendum process, and their consent was recognized as being required for any constitutional change that affects them. The entire set of amendments concerning the Aboriginal peoples in the Charlottetown Accord should be seen, I believe, as bringing the relations between the Aboriginal peoples and the other two orders of government in accordance with the three conventions of trust that underlie the two constitutional paths, Aboriginal and newcomer, of Canadian federalism.[33]

LINGUISTIC AND MULTICULTURAL MINORITIES

It is not only Quebec, the other provinces, and the Aboriginal peoples that share these conventions. The two official linguistic minorities in Canada justify their rights to their language, educational institutions, and varying levels of control over social services by appeal to the same conventions. Their language, education, and social services make up their minority juristic culture, which is protected on the grounds that it should be recognized and continued wherever they live. This is the historical justification for the two-cultures vision, classically formulated by Henri Bourassa by reference to the same convention of continuity that English Canada and Quebec employ. No one has better expressed this vision of the federation, while fully recognizing the jurisdiction of provinces against which it must be constantly negotiated, than Ernest Lapointe in his famous (and unsuccessful) plea of 1916, when Ontario violated the convention:

It has long been the settled policy of Great Britain that whenever a country passed under the sovereignty of the Crown by treaty or otherwise, to respect the religion, usages and language of the inhabitants who thus become British subjects. That this house [of Commons] ... while fully recognizing the principle of provincial rights ... respectfully suggest to the legislative assembly [of Ontario] the wisdom of making it clear that the privileges of the children of French parentage of being taught in their mother tongue be not interfered with.[34]

The application of this convention is deeply woven into the fabric of Canadian constitutionalism. The juristic culture of the English-speaking settlers in Quebec was recognized and continued in 1774 and 1791; Upper Canada was formed as a bilingual colony in 1791 and French-speaking settlers from the Ohio valley were told the Quebec Act would apply to them; sections 93 and 133 continued this tradition in 1867, as did the Manitoba Act in 1870 and sections 16–23 of the Charter in 1982; and every formulation of the distinct society clause makes reference to, or is paired with, the protection of the anglophone minority.

The convention of cultural continuity is extended to other minorities in the Charter in a manner that is manifestly analogous to the official language minorities. Section 27 states that the Charter "shall be interpreted in a manner consistent with the preservation and enhancement of the multicultural heritage of Canadians." Moreover, since 1867 there has been a tacit convention that the views of these minorities will be taken into account in negotiations that affect them, not through direct representatives at the constitutional table, but through lobbying and ad hoc proxies. Throughout the Meech Lake and Canada rounds, organizations representing the two official language minorities and multicultural minorities played this conventional role and advanced the conventional appeals for justice.

But one might ask, "Surely, it is just as important that the juristic culture of political and legal rights and freedoms of *individual* citizens be recognized and continued in sections 1–15(1) and 28 of the Charter on the basis of the same three conventions of justification?" Yes, this is of equal importance.

A further argument might go as follows. For each of the examples given above – Quebec, the other provinces, Aboriginal peoples, official language minorities, multicultural minorities, and individuals – these three conventions have been violated many times. For instance, in his notorious report, Lord Durham explicitly repudiated the principle of continuity on which British policy had rested for seventy years and recommended that the crown should discontinue Quebec's language and customs, on the grounds that British language and customs were racially superior.[35] This provided the basis for the policy of "extinguishing" French Canadianism through the Act of Union from 1840 to 1867. From the perspective of Quebec, the constitution of 1867 was designed to end the policy and secure Quebec against future attempts at assimilation. (Some commentators in Quebec saw the Charter as "Durhamism" in a new guise.) Second, the federal government for a long time denied the western provinces their full section 92 powers, and the triple-E Senate proposal is seen as a way of securing equal footing for them and the Maritime provinces with Quebec and Ontario. Third, the Crown and the provinces also violated these conventions innumerable times with respect to the Aboriginal peoples. The policy of discontinuity was explicitly evoked to justify the genocide of the Mic'mac in the eighteenth century. The successive policies – from the Act for the Gradual Civilization of the Indian Tribes in 1857, through the Indian Act of 1876, to the White Paper on Indian Affairs of 1969 – have been imposed on the Aboriginal peoples without their consent and have sought to destroy their Aboriginal and Métis governments and ways of life, using the same type of racist justification as the Durham Report and forcing them into appalling social and economic conditions. Their treaty and Aboriginal rights have been violated time out of mind.[36] Fourth, the convention of the continuity of the language and education of francophone minorities has been violated, and continues to be violated, by governments of the English-language provinces, from Nova Scotia in 1864 to Alberta, Saskatchewan, and Manitoba today. Even Quebec, which has honoured this convention for centuries with respect to the anglophone minority as francophone communities were being "discontinued" throughout the other provinces, has recently passed some restrictive legislation.

I do not doubt any of this for one moment. My reply to the above argument is only to ask what justifications Canadians conventionally appeal to – whether in conversations, legislatures, courts, demonstrations, or on the barricades at Oka – when they wish to argue that these acts are unjust. Are they not almost invariably the three I have outlined?

As a result of their recognition in the Charter, a number of other actors appeared on the constitutional stage (for example, multicultural groups, women's associations, affirmative action organizations, and civil liberties associations). With the democratization of constitutional recognition, Canadian citizens became directly concerned with constitutional change and demanded a say in the proceedings. As organizations of civil society and individual citizens were drawn into constitutional negotiations in the 1980s, they simply followed the well-trodden paths laid down by the three conventions. That is to say, they justified their demands for justice by appeals to recognition and continuity, asking to have some sort of say in the negotiations that affected them and to be able to express their consent or dissent. For example, the National Action Committee on the Status of Women justifiably objected that the constitution had historically been negotiated without the recognition, negotiation, or consent of women and therefore had to be renegotiated to redress its substantive male bias.[37]

Hence, the blossoming of the constitutional process in the 1980s, from the old middle ground of executive federalism to the new and colourful suburbs of various ad hoc practices of indirect negotiations and deliberations, expanded the middle ground to accommodate the new actors, yet did so in accordance with the traditional conventions. The referendum satisfied the requirement of consent, and the innumerable ways in which the various groups interacted with the negotiations met the test of fair negotiations reasonably well. Of course, those who wanted different arrangements (constituent assemblies and so on) appealed to the same conventions to make their points. The exemplary appeal of the Native Women's Association of Canada that their voices were not being adequately represented in negotiations which directly affected them proves the point.

Even so, are not the conventions of justification so broad and elastic that they do not determine anything? It is as if the constitutional game is almost without bounds. Certainly, the broad boundaries of these three conventions permit a wide range of play with the competing visions. The various Canadian political ideologies of liberalism, communitarianism, conservatism, socialism, and nationalisms can be employed within them. I imagine they could be stretched to accommodate any arrangement, from sovereignty association for Quebec (or whomever) and seats at the United Nations for the First Nations, at one boundary, to a highly centralized Canada at another, as long as the negotiations to get there could be conventionally justified. But to say that the constitutional game is not everywhere bounded by rules is not to say that it is unregulated. This just means that Canadian constitutional culture is not ideological. It has its own conventions of justice immanent in its practice. It is the role of the conventions of a constitution not to impose an ideology but to constitute a just federation in which the everyday ideological struggles of politics can be played fairly.

Nor do these broad conventions need to be reformed in accordance with the latest political theories from the United States or Europe. These may be introduced within the game of politics as one theory among many, but the game does not need to be justified by them (any more than it is in the United States).[38] Canadians are no longer colonials who must subject their thought and practice to the sovereignty of the political thought and traditions of Europe. They have developed, no doubt in spite of themselves, their own genuinely Aboriginal and Canadian conventions of justification and forms of constitutional negotiation.

MIDDLE-GROUND NEGOTIATIONS

The aim of the Canada round was to redress the injustices of patriation, the failure of the four First Ministers' Conferences on aboriginal self-government, and the exclusions of Meech Lake, and to do so through multilateral negotiations in which each voice would be heard and in which (provisional) agreement acceptable to all would be reached. Let us now try to see how an agreement can be reached in negotiations of this middle-ground kind, with convergence on a limited set of visions, the possibility of overlapping consensus on fundamental characteristics among varying combinations of negotiators, three conventions of justification, and various ways of sampling constituents' judgments *en passant*.

One of the apparently impassable objections to the Canada clause was that it did not give full recognition to each of the fundamental characteristics. The Aboriginal peoples objected that their sovereignty was denied; Quebeckers objected to the way the distinct society was whittled down from the Meech Lake Accord; the linguistic minorities were offended by the wording of their characteristic; the National Action Committee protested the wording of the gender equality characteristic; and so on. These criticisms seem warranted by the convention of full recognition and continuity. Canadian constitutional history shows that the full recognition of each member of the federation, in its own terms and traditions, is essential at the outset as the basis for multilateral negotiations. (There are many treaties now being renegotiated because this step was overlooked in the past.)

The Canada clause should set out a full portrait of the members as they recognize themselves, in all their uncompromised, majestic cultural diversity, in order to free Canadians from their dogmatic, one-vision slumber and their attitude of comparative advantage. A portrait of full recognition and continuity, like a portrait of the totem poles in front of a Haida, Kwagiulth, Nisga'a, or Tsimshian village, is a permanent reminder of the fundamental characteristics, with their overlapping federation stories which stand before and continue through all the modifications and accommodations that are made in the middle-ground amendments to the central institutions during the negotiations. If mutual recognition is not achieved at the beginning, then Canadians only recognize the other characteristics if they are presented in terms of, and subordinate to, their various understandings of the federation. The other members are not recognized as they recognize themselves; their dignity and self-esteem are undermined and they feel slighted, insulted, and humiliated. The ensuing and engulfing struggles of *ressentiment* to regain recognition lead to spiralling envy, discord, enmity, and, as Shakespeare explored in *King Lear*, to madness and civil war.

Think of how much of the antipathy in Quebec after the blockage of Meech – and vented in the Citizens' Forum throughout the rest of Canada – was caused by by-passing this first step of full recognition. How much of the drive towards the three solitary nationalisms (Quebec, "Rest of Canada," and Aboriginal) surveyed in Alan Cairns's chapter was fuelled by the same sense of being disesteemed and slighted? The drift towards three solitary nationalisms is an attempt to give oneself the recognition that could not be gained from others through mutual recognition. It is an empty attempt, for the reasons given by Hegel, and it misrecognizes the internal plurality of the three nations themselves, as we have seen. Yet it is tempting to follow this path after the route to mutual recognition has been closed by the moral failure to grant others the recognition one demands for oneself.

This step of self-identification, or dignity-recognition, of listening attentively to the voices of the others, is the first step in just multilateral negotiations, ensuring that no single vision unjustly predominates over the constitution and negotiations at the outset. If one federation story and its forms of expression set the terms of the Canada clause, and thus of the negotiations, then all others are unjustly subordinated by being translated and interpreted in its authoritative language. If a federal structure is then hastily fabricated and rammed through on this unjust foundation, the entire edifice will eventually have to be renegotiated on a just basis, as Canadian history amply illustrates. Just negotiations begin by listening to others introduce themselves and say "where they are coming from" in their own terms and traditions; then they return the compliment. In other words, just negotiations involve speaking *with* rather than *for*.

But in the Canada clause, it looks as if the characteristics are already in negotiated federal relations of interdependency. The way they are set out looks like the result of the negotiations rather than the starting point. It is as if diplomats were ordered to present themselves to a meeting in a manner that mirrored the agreement reached in the meeting. But the portrait of the members in their agreed-upon federal relations of interdependency is the role of the amendments to the central institutions, not of the foreground Canada clause.

The Canada clause should thus portray the first step in the negotiations themselves, each representative presenting its vision of the federation and ways of negotiation in its own terms, ceremonies, and traditions, and listening to the others. The genealogy of constitutional negotiations – from the Aboriginal-crown treaty negotiations to the three years of multilateral negotiations leading up to the 1867 constitution, to some of the tricultural forms at Oka in 1990 – is full of diplomatic ceremonies of recognition and cultural continuity that facilitate mutual understanding and multilateral vision. The *Gus-Wen-Teh* form of mutual recognition is an exemplar of justice for this first and crucial step.[39] The practices and ceremonies of the Beaudoin-Dobbie commission and of the seventeen negotiators also facilitated

184 Constitutional Predicament

this first step to some degree. The representatives had an opportunity to present their vision, to observe, listen to, participate in, and over time and close interaction to come to appreciate the stories of the other members of the federation. The more the negotiators were able to see the others' points of view through interaction, the more they were able to negotiate a way round apparent impasses.

All this is an example of the activity of engendering diversity awareness, which Aboriginal peoples have always practised in their forms of government: to tell and exchange stories of one's family, clan, nation, and federation (*ada'ox* in Gitksan) at public feasts in order to acquire a multiple vision of reality. The practices of exchanging federation stories are as necessary to the health of a diverse federation as market exchanges are to a diverse world economy.[40]

Canadian citizens did not have the same interactive experience to free them temporarily from their own background understanding. A gap between the negotiators and the deliberators opened up as the negotiations proceeded. Canadians need to engage in more exchanges and become a little more intercultural, in addition to multicultural, in order to surmount the impasse. The inability to appreciate the other ways of participating in the federation and imagine how just relations among them might be negotiated is the first cause of the impasse. This first step is not easy in the best of circumstances. It requires an act of the imagination – the ability to imagine the federation from other points of view and overcome diversity blindness. Like all abilities it is difficult to acquire, yet it is the indispensable requirement of just multilateral negotiations and deliberation. The queen of the federal abilities is diversity awareness.

THE DISTINCT SOCIETY CLAUSE

A second example is the apparent impasse caused by the conflict between the distinct society clause and the official language minority in Quebec. In 1982, Prime Minister Trudeau entrenched the right of the official languages minorities in the Charter and shielded these sections from the notwithstanding clause. Section 23(1)(a) states that citizens of Canada whose first language learned and still understood is that of the English or French linguistic minority population in which they reside have the right to have their children receive primary and secondary school instruction in that language in that province. If this were enforced, it would discontinue Quebec's jurisdiction over the language of education of immigrants. Accordingly, section 59 (2) reads that this right will come into effect only with the consent of the legislative assembly of the Government of Quebec. Thus, even

Prime Minister Trudeau acknowledged that the minority language rights of the Charter were limited by the character of Quebec as a distinct society and that they required Quebec's agreement.

Of course, there is no solution to the conflict. It is a constitutive tension between two claims to continuity (as Ernest Lapointe's earlier quotation neatly illustrates) that has been continually negotiated since 1774. A path to conciliation is illuminated in the case of *Quebec v. Ford et al.*[41] The French-only sign legislation of Bill 101 was challenged on the ground that it limited the freedom of expression in section 2(b) to an extent that could not be justified in terms of "such reasonable limits ... as can be demonstrably justified in a free and democratic society" (section 1). The Quebec court ruled that the sign law violated the freedom of expression in Quebec's Charter, and then the Supreme Court ruled that it violated freedom of expression in the federal Charter.

The reasoning of the Supreme Court was twofold. First, it gave full recognition to freedom of expression. The right to communicate in one's language is said to be entailed by the freedom of expression because language is inseparable from individual identity. The court inferred that commercial signage is an instance of freedom of expression, and it went on to ask what limits could be placed on this in a free and democratic society. Second, the court fully recognized that the continuity of the "French face" of Quebec was "a pressing and substantial objective," sufficient to warrant limiting a constitutional freedom. Next, the three criteria of the Oakes test were employed to determine to what extent the freedom of expression could be limited: (1) The means should not be arbitrary and must achieve the objective; (2) the means should impair the freedom as little as possible; and (3) the costs should be proportional to the benefits. The court concluded that it was not necessary to require French-only signs to achieve the objective of the continuity of the French face of Quebec. This could be achieved by requiring the French language to have a "marked predominance" on commercial signs, rather than exclusivity, thereby permitting the proportionately smaller expression of English and other languages on commercial signs.

The reasoning of the court illustrates one of the central features of multilateral federalism – that seemingly irreconcilable fundamental characteristics (the distinct society, minority languages, and individual expression) can be conciliated by forms of reasoning that employ rules of thumb such as the Oakes test to accommodate competing claims of recognition and cultural continuity in particular cases. (If Premier Bourassa had accepted this decision rather than introducing the contentious Bill 178, the Meech Lake Accord might well have passed, for Bill 178 was cited as the main objection to the accord outside Quebec.)

The distinct society clause in the Charlottetown Accord is set up in a similar manner. It consists of three characteristics: a French-speaking majority, a unique culture, and a civil law tradition, preserved and promoted by the government and legislature of Quebec. This is immediately followed by row (d) which states that Canadians and their governments are committed to the vitality and development of the official language minorities. It is difficult to see in this anything other than an attempt to make explicit the kind of implicit considerations of conciliating competing fundamental characteristics that are already typical, and indeed conventional, in the legal reasoning of *Quebec v. Ford* and other cases, such as *Sparrow v. Regina*.[42] This distinctively Canadian form of reasoning is not based on individual *versus* collective rights, but, as we have seen throughout, on considerations of overlapping identity-related cultural differences and on the appropriate forms of their compossible recognition, continuity, federation, and *épanouissement*.

The distinct society clause was also criticized because it is allegedly irreconcilable with the fundamental characteristic of provincial equality. The Canada clause sought to make this seeming impasse passable by drawing attention to a third and intermediate fundamental characteristic on the same row – provincial diversity. The point of the juxtaposition is to free provincial egalitarians from captivity to a vision of Canada based on one fundamental characteristic of provinces (equality) and enable them to see the diverse characteristics as well, thereby disposing them to think analogically of the distinct society clause as an aspect of Quebec's provincial diversity. Presumably, the negotiators conciliated provincial equality and the distinct society by employing provincial diversity as an "intermediate case," or object of contrast, in this analogical fashion, and many commentators supported them by pointing out the great diversity among the provinces recorded in various parts of the constitution.

However, this is to misrecognize the nature of the distinct society as a fundamental characteristic. It is not based on Quebec's characteristic as a province; as we saw above, it is based on its character as one of the two non-Aboriginal founding nations, constitutionalized first in 1774 and 1791. The reasoning here is that each of three characteristics in the distinct society clause render Quebec analogous to all the other provinces taken together, not to any other single province. The language of the majority is French, whereas it is English in all the other provinces. The culture is pluralistic and predominantly French, whereas it is pluralistic and predominantly English in the other provinces. Quebec has a civil law tradition, whereas the other provinces have only the common law tradition. By virtue of precisely these three characteristics, Quebec is analogous to the other provinces taken together.

What follows from looking at Quebec-Canada from the aspect of two non-Aboriginal nations or two distinct societies? It is unquestionably the case that the majority English-language provinces as a whole take measures to preserve and promote their language, culture, and common law traditions. There are hundreds of laws limiting the rights of individuals and groups in the rest of Canada (in relation to the United States and other cultures, to trade, and to laws), all justified on the ground of preserving and promoting the English language, Canadian culture, and legal systems. Throughout the Americas, the majority English-speaking United States, the predominantly Spanish-speaking countries, and the predominantly Portugese-speaking Brazil all do the same. Quebec is making the analogous case for the preservation and promotion of its majority language, culture, and legal system.[43]

These are the uplifting analogies to keep in mind when negotiating and deliberating the distinct society clause, rather than the illiberal misanalogies that Alain Noël calmly exposes in his comment on Barry Cooper's chapter in this volume. (If the 85 per cent of anglophone Quebeckers who voted Yes can affirm these dignifying analogies, why can't the majority of Canadians west of Ontario be as generous, especially since they demand an equitable form of reciprocal recognition?) Consequently, the argument that the distinct society clause violates provincial equality is based on a misrecognition, or a refusal to recognize, the fundamental characteristic on which the clause is based.

A second objection to the distinct society clause was that it would be used to discontinue the various juristic cultures of the eleven First Nations of Quebec and the allophones and anglophones of Quebec. The negotiators responded by placing these three fundamental characteristics snugly around the distinct society in the Canada clause itself so that citizens and justices would bring them to mind, and take them into consideration, in the same panorama as the interpretation of the Charter in the light of the distinct society clause. In addition, this objection seems to rest on a misunderstanding of the distinct society clause itself. It presumes that the clause is a mask for the unilateral assimilation of the First Nations, allophones, and anglophones to a homogeneous national culture – a reverse Durham Report. This is the unilateral vision of a minority of Quebeckers. For example, Jacques Parizeau has said that it is impossible to promote the French language and culture and at the same time to preserve the anglophone minority.[44]

However, the vision behind the distinct society clause for most Quebeckers is multilateral, of Quebec as a *société globale*. Quebec is seen as a society analogous to the rest of Canada as a whole by virtue of being an overlapping plurality, as we saw above. The *autonomie* and self-government of the eleven First Nations are recognized and affirmed, the anglophone juristic culture and allophone polyethnicity are protected and celebrated, individual rights are entrenched in the Charter, and the citizens of Quebec have all the considerable advantages of participating in the Canadian federation with a partner *société globale* whose predominant public language is English and who, after all is said and done, is *dans la peau*. This is what most Quebeckers, or at least most Montrealers, mean by "unique culture" in the distinct society clause. A fully modern life of work, politics, and culture in a multinational and multicultural society can be lived in French in Quebec, just as such a life can be lived in English in the rest of Canada. The French language can be justified in Quebec, as English is in the rest of Canada, on purely utilitarian grounds. It is the language that enables citizens to participate fully in the life of their society. Nowhere else in the Americas is this possible. The irony of post-Trudeau Quebec is that while nationalists continue to repudiate Trudeau's pan-Canadian nationalism, they are reconceptualizing Quebec nationalism in a more liberal pluralist form than Trudeau's Charter.[45]

Negotiation, then, need not consist in imposing the distinct society over other fundamental characteristics. It can consist in either placing the other characteristics in the distinct society clause, as in the Meech Lake Accord and the Beaudoin-Dobbie Report, or arranging the characteristics alongside each other, as in the Charlottetown Accord, and so incrementally negotiating agreement by means of overlapping consensus, and ongoing appeals to conventions of justification at each step, with the proponents of the other characteristics.

EQUALITY AND ASYMMETRY

Another impasse was the conflict between the equality of provinces and Senate reform. The western provinces were justified in pressing for provincial equality. The provinces are equal in a fundamental sense (the sense given by Lord Watson and embodied in section 92) as autonomous representative democracies in their own jurisdictions, in relations of coordinate sovereignty with the federal government. Yet in practice the western provinces have been dominated in the central institutions, both by the federal control of their natural resources until 1930 and by the weight of the eastern provinces. A Senate in which each province has equal representation was advanced on the principle of equality and as the means of blocking further domination. A quick calculation of voting in such a Senate showed that it would not have the desired effect. Accordingly, the western provinces demanded and received a Senate veto over any tax legislation affecting their natural resources. This is a just demand by virtue of the convention of consent over what touches a member, but it is separate from provincial equality. The western provinces could have gained this in exchange for the double-majority rule for Quebec senators on legislation affecting French language and culture (justified by the same convention of consent) without altering the regional composition of the present Senate. Moreover, the characteristic of provincial equality is already embodied in the conventions of constitutional amendment and in the institution of annual First Ministers' Conferences. The latter is a powerful institution, and the western provinces might have been better off seeking to strengthen it, rather than to reform the Senate.

The reform of the Senate in accord with the equality of provinces knocked out Quebec's fundamental characteristic of roughly 25 per cent representation (based on population and region). This was a symbolic loss, as Quebec commentators pointed out, because the old one-quarter representation of Quebec, along with new Aboriginal representation in the Senate, looks like a fair compromise expression of the "two non-Aboriginal nations" vision. The negotiators thus realized that they had to find a place to preserve this fundamental characteristic in the central institutions. They then carried it down to the House of Commons, giving Quebec a threshold of 25 per cent of the seats. This was a disaster, because the House of Commons is one of the fundamental characteristics that is shared by everyone in the same way. Everyone shares the public good that the form of participation in the House (currently representation by population) should apply equally across the country. Given this sturdy Canadian consensus, there is no way that another conflicting fundamental characteristic can be carved into the face of the House. Some who voted Yes replied that it would make no difference in practice, since Quebec has (and will continue to have for at least a century) 25 per cent of the population of Canada. But this pragmatic "nose holding" ignored the extent to which Canadian constitutional politics is a serious game of principles and values; of keeping the public goods and principles carried by the fundamental characteristics in a just arrangement.

One of the biggest impasses to agreement was the perceived incompatibility of provincial equality and Quebec's demand for asymmetrical federalism. On closer inspection, the incompatibility seems to stem from the way these two characteristics were envisioned. Most of the powers Quebec requested are provincial powers that have been taken over by the federal government through the expansion of the federal spending power, especially since 1945. Quebec wished to limit the expansion and regain exclusive or paramount jurisdiction over at least six provincial powers.

The federal government has sought to set up federal programs to ensure the basic needs of all Canadians. However, the powers to do so fall under provincial jurisdiction in section 92, making it unconstitutional for the federal government to exercise these powers. Yet Ottawa has the right to raise taxes for, say, health care, even though health care is a provincial jurisdiction. So Ottawa says to the provinces that they will get the money required to administer health care programs if they follow the federal standards. By this means, of dubious constitutionality, Ottawa has extended its spending power into several provincial jurisdictions. The Charlottetown Accord would have validated federal spending in exclusive provincial jurisdictions, something the provinces have never agreed to before. In exchange, Ottawa would agree to provide the money necessary for a province if it wished to offer its own program as an alternative to a national program, as long as the program met the objectives set down by the federal government. This compromise solution, which leaves the federal government with considerable control over provincial jurisdictions, is misleadingly called provincial "opting out."

The option of opting out meets the standard of provincial equality because it is available to each province equally. Although it may lead to asymmetry in practice, since not all provinces may choose to exercise the same options, it is based on the equality of provinces and the convention of consent. Some of the objectors spoke of this as a "special privilege" for the provinces. Nevertheless, it is the federal government that has the special privilege of exercising powers, and setting objectives for others, which belong to the provinces by the conventions of consent and continuity. Others objected on pragmatic grounds that opting out would lead in time to a decentralized, crazy-quilt, and unworkable federation. The accord's proposal for future negotiations on an economic, social, and environmental union was the response to this objection. However, if this objection has some validity, rather than being simply an unexamined prejudice for symmetry and central control, then the only way to move justly towards greater centralization is through the force of better argument, further negotiations, and consent. If English-Canadian nationalists can convince the provinces other than Quebec of the value of centralization, they can agree among themselves to centralize their powers under sections 94 or 38(2) and (3) without Quebec's consent. The federal government cannot decide on its own prerogative to centralize the federation, for, as we have seen, it has no prerogative to impose such a Norman yoke by conquest and discontinuity. Even John A. Macdonald proudly upheld the conventions of continuity, negotiation, and consent, which have been the guardians of constitutional liberty since 15 June 1215.

ABORIGINAL PEOPLES AND THE ACCORD

Did the agreements on Aboriginal self-government constitute a closed impasse for Canadians? The understanding of the Aboriginal peoples as inherently self-governing nations, consisting of 750,000 citizens who live off reserves from time to time, has not been widely disseminated among non-Aboriginal Canadians in the late twentieth century. It began to come to their notice through Aboriginal writings and protests in the 1960s, through the courts after the landmark *Calder* case in British Columbia in 1973, through the land claims, demonstrations, commissions, and legal research of the 1980s, and through the recognition of nationhood in international law. Unless one was involved in these occurrences in some way or followed the events and writings closely, it was difficult to question and criticize the habitual stereotypes and misinformation that continued to inform non-Aboriginal culture.[46] Consequently, there was little middle ground to begin with and few occasions to imagine, let alone appreciate, the negotiations and final agreement from Aboriginal points of view. This stultifying obstacle to recognition, affirmation and renegotiated relations of interdependency is not impassable, but it was surely naive to presume that it could be dislodged in a short referendum campaign.

The Aboriginal peoples themselves were deeply divided over the Charlottetown Accord. The four Aboriginal negotiators all supported the accord. Three of the four had the support of their organizations: the Native Council of Canada, which speaks for Aboriginal people living off reserves; the Inuit Tapirisat of Canada, and the Métis National Council. Even if the accord did little more than constitutionalize a process already underway for Métis and Inuit self-government and land reclamation, the recognition of the continuity of the juristic culture of Aboriginal peoples living off reserves, and the unanimous recognition of *kitipanimissinow* (Aboriginal self-government), however mitigated, were seen as the basis of a better relationship of trust with non-Aboriginal Canada.[47] However, 60 per cent of the Aboriginal citizens who live on reserves and who voted, voted No, even though their negotiator, Ovide Mercredi, the chief of the Assembly of First Nations, was the most visible Aboriginal negotiator and the most outspoken Aboriginal supporter of the accord. There are several reasons why this impasse developed.

The first is that in the *Draft Legal Text*, the phrases "in Canada" in the Canada clause and "within Canada" in section 35 both make it appear that the inherent and independent Aboriginal governments exist only within a Canadian legal framework. It is not clear how the Aboriginal peoples can justly move from being "the first peoples to govern this land" at the beginning of the Canada clause to "one of three orders of government in Canada" at the end, without some explanation of the intermediary step: namely, the conditional *Gus-Wen-Teh* mutual entrustment treaties. This subordination is reinforced by 35.4(2), which states that no exercise of inherent self-government "may be inconsistent with federal or provincial laws that are essential to the preservation of peace, order and good government in Canada," which makes the Aboriginal "order" appear subordinate to the other two. The treaties between the First Nations and the crown appear as intranational rather than international treaties, thus breaching the convention of recognition and continuity. One of the chiefs of Kahnawake, Billy Two Rivers, pointed out this misrecognition when the accord was first made public, and many traditional chiefs followed his lead.

Another objection voiced by many chiefs was that the process was too hurried to engage in their consensus practices of negotiation, thus disregarding the convention of fair negotiations. When Chief Mercredi sought the support of 435 chiefs in Vancouver, most walked away without a vote, signalling their dissent in Aboriginal style and giving the failure to respect Aboriginal forms of negotiation as the reason.[48]

A widespread objection, accounting for much of the rift in the Assembly of First Nations, was the distrust of the federal government. As a result of treaty and other formal obligations incurred by the taking of Aboriginal lands and by pushing Aboriginal peoples onto tiny, polluted reserves, the federal government owes the Aboriginal peoples over $4 billion a year. While this is a pittance relative to the profits Canadians have reaped from the land and the damage they have done to the Aboriginal peoples, it looms large in a recession. There was reason to believe, especially with a history of lying and broken promises, that the offer of self-government was a stratagem to offload federal fiscal obligations. This distrust was reinforced by the objection, advanced by Elijah Harper, that the accord did not bind the federal government to turn over the Aboriginal land or finances necessary for the practice of self-government.[49]

Distrust also developed between Chief Mercredi and other chiefs as the negotiations proceeded. Many traditional chiefs do not consider that the assembly represents them, but even band council chiefs moved away from their negotiator. Part of the explanation lies in the division of Aboriginal societies throughout Great Turtle Island (North America) between Aboriginal peoples based on the reserves, such as the reserve chiefs, and Aboriginal people who spend little time on a reserve, such as Chief Mercredi and many of his advisers. In addition, the distrust is one aspect of the general crisis of representation between all negotiators except the other three Aboriginal negotiators, and their respective constituents. The prime minister was distrusted from the beginning, and even those premiers who were trusted initially came away badly tarnished.

An agreement cannot be reached unless relations of trust between representatives and citizens are sustained throughout the negotiation and referendum period. As we have seen, Aboriginal and non-Aboriginal elders, from Deganawida to Lord Watson, have been of one mind that negotiations are suspended in bonds of trust. When they do not exist or are severed, the talks break down. The delicate sentiments of trust can be preserved and strengthened only by an intermediate consultative process in which the negotiators report on each stage of the negotiations and receive advice from their constituents. The various advocacy organizations of civil society could also play an important mediating role. Diplomatic practices of holding informal meetings in the "bushes" with constituents enable the negotiators to explain their view from within the multilateral negotiations and the citizens to explain how things look from their perspective, thus clarifying each other's vision and clearing the path for further talks.[50]

The most intractable impasse was between the Aboriginal supporters of the Accord and the Native Women's Association of Canada. Although the Charter of Rights and Freedoms applies to Aboriginal governments (section 32), a number of exceptions are written into the *Draft Legal Text*. Like the federal and provincial governments, Aboriginal governments have access to the notwithstanding clause to override sections 2 and 7–15 of the Charter. In addition, the Aboriginal and treaty rights of section 25 are strengthened, thus shielding Aboriginal peoples from the application of the gender equality section 28 of the Charter. The sections of the Charter on the right to vote and to stand for election are written so that they do not apply to Aboriginal governments. The inherent right of Aboriginal self-government in section 35 is moved so that the gender equality clause at 35(4) will not apply to it. On the other hand, there is a guarantee of a conference on gender equality in 1996.

The Native Women's Association of Canada argued that the entire Charter should apply to Aboriginal governments. The present Aboriginal governments are dominated by males and there is a high incidence of male violence against women on the reserves. If the accord were passed, Aboriginal women, especially Aboriginal women coming onto reserves from the cities, would be excluded from Aboriginal governments and discriminated against, as they were in the 1970s and 1980s over Bill C-31; the violence would continue, and they would have no means of redress.[51]

Defenders of the accord, including a leading Aboriginal feminist adviser and two Aboriginal women negotiators, argued that the Aboriginal governments, values, and traditions needed to be recognized and continued against the imposition of the Charter, with its antagonistic Western values. They conceded that although the present band council governments are dominated by men, they have been imposed by the administrators of the Indian Act. As Aboriginal governments evolve, they will develop their own practices of gender equality by drawing on and reforming traditional forms of Aboriginal government that predate the Indian Act. These forms have a richer repertoire of gender equality and empowerment, such as the clan mother system, than the patriarchal Canadian legal and political system has.

As Canadian feminists have argued, the guarantee of gender equality in section 28 of the Charter has done little to alleviate violence against women, and it has disguised the underlying substantive inequality of women in Canadian society. Moreover, as Europeans have long observed, the Aboriginal consensus forms of government are generally more egalitarian and participatory, and permit a far greater degree of uncoerced individual freedom than the majoritarian, representative, and stratified Canadian system. Charter imposition would undermine the evolving Aboriginal governments and justice systems, which are based on the values of shared responsibility to, and care of, mother earth, family, community, and the seventh generation. These culturally based governments and justice systems will provide the social basis of self-respect needed to root out the underlying causes of alcohol abuse, suicide, and violence; namely, the dependency, self-depreciation, and helplessness caused by the imposition of Western values through the Indian Act and through the destruction of Aboriginal cultures.[52]

Is this impassable? Both sides agree on political participation and gender equality but disagree on the means. To mediate this conflict, Aboriginal peoples are working on middle-ground institutions that could be phased in gradually as the Indian Act and federal and provincial laws are phased out. One is tribunals, based on Aboriginal forms of justice and conflict resolution, in which grievances can be heard and redressed by the community, and by which appeals can be made to the international law of Aboriginal peoples. Another is Aboriginal charters, which express the Aboriginal values of strength (cultural rights), kindness (social rights), sharing (economic rights) and trust (political and civil rights). The checks on the Canadian Charter in the Charlottetown Accord are designed to ensure that the genuinely cross-cultural values underlying the Canadian and Aboriginal charters – such as participation and equality – will be realized in a culturally sensitive manner, just as the distinct society clause works for Quebec.[53]

One of the most promising developments is the dawning awareness among legal scholars since the Supreme Court ruling in *Québec v. Regent Sioui* (1990) that the totality of Aboriginal laws and customs was understood, prior to the twentieth century, to constitute part of the Canadian common law. These laws and customs form, so to speak, one of the three orders of jurisprudence in Canada's tricultural legal system. Thus, Aboriginal cases can be tried in Aboriginal ways by Aboriginal justices in Canadian courts. Once Canadian common law is seen as a federation of Aboriginal and non-Aboriginal legal systems, the threat of domination posed by the expression "within" Canada is dissolved.[54]

Although this middle ground is more of a working promise than a reality at the moment, it does show that one of the most difficult and important impasses of the entire Canada round is not impassable. Now, I am aware that although I have given several examples of negotiating multilaterally on the intercultural middle ground in order to keep the fundamental characteristics of Canada in a just arrangement, I have not presented a theory of this form of federalism. How, one might ask, can one understand the concept of multilateral negotiations without a theory? To this, I would reply that you learn the concept of multilateral negotiations by following and going against the examples, and thus acquiring the abilities to carry on yourself, just as you learn the activities of negotiating and deliberating multilaterally by engaging in and going against them in practice. In giving one example after another, I have put forward no less than I know myself. A theory is neither possible nor necessary here. A theory is always an example or two mis*taken* as the comprehensive view of all possible examples.[55]

CONCLUSION

The activity of keeping the fundamental characteristics of Canada in just relations one with another by means of multilateral negotiations over time in accord with the three conventions constitutes the living character of Canada as a federation. In the last few decades all Canadians have been thrown into the activity and held responsible for keeping the character of their federation alive. In the Canada round they were invited to imagine a further dimension to this complex game. They not only have to recognize that there are competing visions of the federation that need to be accommodated along with their own – and this is difficult enough – but they also have been invited to recognize and affirm the diversity of the federation as a fundamental characteristic itself. This is a new way of seeing Canada. No one spoke of Canada as a diversity of aspects or of diversity as a good until recently. This characteristic was hidden or suppressed by each of the visions and by the competition among them for predominance. One might speak of the change in vision as the dawning of diversity awareness.

Seeing Canada as a diversity dissolves the earlier puzzle of envisioning the federation without at the same time imposing one point of view over the others. For "diversity" justly names the negotiated arrangements of the members over time. Canada is indeed a diversity, like the diverse ecosystems on which it depends and in which it has its being. The term began to be used in the early 1980s and entered constitutional discussions around mid-decade, receiving its first influential interpretations after 1990.[56] Diversity shows its enigmatic face in three places in the Charlottetown Accord.

The first appearance is in the recognition of Métis self-government after more than a century of oppression and racism. The Métis are the true exemplars of Canadian cultural diversity. Their long-overdue recognition was an invitation to other Canadians to look on them, in diversity's enlightenment, with respect and pride. Second, in the Canada clause, the provinces are said to have "diverse characteristics." The expression invites us to see a province not only as a home, a way of experiencing Canada and a form of self-rule, but also as a diversity of characteristics – a microcosm of the federal diversity.

Last but not least, cultural diversity appears in the multicultural statement of the Canada clause. "Canadians are committed to racial and ethnic equality in a society that includes citizens from many lands who have contributed, and continue to contribute, to the building of a strong Canada that reflects its cultural and racial diversity." Generically, this characteristic refers to the diversity of all the overlapping cultures and citizens that constitute Canada. Specifically, it refers to the cultural diversity not covered by the other fundamental characteristics of the Canada clause. This comprises the Canadians who choose not to identify culturally with Aboriginal peoples, francophones or anglophones: African Canadians, Jewish Canadians, Asian Canadians, Indian Canadians, Latin American Canadians, Mennonites, Ukrainian Canadians, and all the other contributors and builders. Their often-disregarded or suppressed histories and social movements enrich Canada, and they too have every right to negotiate their cultures into the character of Canada.

To see the change in the form of expression of multiculturalism here, compare it with section 27 of the Charter in 1982. There, multiculturalism was justified by the traditional convention of continuity of cultures. Diversity does not appear. In the Canada clause, the convention of continuity is not even mentioned. The cultural diversity of Canada is justified in terms of diversity itself. A strong Canada is described in turn as nothing more (or less) than the "reflection" of that diversity. Hence, the growing constellation of multicultural oldcomers and newcomers who are rapidly diversifying the character of Canada, especially its cities, is given an exemplary place in the accord. They are the specific bearers of the new fundamental characteristic of diversity which stands as the symbol for the entire federation. As a result of this multicultural passage, therefore, the traditional seating in the constitutional longhouse was quietly rearranged and a place of great honour prepared, Tuscarora-style, for the newest and fastest-growing member of the federation.

Symbolizing this entire reinterpretation of Canada, diversity was given artistic recognition in the middle of the Canada round. The awe-inspiring celebration of diversity, the black canoe entitled "The Spirit of Haida Gwaii" by the Haida and Canadian sculptor Bill Reid, was placed in front of the Canadian embassy in Washington, D.C., as the symbol for Canada as it enters the uncertain dawn of the twenty-first century. Xuuya, the Raven, the wonderful spirit of diversity, is at the helm.[57]

So, in addition to the differentially shared goods carried by the fundamental characteristics, it seems that there is a common good which the federation preserves and promotes after all – the diversity of the members (*ex uno plura*). For the representatives and citizens to have come to an agreement on an accord, they would have had to do more than catch these first glimpses of diversity's youthful smile. They would have had to acquire the federal abilities to imagine and appreciate Canada from the point of view of diversity in order to negotiate their way through the structural impasses. This was the gambit they declined.

À la prochaine. Until we meet again. For we, the people, are just finding our feet on the middle ground and learning how to play this Canada game.[58]

7 Globalism and Localism: Constitutionalism in a New World Order

PETER EMBERLEY

"The constitutional odyssey must end," Peter Russell argued in a recent article in the *Globe and Mail* (4 October 1992), "to secure Canada's sovereignty." There is really only one essential question, Russell contends, underlying our constitutional wrangles: whether we can be a people sharing a common constitution. "Is it too much," he challenges, "to seek closure on that question?"

Seek *closure*? Is it accidental that one of Canada's most respected political scientists would express his desire for unity with a term that resonates deeply with the deconstructive tactics of progressive intellectuals all over Europe and North America? And though Russell *seeks* closure while those intellectuals *vilify* closure, is it not curious that each sees the task of politics in relation to the closure of discourse? And does Russell's desire for closure not finally vitiate his own liberal politics?

In this essay, I am suggesting that the convergence of language is neither accidental nor merely semantic. I shall argue that the *problematique* of contemporary politics is one necessarily characterized by ambiguity, paradox, and disjunction. Russell's malapropism is repeated by many, from those who are committed to democratic pluralism but use the language of Derridean difference, to environmentalists who, in the interests of a less destructive relation to nature, desire more effectual "resource management"; to Aboriginal people who wish to live by their ancestral traditions, which they have come to know as their "cultural values"; to marginal populations who seek political recognition but denounce Western power; and to legislators who cannot distinguish between political, social, and administrative issues, reckoning that each has a place in the constitution. The obvious difficulty of these positions is that each is composed of metaphysical postulates contesting with one another, rendering the amalgam incoherent and even comical: early modern (Newtonian) liberalism with postmodernist renunciation of the subject; traditional metaphysics of nature with the technological act of seeing the world as object; premodern cosmologies with the radical historicist denial of order; a humanist desire for "self-empowerment" with Heidegger's anti-humanist "fundamental ontology"; and premodern and modern *diaresis* of different dimensions of reality with contemporary suspicion of distinctions.

These strange fusions are indicative of the fact that we are living through a complex time. The paradoxes betray a deep crisis in the self-interpretation of contemporary man: we are attempting in a seminal manner to express the experience of participating in a dynamic that is radically transforming the bearings defining us as modern beings, while having as compass points only the political language of that modern period. Part of us is gravitating towards a centre while as great a part is shifting to multiple peripheries. Some explanations of this motion even suggest that the present dynamism is exploding centre-periphery relations.[1] In desperation to express what it is we are experiencing, we are grasping into the vocabularies of the premodern and non-Western. But what is peculiarly contemporary about these combinations is not simply their inconsistency – for when has the everyday world ever been free of contradictions and paradoxes? – but that these inconsistencies are wholly acceptable to us. Indeed, they are not seen as inconsistencies, nor do we question their coherence because the difference between surface and ground is becoming obscure to us. We live in a time when the demand for consistency and coherence no longer has any standing and when the simple fact that we are aroused, agitated, or tantalized by images and signs is sufficient justification for these pastiches of political declaration to be the mainstay of our political debate.[2]

Permit me to establish the parameters of this paper's argument as follows: decisive watersheds in the history of the West are marked by a dissolution in the primary political unit. This dissolution coincides with efforts to resymbolize order, efforts which can occur across the spectrum of human activity. Our times, it has been suggested, are reproducing the form of the political mobilization, intellectual realignment, and spiritual perplexity occasioned by the decline of the Greek polis in the fourth century B.C. and the ecumenic empire in the thirteenth century. In our case it is the nation-state that is losing its status as the symbol of order, as the symbol that focuses our ambitions and hopes, our desires and thoughts. Its dissolution has both a theoretical and a pragmatic dimension.

Let us look first at the theoretical dimension. Modern constitutionalism, and the moral principles it safeguarded, was sustained by a theoretical foundation that had its birth in the symbolic reconstellation of the Renaissance and Reformation. However, at its core, modern constitutionalism also reaches back to the metaphysic of Plato and Aristotle. In the new science projected by Francis Bacon and René Descartes, which built on the achievements of the Renaissance and the Reformation and whose theoretical conceptualization underscores modern constitutionalism, that metaphysic is still present. However, in the desire to give that metaphysic an immediate political efficacy, early modern thinkers dogmatized certain features of it. In Hobbes and Locke, for example, the symbols "rational man" and "social man," which in the past articulated complex and fluid tensions within human existence, could become the authoritative bases for concepts of political sovereignty, political power, and the juridical person. In application, these ideas historically lent themselves far too conveniently to harsh, crude, and oppressive practices. Many have pointed out how, in the interests of efficacy, these thinkers offered reductionist and vulgar accounts of human longing. However, there was also a restraining feature to modern thought: it has to be admitted that these modern thinkers retained the restrained anthropomorphism of the ancient metaphysic: man, for Plato as for Hobbes, is the measure of all things.[3] This meant that reflection on the whole – nature, the universe, the world – was mediated by a conception of what was good and useful for man.

But four hundred years of subsequent deconstruction of these dogmatisms, in the hands of Kant, Hegel, and Nietzsche, has led to a progressive, and finally, radical repudiation of all the forms of the traditional metaphysic, the denunciation of the humanism it had sanctioned, and the rise of a situation in which traditional moral and political categories of analysis increasingly no longer have standing. The ease with which individuals feel they can jettison or creatively manipulate their identity – regardless of historical or cultural matrices, not to say natural ones – as well as the evident impotence individuals experience in affecting the essential features of mass society (evident both at a pragmatic level and in intellectual fashion) and the widespread acceptance of a self-interpretation that sees human beings as part of a universal process signal that what we take persons and society to be is under radical revision. In an age in which tremendous technological forces can be unleashed, whose power exceeds human measure, and in which many see the "person" less as an initiator of action than as an effect (often an accidental or arbitrary one), a fundamental reassessment of the modern self-interpretation seems to be occurring. My view is that the current situation is one where central modern concepts such as agency, intentionality, power, identity, and causality – which had been keyed in to an epistemological structure whose source was Newtonian physics and Cartesian subjectivism and rationalism – no longer appear to have sufficient explanatory power. An atavistic residue of these remains in legal and political speech, where the fiction of sovereignty, responsibility, and representation is maintained but the concrete evidence of social life, I suggest, belies this speech.

Simultaneously, the organization of independent nation-states is being replaced by a system of interdependencies whose "anarchic" form of power defies control or regulation by single actors, be they individuals, groups, institutions, or governments. The web of power has neither centre nor periphery; its relations are neither continuous nor causal; its motions are neither sequential nor uniform. We are witnessing complex and contradictory forces, which on the one hand are apparently integrating and homogenizing global culture, social policy, and technological programs and, on the other hand, are evidently disseminating production processes, proliferating social identities, and valourizing localized initiative. A situation is emerging where concerted, globally cooperative participation is required (in response to an increasingly fragile ecosystem, to potential nuclear terrorism, to the threat of regional wars) and yet where the possibility of agreement on criteria or measures of what is reasonable, just, or appropriate is being flatly rejected under the guise of a new pluralism. I suggest, however, that this pluralism has none of the substance or critical potential of classic democratic pluralism (as is still evident in C.B. Macpherson, Carole Pateman, and Robert Dahl). It is instead a mere multiplicity or heterogeneity of deracinated voices (or "discourses"), constituted in great part through the communications media, and distanced from any reality commonly attested to, other than that which is the product of subjective grievance or private fantasy. This radical heterogeneity and fragmentation is the context in which contemporary efforts to reappraise and renew constitutions is taking place, and it is placing burdens upon courts and legislators which the "metaphysic" of modern constitutionalism cannot bear.

The Canadian discord is an example of this world crisis. From Meech Lake to the Charlottetown Constitutional Accord, a plethora of recommendations and detractions, options and grievances, has been aired; each voice has been granted legitimacy and been permitted to be fully recognized as necessary to the political debate. The new constitution was to speak authentically to different voices, and it was to resonate with the radically transforming dynamics of contemporary life. The language of this amalgam is confusing and discontinuous: "founding nations," "empowerment," "global competitiveness," "distinct society," "effectiveness," "parliamentary supremacy," "managing culture," "special responsibility," "asymmetry," "affirmative action," and so on. It is remarkable that anyone would assume that all these voices could and should be accommodated. The debate quintessentially exemplifies the novelty of the contemporary world. Images and signs of ancient Greek practice, Roman theory, medieval organization, early modern reform, and late modern praxis float and circulate around; politics (which, incidentally, is no longer differentiated from legal, social, economic, or administrative dimensions) is a grand play of the surface. What is absent is the assumption, which governed both the ancient and the modern world, that politics needs a ground; or better, that political reform should be grounded in rational justification, or experience, or a philosophy of history, or the self-evidentness of political or moral principle.

Perhaps we should not be surprised. That we would proceed in the absence of a ground has been prepared for us by predominant philosophers of this century, who witnessed, participated in, and attempted to symbolize the dynamic of world transformation that is currently underway. In a lecture given in 1956, Martin Heidegger undertook a radical deconstruction of Leibniz's principle of sufficient reason. The lecture, entitled "Der Satz vom Grund," or "The Principle of Ground," was an effort to shift subsequent philosophy away from the traditional premises of rational inquiry: namely that everything has a ground, everything that is real has a ground for its reality, every behaviour has a foundation, no judgment without justification, no truth without proven correctness, no event without a cause that is a kind of ground; in sum, nothing without ground. Liebniz's principle of sufficient reason, the principle that nothing exists for which the ground of its existence cannot be sufficiently presented, he argued, only encapsulates what is expressed in all philosophy to date. But there is a more authentic relation, Heidegger challenged, that the essence of man can have to Being. Calling that thinking which requires a ground a "madness," Heidegger looked to a future in which the Western error would be overcome.

Thirty-six years later, I want to argue, we are participating in such an overcoming and are beginning to catch the faint outlines of an era that finds its self-interpretation in that primordial genesis of perpetual becoming which Heidegger took to be the more authentic resonance with Being. What was meant to be an ontological analytic – or, to give it the most generous recognition, a reformulation of human consciousness – has become for us the concrete actuality of our everyday lives. I suggest that if we wish to understand the distinctive modalities of contemporary constitutionalism, and the Canadian situation in particular, it is to Heidegger and his epigone that we must turn to observe with them the unfolding of the dynamic to which they were witness.[4]

I would like to focus my discussion on the crisis of the nation-state. To understand the character of the nation-state thoroughly, one must attend not only to its pragmatic historical reality but also to both the logic of its conceptual organization – as this is elaborated in the works of Thomas Hobbes and John Locke and completed in the thought of Immanuel Kant – and to the perception of the order of reality it was meant to represent. In her book *The Origins of Totalitarianism*, Hannah Arendt has set out the former with great clarity. I shall summarize this account only briefly before turning to the latter topic.

Throughout the seventeenth and eighteenth centuries, nation-states developed under the direction of absolute sovereigns. These forms of political association were highly unstable, because they linked together two opposing forces: the state, with its focus on freedom of the legal person and equality before the law, and the nation, with its demand for conformity to its ethos and exclusivity. The recurring conflicts within them was a consequence of attempting to graft national interest onto legal institutions. Either the state was an instrument of the law or it was an instrument of the nation. Conceptually, the nation-state was organized, on the one hand, around the ideas of sovereignty and the juridical person and, on the other hand, on the principle of the equal recognition of particularistic or ascriptive relations under the law and the act of representation whereby these relations could acquire a public persona.

The state is an enactment of sovereign legislation, and its form assumes the existence of autonomous individuals who can reproduce the act of sovereign legislation within themselves. The principle of the state's authority is not bonds of family or blood ties, but consent to the enactment of the rule of law. The sovereign establishes a public domain regulated not by a substantive vision of what humans think good, for on that no agreement is possible, but by certain procedural criteria of right, which safeguard the security and rights of the person. The authority held by the state is legitimate by virtue of each individual's rational ratification of the contractual relation he or she has to the state. This is either a calculation of how one's rational self-interest is preserved by obliging oneself to the principle of contractual relations; or it is a situation where the political contract is dignified by the moral act of affirming the law as the universal form of respect for all rational persons. In either case, no primordial or innate bonds to one's people, or land, or tribe provides the distinctly rational principle of obligation. In other words, political organization rests on the distinctions between state and society, and between the political and the social. The understanding of equality, identity, and freedom are all defined by these distinctions. The individual recapitulates the form of political sovereignty in the act of self-division: his particular will is surmounted by a general will that is the expression of rational calculation. Sovereignty at the level of world organization means that the world is a system of states, a collection of distinct powers, whose legislative enactments give them absolute control of the territory and people within their boundaries, and who in principle are independent of each other. The world situation is one of a tenuous and fragile balance of powers.

The imperative of formal equality under the law means that the task of government is to ensure a homogeneous population. It must integrate distinct individuals to accept and respect one another as legal persona and to see the rational necessity of a common law. The only way that government will be able to integrate a differentiated body politic is by enforcing consent to principles of right rather than to substantive notions of justice. Its legitimacy will nevertheless recurringly be questioned. This is why a civil service that is economically independent and politically neutral is central to a state's persistent ability to legitimate itself. The state's authority depends on it. To speak of "authority" is to recognize a power above the state: its constitution, a paradigm of order that stipulates the character and accompanying procedures for the maintenance of political liberty and sovereignty and is the rational standard for all political practice.

The second term of the "nation-state" hybrid pulls in the opposite direction. The nation is partial and exclusive. It grounds the legitimacy of its principles on a commonality of innate characteristics, or tribal allegiances, or a shared destiny, which is to say that it defines human essence by its rootedness and irreducible belongingness to a place and to a history. Human experience is not simply within universal space and time; these are instead invested with human meaning, located and dignified by stories of memorable events and exemplary persons. A nation operates by a substantive vision of virtue and the good, and finds the principle of obligation in culture, language, religion, or race. Integral to the nation's principle, then, is privilege. It sees the law as the outgrowth of its unique national substance and as something that is not valid beyond its own people and the boundaries of its own territory. The nation is a contained entity; it has to be added that expansion is not inherent to its principle.

When nation and state combine, the result is obviously unstable. The nation-state must balance rootedness and belongingness with equality under the law. It must balance exclusivity with fairness, substantive justice with respect for difference. The two poles between which the nation-state is situated produce a field of tension structured by forces tending on the one hand to identity and on the other hand to difference. Another way of saying this is that one of its forces pushes for universality; the other, for particularity. As state, it must maintain equality of rights for all, even beyond its own boundaries, but as nation, it will make nationality a prerequisite of citizenship. The state machinery must rule above nationalities, but its legitimation depends on consciousness of national identity. Internally, the nation-state will be subject to conflicts in which its efforts to establish national consciousness will splinter, and a multiplicity of nationalities will desire distinctive sovereignty. Every group must be respected as equal, but there are inevitable conflicts between different groups, each reluctant to grant the other this basic recognition of equality. The nation-state will have to make continuous efforts to assimilate, rather than integrate, the population in order to ensure active consent to its government. It cannot allow things to degenerate into simple facts of birth, and it has to maintain the elaborate artifice of the political state; but the substance of the regime comes from forces denying these efforts. The contradiction between equality and privilege can be resolved only by an ideology of respect and self-respect. Even if that result can be produced, the nation-state cannot avoid tension, political agitation towards one pole or the other, the recurring threat of dispersion of national focus, and the mobilization of support behind either extreme unity or extreme divisiveness and fragmentation.

Historically, this tension and unrest were not always a bad thing. For one, they ensured a politics of continual self-questioning. More importantly, they constituted the ingredients of the most essential character of a body politic – plurality. Where the nation-state could balance its contradictory forces, it produced a politics of reciprocity, in which identity was harmonized with difference. A politics of plurality, which is more than simple multiplicity of the same view countless times over, testified to the uniqueness of essentially different perspectives.

The nation-state was an historical achievement. That is to say that the nation-state was a chance combination of political expedience and insight into the grounds of human order. Now, as even Plato understood, these chance combinations cannot be expected to be everlasting. Arendt is particularly vivid in her demonstration of how its contradictions have torn the nation-state apart; it cannot be said to be our primary political unit, for the nation-state increasingly now fails to focus our self-understanding.[5] Two processes emanate from our historical experience of the nation-state: the aggregation of some phenomena into a universal pattern and the dissemination of others towards the minutely particular. Released from the limits imposed by the humanist science of politics that attempted to harmonize them – and to ground them in a science of order – these processes are now producing a wholly novel array of identities and interdependencies which are quite outside the practices, institutions, and ethos of the nation-state.

THE DISRUPTION OF MODERN CONSCIOUSNESS

The historical particulars of the gradual inanition of the nation-state has been widely documented by international-relations theorists. The names Richard Ashley, James Der Derian, Michael Shapiro, Rob Walker, and Henry Kariel are well known, as are the general arguments made by many writers in the journals *Alternatives* and *Millennium*. These theorists have argued that such phenomena as direct foreign investment, trade liberalization, tied capital and debt flows, the international division of labour, the dissemination of production processes, the disappearance of dominant poles structuring central and peripheral relations, the growing presence of multilateral institutions such as GATT, the proliferation of a vast array of old and new nationalisms, and the effect of mass culture have significantly diminished the sovereignty, territorial integrity, and symbolic order of the nation-state, not only vis-à-vis other states but also domestically. In a global economy, it is argued, management and administration of system-norms are gradually replacing traditional nation-state performance.[6] Moreover, as these international-relations theorists also point out, the unfolding reality is making mockery of modern forms of political analysis: developmental theories, group theory, rational actor models, deterrence theory, and interpretations of structures of dominance and subordination. In the absence of those visible poles which, during the modern period, structured the various political terrains – two distinct empires, East and West, state and society, centre and margin – and in the emergence of mass, global society interconnected by sophisticated information and communications technologies, modern concepts seem to be faltering. The new world "order," it is argued, is a radical disruption of the modern organization of power and ideas, a revolutionary sweep of the ground upon which modern practice and theory stood.

We need, however, to add a further element to this account by international-relations theorists. The organization of power under the symbol "nation-state" was more than the conjunction of social/economic relations and ideas. It was also the expression of a perception of the order of reality. The construct of reality upon which the nation-state's distribution of political actors, social relations, and authorized knowledges rested can be apprehended by an audit of its epistemological presuppositions.[7] What held the symbolic structure of the nation-state together was a specific ordering of human consciousness, distinctive to the modern era, namely, the coordinates of space and time derived from the Newtonian-Cartesian paradigm. The understandings of politics, culture, and power of the modern period are based on notions of space as enclosed, homogeneous, and exclusive, and on notions of time as linear, successively durational, and irreversible, constituting the human experiences of sequentiality, causality, and continuity. This is a view of the world which sees its forces as mechanical and its phenomena as mutually exclusive. Each compartment or departmental boundary is seen as having a separate order of constitutionality, a regime understood as having a singular purpose or end.

Politically, a consciousness ordered by the Newtonian-Cartesian perspective will identify the relevant phenomena as structured by the problems of sovereignty and freedom of self-definition. How is power distilled into authority? What vector of force causes the effect of constraint? How can human relations be seen within the series of objectification, alienation, resistance, and reconciliation? The traditional causalities and sequences constituting the activity of autonomous states, the contract relations between self-interested agents and groups, the coordination of centres and peripheries of control, or the composition of political personae are recognized to be stable and secure. The durable coordinates of uniformity and repeatability, homogeneity, and distance, which constitute distinctive "points of view," underlie the formal equality and recognition of plurality of legal persons under the law.

It is within this paradigm, which sees the world as a taxonomic grid of distinct and separate entities, each structured by the idea of independent sovereignty and each located at a specific conjuncture of history and place, that the questions of ethnicity, nationalism, cultural right to self-determination, economic control, and ideology

– and the constitutional separating out and uniting together of these elements – are still, in great part, being posed. Seeing the world as a mechanical interaction of spaces and durations legitimates certain types of questions while ignoring others. In an important way, it sees the problems of politics and culture exclusively as being confined within specifiable boundaries and as being characterized as a specific, localizable set of phenomena and a logic distinctive to an established form of social existence, such as labour, class, religion, or art.

This problematization of culture and politics assumes that power is something held, appropriated, transferred, and exchanged; in other words, that there is a fixed quantum of power within which political relations are formed. Power, in this perspective, is an opaque force emanating from a subject (an individual, group, class, state, or nation) through knowable dramas of history within the evident experience of a place. The task is to acquire power and to turn it to one's advantage. This same problematization also assumes that there are reasons and justifications that legitimate action, that any rational person could be brought to recapitulate for himself. There are forms of inquiry and objects of cognition that can rationally substantiate the exercises of power. Power and knowledge (as Michel Foucault depicts in *Discipline and Punish*, his study of lawlessness within and beyond the juridical state) articulate themselves on one another, forming the distinctive tensions and ambiguities of this political history.[8]

The dynamic in which we find ourselves today, however, cannot be confined conveniently by this Newtonian-Cartesian system of boundaries. The world in which the problems of identity and difference arise is one that is traversed by a new form of power whose fluidity, non-localizable episodes, and non-linear generative order is breaking apart centre/margin relations, cause/effect sequences, and traditional models of intentionality, agency, and responsibility. At a pragmatic level, once the ascending forces of existence manifest themselves as global information networks, disseminated production modes, bio-technological interventions and simulations, and optimalizations of life forms, the regulative parameters and symbolizations of order of modern constitutionalism are left far behind. The projected scope of the new developments is even taking us beyond an era of *international* political economy or *multinational* corporate enterprise, at least as these have traditionally been mediated through the interests of a sovereign nation-state, to a global and mass process with its own internal dynamic. The current realignments and unending readjustments of the defined limits of what we have taken the human to be – singularly, politically, economically, socially – simply exceeds the still considerably "humanistic" boundaries of an industrial, materials-based society. Indeed, the "personal," "political," "economic," and "social" can hardly be kept conceptually distinct. We are required to think of a globally transformative process of a new "order."

What is this new process? From within liberalism and from within the regulative principles of modern constitutionalism has emerged a dynamic (variously called global realignment, systems-management, the consumer age, the information and communications process) whose vitality, I wish to argue, is corroding those political and economic parameters of modernity which, since the Industrial Revolution, have limited that dynamic. The era of the nation-state and the confinement of questions of economics and social existence to the political form of sovereignty is nullified under the realignment effected by the globalizing transformation of this dynamic, which, to give it its most general name, is technology.

This needs explanation by our expanding on what is meant by "technology." Technology is more than an aggregate of techniques, instruments, machines, and organizational procedures. It is a way of seeing human and non-human nature as something to be controlled and managed. It is not even just a perspective or mind-set; increasingly, it is the ontological basis of our being, a development that can be thoroughly thought through only by bringing together the work of Hegel and Heidegger, a task that can be started by reading Jacques Ellul's seminal work, *The Technological Society*.

For our present purposes, technology (that is, the appropriation, mastery or domination, and correction of human and non-human nature) is not merely applied science but is the modern form of science and thus our sole mode of legitimate rationality. Prior to modernity, knowledge came from practical experience or through thoughtful wonder at, and consent to, the eternity of what is, but since Galileo and Descartes modern knowledge has been a type of making: the world must be reordered to reveal its inner structure and laws. Instruments must disturb and break down the compounds in which existence appears in the everyday. Knowing requires an extracting of phenomena as objects. Reason is technical, regulative, and interventionist, rather than receptive. Science itself has become inherently technological – to know is to control and master ambiguity, contradiction, and tension in existence. Technology is increasingly our way of revealing and understanding our being – displacing philosophy, art, religion, and politics, which were the traditional indices of what human limit and possibility are. In technology we expect to find both the fullest expression of our freedom and the highest form of our rationality.[9]

Now, technology, as reading Descartes and Bacon makes clear, is also an interventionist and regulative mode of world organization. Our hopes for freedom and understanding can advance by this account only through constant re-creation and experimentation with reality. Descartes' method, whose imperative of world-denial and world reconstruction leads to this, is important for another reason: the resolutive-compositive method demands universality and homogeneity, not only because Descartes understood it to be applicable transculturally, but because it assumes a reality that is essentially unidimensional, clear, and simple, its parts equally commensurable to one another. World events are subject to universally valid laws. The suspension of trust in the senses and their images is at once the occlusion of the entire existing intellectual tradition, popular opinion, and common sense. Henceforth, man would see himself as a universal being, with no fixed centre.

This universality means a number of things. Technology refers to a "systematic" deployment of instruments, procedures, and skills under organized rules to achieve the effect of optimal efficiency. "System" suggests a process of growing interdependence of controlled environments whereby single components are "rationalized" and thereby rendered equivalent and substitutable. Industrial, social, cultural, and psychological phenomena are ordered into subsystems and installed within an interrelated and interdependent web. Separate and distinctive techniques tend to integrate and function within continuous processes. The emergence of supply networks, multinational production cooperatives, and information networks indicates a correlation of manifold technologies in which diverse techniques are coordinated to function according to overall processes of development that are internal to the system. The density and complexity of the world is reduced and contracted to resemble the perfect workings of a machine and the mathematical logic of perfect relations and proportions. Moreover, all systems function by the process of "dynamic disequilibrium": as long as they continue to be challenged by countervailing tendencies and by margins of indetermination they are vital, for the system's strength is measured by its capacity to grow in power. Thus, such systems are expansionary: to avoid internal dissonance, a system, coming up against other systems, will enhance itself by competition and then incorporate these or demand their realignment in conformity with its own logic. "Organization" refers to the progressive deployment of a single logic of abstraction, optimalization, and idealized reconstruction at every level to maximize management. The conjunction of systematization and organization universalizes all internal processes to a single logic and then expands the system to incorporate other ensembles.

When systematization and organization proceed together and maintain the dynamic self-modification of recurring innovation, technology displays a single end: efficiency. "Efficiency" suggests the *telos* of technological development: taking the plurality of ends and means and reducing them to one system of means – the most efficient. When this is achieved, all dissonance and asymmetry has been eliminated, a situation we now term "user-friendly." User-friendly technology is an example of pure efficiency, a state in which all the components are in tensionless coordination.

This systematization and rationalization of all the dimensions of human reality, where even the characteristically human experiences of the self, politics, social life, and reason become technicized and optimalized through the medium of technology, leads Jacques Ellul to write that technology is "the totality of methods rationally arrived at and having absolute efficiency (for a given stage of development) in every field of human activity." Technology, he claims, has become automatic, self-augmenting, monistic, universal, and autonomous.[10] Wherever man goes, he sees and participates only in a technological system whose imperatives proceed by their own accord.

This process entails more, though, than the mere replication of the same thing worldwide. In its current phase, technology is producing what Marshall McLuhan has called a "global village." McLuhan does not mean by this that the world has simply been homogenized. He is instead pointing to a development within technology which brings wholly new fusions and interdependencies into existence, modalities which decisively shatter the Newtonian-Cartesian order of reality. The new communication and information technology, he argues, is underwriting novel forms of power, relations, senses of identity, conceptions of action, and entanglements of social, economic, and political force. What makes McLuhan's characterization of the global village unique is that he writes of *isolated* individuals simultaneously and multidimensionally connected with every other being through the medium of electronics and information transmission. For example, in *The Gutenberg Galaxy* he writes of a new global embrace which "abolishes both time and space," in which a new mythic tribalism has emerged. Boundaries and separations, fixed points of view, and sequential causality will be dissolved. In a world of circuits and integral patterns, of total environments and fused interdependencies, the space between individuals will be overcome, he predicts. McLuhan does not see this as merely a vast universal homogeneity or as something that modern science can explain. He claims "our speed-up is not a slow expansion outward from centre to margins but an instant implosion and an interfusion of space and functions." An "implosion" means a "bursting inwards" in which each person withdraws from the mediated relations and forms of everyday life and, with perhaps a small band of like-minded fellows, experiences via the electronic communications network an immediate affectivity with the whole globe. "General cosmic consciousness," as McLuhan identifies it, is at the same time isolation and universal resonance.[11]

Earlier, I referred to the pattern of contemporary motion as simultaneous gravitation towards a centre and towards multiple peripheries. Nowhere is this more evident than in politics, where the conjunction of highly sophisticated executive-management skills on behalf of "global competitiveness" and the activation of a plethora of nationalisms or "identities" (based on ethnicity, gender, religion, race, and sexual preference) is redefining political action. The phenomena produced by these processes do not seem to be explained readily by modern notions of causality, of representation and reiteration, of localizable power, or of direction. What we are observing instead is, I think, the emergence of a new paradigm of interaction and energy, of nonlocal connections and simultaneity. Speaking very generally, the network that is emerging has an uncanny resemblance to what one might speculate is a practical application of Heidegger's "fundamental ontology," or of the postmodernist's "philosophy of difference." Needless to say, the effort to characterize what this means must usually have recourse to metaphor, though modern science is attempting to find a vocabulary to express "nongenerative order." Looked at in terms of its political appearance, the network is one that links a kind of retribalized existence with instantaneous reactivity to the whole globe. This situation is one in which the imploded "identity" confronts directly and without mediation the powerful dynamics of the global environment. Monad and global force resonate with one another without any dialectical intervention, without any of the everyday forms of political or social causality, and without political or legal protection. No distinctive modalities of mediation arise in this pure affectivity. Jean Baudrillard is one who has tried to express what the implication of this is. In his *In the Shadow of the Silent Majorities – or The End of the Social and Other Essays*, he writes:

The medium also falls into that indefinite state characteristic of all our great systems of judgment and value. A single model, whose efficacy is immediacy, simultaneously generates the message, the medium, and the "real." In short, *the medium is the message* signifies not only the end of the message, but also the end of the medium. There are no longer media in the literal sense of the term ... – that is to say, a power mediating between one reality and another, between one state of the real and another – neither in content nor in form. Strictly speaking, that is what implosion signifies: the absorption of one pole into another, the short-circuit between poles of every differential system of meaning, the effacement of terms and of direct oppositions, and thus that of the medium and the real. Hence the impossibility of any mediation ... circularity of all media effects. Hence the impossibility of a sense (meaning), in the literal sense of a unilateral vector which leads from one pole to another.[12]

The implication of this is that in the context of making and revising constitutions, it now becomes increasingly inappropriate to speak of the questions of sovereignty, commonality, political power and economic control, and the recognition of identity as if these were phenomena still linked to political entities defined within the boundaries and the political *problematique* of the juridical nation-state. The new empowerments, fusions and interdependencies, experiments, and strategies that we are witnessing are taking place within a field of energy which, linking enormous technological capacity (nuclear power, recombinant DNA engineering, and simulation technology) and intense commitment to images of identity (the "black-Athena" movements, the "age of the goddess" movements, the "men's rights" movements) produce motions which exceed the measures of modernity (its humanism, its standards of utility and protection of the individual) and which perhaps cannot be predicted or controlled.

Since it is germane to the issue of the Canadian constitutional debate, permit me to focus briefly on the trajectory which some are calling the "new pluralism." From the perspective outlined above, what characterizes the distinctiveness of the contemporary appeals to religion, race, locality, and gender is twofold: first, that the juridical and political parameters within which these had been defined as issues associated with pluralism are evaporating, leaving these allegiances and commitments as free-floating phenomena that can be attached to any globally mobilized movement. Secondly, they are increasingly defined through technology. By this I mean that they are highly technicized phenomena – emanations of communications technology, signs manipulated by those who have access and resources to mobilize masses, forms not so much of particular culture but rather of marketing strategy and effective communication.

I do not think that we can see the regional activation of tribal allegiances as genuine forms of attachment and obvious options and points of resistance to the age of globalizing transformations and realignments. Jean Baudrillard, in a series of devastating critiques of contemporary society, suggests that they must be understood as signs of nostalgia and simulation within the peculiar processes of the contemporary information order. He repudiates the view that the discovery of ethnic and cultural wholeness is a continuation of the humanist affirmation of enriched subjectivity in the face of technology's objectifying processes. Baudrillard suggests that the information age produces a consciousness wholly unlike that of even late capitalism. The commodity form, he challenges, no longer prevails. Instead, the environment is constituted by a constant dispersion of signs. No stable value orders the commutability of these signs. The infinite metamorphosis of signification means that there is no "real." We consume images that appear intelligible within no political horizon or rational understanding. These images are, Baudrillard suggests, "hyper-real": they are ones where the real has withdrawn and returned as highly stylized, formalized simulations. (Members of the environmentalism movement use the idea of "sacred nature" in this creative manner.) They are refurbished "copies" though the original may never have existed, or where the "original" lived-context itself is utterly refabricated. (The Puritan ethic of hard work and honesty survives because Plymouth Plantation exists.) Past cultures become eclectic signs that have lost their referents in the service of mass consumption and innovative marketing strategies. Their use and deployment in the media as circulating signs permits of no recollection or reminiscence to a primal point, an *arche*, which would endow them with meaning. Under the global transformation which information technology activates, culture becomes wholly abstracted, reduced, and processed as manipulable data. Everything becomes a stylistic variation of the same.

Abstracted from contexts of meaning, culture then becomes an arbitrary horizon, and it can provide no substantive basis for meaningful action. Discrete and singular practices, ways of life, and understandings have been made over to participate in the overall functionalism of the system. Culture can no longer be seen as a set of practices from which resistance can proceed, or as a structure that confers meaning on the processes unleashed by technology; instead, it is seen as an ancillary to technological functionality. It is just more information that can be arranged and rearranged into repertoires. As Baudrillard suggests, the symbols of culture simply become masses of detritus and excess, dead signs where at best everything is made available to everyone.

Seen in this light, the dispersion and proliferation of identities in not as great an object of hope as it may at first appear to be. If we accept Baudrillard's argument that the general form of our consciousness is becoming structured by the logic of the information age, then while we may seem to be more receptive to diversity and while we encourage multiplicity, we have left no measures which would contribute to our understanding of the distinctions within that differentiation. It is the proliferation of difference in the same mode and through the same medium, namely communications. In a state of uniform heterogeneity, or mass differentiation, a more intrusive reductionism and trivilialisation has occurred. We have before us the spectre of anonymous global processes combined with tribalism and isolationism; and the preponderant part of the initiatives being undertaken today – politically, socially, and economically – celebrates this double process.

The Charlottetown Accord cannot, of course, be accused of merely falling in line with the contemporary development. In a magisterial tone it recognizes the main structures and practices of the modern nation-state: the primacy of the rule of law, the recognition of the legal person, the supremacy of a sovereign parliament, territorial integrity, and so on. However, both within the document and during the accompanying debate, powerful dissenting voices also created the conditions for Canada's participation in the double process of globalism and localism. The agreement attempted to be all things to all people, uniting regional "empowerment" with economic competitiveness, Aboriginal demand for self-determination with effective resource management, the rule of law with the prerogatives of birth. The process was one attempting to reconcile features of the Meech Lake Accord, the Beaudoin-Dobbie Report, and the Allaire Report, while taking seriously the Bélanger-Campeau Commission, the triple-E Senate proposals, and Ontario's desire for a social charter, without recognizing that there were fundamental theoretical incompatibilities between them. The result was not a simple compromise package reflecting the give-and-take conciliation of modern pluralism. Instead, its incoherent amalgam of remnants of earlier historical periods, future possibilities, localized grievances, and global pressures reflects the contemporary quandary of constitutionalism in a new world "order." On the one hand it diversifies and fragments, disseminating cultural identities into multiple contingencies, decentralizing federal spending power and shared cost programs, and localizing constitutional entitlement on the basis of declared identity. On the other hand, it commits the new machinery of federalism to working effectively to use the institutions of government to produce a single market initiative in the interests of global competitiveness. For example, local procurement practices, agricultural supply marketing boards, local hiring policy, all "means of arbitrary discrimination" or "disguised restriction of trade across boundaries," are to be administratively regulated against, in effect, by an extension of the free trade agreement internally for a more effectual participation in the global economy. Apart from the obviously inevitable contradictory results of these two pulls (for example, what happens when Aboriginal peoples, using their resources as they see appropriate to maintaining their "traditional culture," come up against the regulations of "environmental management"?), what is apparent, in the erosion of national focus, in the evident mistrust of parliamentary federalism, and in the renunciation of the liberal democratic principles of representation and equality of political rights is that Canada is aligning itself with the powerful dynamic of the contemporary era.

The Charlottetown Accord was, of course, defeated. The No vote of the referendum was not surprising, because it simply continued the process unleashed by the accord itself: having legitimated a plethora of irreconcilable voices, it was predictable that an infinite regress down to the most minute grievance, extravagant expectation, and expression of cynicism would occur. The broadcasting of results before all the votes were in ensured that voters acted on any number of projected scenarios. Indeed, the No was a perfect example of the peculiarities of the contemporary postmodern condition: the "global" result of radically contradictory positions created the "hyper-reality" of agreement by valourizing every particular disappointment and fantasy (by giving each media coverage) and aggregating them into a "totality." The accord did not establish or recall us to commonality; it did not testify to or evoke plurality. What it affirmed was multiplicity – many different voices under the single sign of communications.

Our future cannot be that hoped by Peter Russell. There cannot but be a rise in paradox and ambiguity, because that is the modality of the process in which we are now situated. Russell's desire for closure can no longer be satisfied, short of the massive employment of social and behavioural technologies. Sovereignty and the closed world of territorial integrity are no longer options for us either. As we participate in the ascendance of a new world disorder, our only hope is that a sufficient reserve of common sense and common decency remains immune to the transformations reconfiguring our world.

COMMENTS ON
PETER EMBERLEY'S PAPER;
OR, THE CRISIS OF THE STATE
DAVID HENDRICKSON

Peter Emberley's paper is a provocative and disquieting examination of the contemporary world crisis. It is sufficiently wide-ranging that no thorough or systematic response is possible. I shall focus my remarks on Emberley's thesis that we are living through a decisive watershed in which the primary political unit of our time – the nation-state – is losing its status as the symbol of order.

As Emberley suggests, there are underway powerful tendencies of both integration and disintegration in international society. A variety of tensions come to mind in characterizing this phenomenon – between aggregation and disaggregation, integration and fragmentation, globalism and localism, homogeneity and particularity. The state, as Daniel Bell said many years ago, is too small for the big things in life and too big for the small things. States acting alone are incapable of dealing with certain transnational problems such as the environment or the management of the world economy. At the same time, they are often experienced as alien structures that have no responsiveness to the needs of ordinary people. I do not doubt the existence of this phenomenon. It certainly shows that, in some respects, existing state structures are under serious strain. However, I do think it is mistaken to conclude from the existence of these forces that the nation-state is on its way out as the primary political unit of our time, or to speak of its growing "inanition."

A thorough analysis of this problem of simultaneous "globalization and localization," to use Emberley's terms, would require an examination of the various subnational, transnational, and supranational forces affecting the state, along several different axes or dimensions (political, economic, environmental, cultural, and so on), and in various geographical regions (on the assumption of considerable variety in the significance or strength of these various forces). That analysis obviously cannot be attempted here, but it is useful at least to establish the framework which such an analysis would attempt. I shall instead make a few general observations bearing on the topic.

First, the continued vitality of the state may perhaps best be demonstrated by the G.E. Moore test. Moore, you will recall, in a famous lecture before the British Academy, gave as a good argument for the existence of an external world the fact that we can point to objects in it. Thus, he held up his hands saying, "Here is one hand, and here is another," to prove the existence of an external world. We can do something similar with the state. Compare the size of state institutions with what they were eighty years ago, and one must be impressed by their extraordinary growth and continued vitality, even in the face of contrary pressures. On most indices that I can think of – the number of laws or bureaucrats, the areas of social and economic life that go on under the watchful eye of the state, the level of military expenditures – the state seems to be fully alive, if not always in full control of its senses. It may be true that the state in the advanced industrialized democracies, and perhaps elsewhere, is no longer the primary focus of human loyalty in the sense in which it once was. But we still need what it can provide, and we continue to make enormous and growing demands upon it, even if we are not entirely happy with its response.

Second, there is a sense in which the full working out or acceleration of these processes of disintegration and integration would lead to both smaller and larger states but would not challenge the centrality of the state as such. All the new republics in the former Soviet Union and Yugoslavia are busily engaged in the task of state creation – forming armies, asserting control over borders, introducing (worthless) currencies, and, as often as not, oppressing minorities. The renewed importance of claims to national self-determination, far from challenging the primacy of the nation-state, seems rather to confirm its central position in world politics. The same may be said of at least some integrative tendencies. Project them out, and you still have states – larger in size and fewer in number, to be sure, but still states. The achievement of a federal Europe would be a highly significant development both for Europeans and the world, but it would not noticeably alter the state-centric character of international politics.

A somewhat different point may be made with respect to some of the supranational institutions, such as the United Nations and the GATT, whose increasing importance might be held to show the crisis of the state. If we look at the United Nations and at the doctrine of collective security that has been identified with the new world order, perhaps its most interesting feature is its conservative character. Collective security would represent a radical innovation in the governance of international society that is nevertheless intended to preserve the territorial integrity and political independence of states. Other international institutions, such as the GATT, also rest on the support of states. It is states that negotiated the rules of international trade and with whose consent we either go forward to a more liberal regime or step back into a more protectionist one.

Third, there seems to be an assumption in Emberley's essay that these contradictory forces of globalism and localism have the state caught, as it were, in a crossfire. Let us entertain the possibility, however, that each manages to miss its target and hits the other. Rather than reinforcing one another, these processes of globalization and localization may instead cancel each other out. One might even claim, to vary the metaphor, that each trend might paradoxically serve as flying buttresses to maintain the edifice of state power – with localism checking the trend towards globalization, and vice versa. The Canadian experience itself is illustrative of this tendency, for surely one of the most important factors operating to preserve Canada as a single country is the fear that its division and breakup would ultimately come to mean increased domination or even absorption by the United States, with all that implies for the maintenance of a distinctive Canadian cultural identity.

Emberley writes at one point that "a situation is emerging where concerted, globally cooperative participation is required (in response to an increasingly fragile ecosystem, to potential nuclear terrorism, to the threat of regional wars) and yet where the possibility of agreement on criteria or measures of what is reasonable, just, or appropriate is being flatly rejected under the guise of a new pluralism." Part of this argument has considerable merit. It does seem to me true that there are certain problems that require global cooperation; I doubt, however, that what Emberley calls the new pluralism is the factor most responsible for blocking it. On the environment, for example, there is a genuine conflict of interest between developed and developing states, just as there is a sneaking suspicion on the part of many developing countries that the existing nuclear powers wish to preserve their own nuclear weapons but deny them to others. This kind of disagreement is endemic to the state system; even international systems that were far more homogenous than our own, such as the European concert after the Napoleonic Wars, had considerable stresses and strains. I suppose that one could argue that the problems we face (either in the form of environmental or nuclear apocalypse) are far more serious than those faced in earlier epochs, that we have far greater need of international cooperation. But the existence of pluralism in the system of states is not at all novel, and one need not resort to new developments in the philosophy of knowledge to account for it.

With regard to transnational institutions such as the multinational corporation, the matter is still more complex. After declining in relative power vis-à-vis the state during the 1960s and 1970s, when it was forced to suffer nationalizations, expropriations, and other indignities, the multinational has staged an impressive comeback in recent years. Both the collapse of communist command economies in the former Soviet bloc and the discrediting of import substitution strategies in Latin America have sharply weakened the attractions of economic autarky, and it is the multinational that is normally in the best position to exploit the new opportunities opened up by these changes. But rather than seeing this as a case of transnational forces rendering the state obsolete, it is better to conceive of this change as a shift in the balance of power between the two.

Let me finally turn to some of the broader philosophical implications of Emberley's paper. Although I have difficulty in assenting to many of the philosophical propositions contained in the essay, I do not doubt that were such propositions to become widely accepted, they would have political consequences. The new pluralism may not cause the state as such to disintegrate; but it may well aid in the disintegration of multiethnic states such as Canada. The analysis has ominous implications for the United States as well. As Emberley argues, "From within liberalism and from within the regulative principles of modern constitutionalism [there] has emerged a dynamic ... whose vitality is corroding those political and economic parameters of modernity which since the Industrial Revolution have limited that dynamic."

This argument, with which I have considerable sympathy, bears a structural similarity to many other views that have been put forward to explain the dissolution of political and economic structures. Many arguments about capitalism – one thinks of Marx and Schumpeter or, more recently, Daniel Bell and Fred Hirsch – postulate a similar dynamic, in which capitalism generates certain consequences in the economic or social order which prepare the way for its subsequent collapse. As Albert Hirschman has shown in one of his marvellous excursions into intellectual history, the structure of the argument recalls a "well-known, much older morality tale: how the republican virtues of sobriety, civic pride, and bravery – in ancient Rome – led to victory and conquest which brought opulence and luxury, which in turn undermined those earlier virtues and destroyed the republic and eventually the empire." Our discussion in this collection of papers suggests that our societies are acutely vulnerable to a similar dynamic, one in which liberal societies committed to the principle of equal citizenship and to individual rights find that their citizens cannot be guaranteed true equality without their demarcation into groups and the intervention of an activist state – an argument, as

James Tully suggested (in chapter 6, above), which has a plausible link with liberal premises but which nevertheless tends to end in dividing the society into self-conscious minorities who seem increasingly to be at one another's throats. The major challenge of modern constitutionalism, in my view, is to figure out a way of preventing that dynamic from playing itself out.

Appendix

Consensus Report
on the Constitution

Charlottetown

AUGUST 28, 1992
FINAL TEXT

TABLE OF CONTENTS

NOTE: Asterisks *in the table of contents* indicate areas where the consensus on some issues under the heading is to proceed with a political accord.

PREFACE

This document is a product of a series of meetings on constitutional reform involving the federal, provincial and territorial governments and representatives of Aboriginal peoples.

These meetings were part of the Canada Round of constitutional renewal. On September 24, 1991, the Government of Canada tabled in the federal Parliament a set of proposals for the renewal of the Canadian federation entitled *Shaping Canada's Future Together*. These proposals were referred to a Special Joint Committee of the House of Commons and the Senate which travelled across Canada seeking views on the proposals. The Committee received 3,000 submissions and listened to testimony from 700 individuals.

During the same period, all provinces and territories created forums for public consultation on constitutional matters. These forums gathered reaction and advice with a view to producing recommendations to their governments. In addition, Aboriginal peoples were consulted by national regional Aboriginal organizations.

An innovative forum for consultation with experts, advocacy groups and citizens was the series of six televised national conferences that took place between January and March of 1992.

Shortly before the release of the report of the Special Joint Committee on a Renewed Canada, the Prime Minister invited representatives of the provinces and territories and Aboriginal leaders to meet with the federal Minister of Constitutional Affairs to discuss the report.

At this initial meeting, held March 12, 1992 in Ottawa, participants agreed to proceed with a series of meetings with the objective of reaching consensus on a set of constitutional amendments. It was agreed that participants would make best efforts to reach consensus before the end of May, 1992 and that there would be no unilateral actions by any government while this process was underway. It was subsequently agreed to extend this series of meetings into June, and then into July.

To support their work, the heads of delegation agreed to establish a Coordinating Committee, composed of senior government officials and representatives of the four Aboriginal organizations. This committee, in turn, created four working groups to develop options and recommendations for consideration by the heads of delegation.

Recommendations made in the report of the Special Joint Committee on a Renewed Canada served as the basis of discussion, as did the recommendations of the various provincial and territorial consultations and the consultations with Aboriginal peoples. Alternatives and modifications to the proposals in these reports have been the principal subject of discussion at the multilateral meetings.

Including the initial session in Ottawa, there were twenty-seven days of meetings among the heads of delegation, as well as meetings of the Coordinating Committee and the four working groups. The schedule of the meetings during this first phase of meetings was:

March 12	Ottawa
April 8 and 9	Halifax
April 14	Ottawa

April 29 and 30	Edmonton
May 6 and 7	Saint John
May 11, 12 and 13	Vancouver
May 20, 21 and 22	Montreal
May 26, 27, 28, 29 and 30	Toronto
June 9, 10 and 11	Ottawa
June 28 and 29	Ottawa
July 3	Toronto
July 6 and 7	Ottawa

Following this series of meetings, the Prime Minister of Canada chaired a number of meetings of First Ministers, in which the Government of Quebec was a full participant. These include:

August 4	Harrington Lake
August 10	Harrington Lake
August 18, 19, 20, 21 and 22	Ottawa
August 27 and 28	Charlottetown

Organizational support for the full multilateral meetings has been provided by the Canadian Intergovernmental Conferences Secretariat.

In the course of the multilateral discussions, draft constitutional texts have been developed wherever possible in order to reduce uncertainty or ambiguity. In particular, a rolling draft of legal text was the basis of the discussion of issues affecting Aboriginal peoples. These drafts would provide the foundation of the formal legal resolutions to be submitted to Parliament and the legislatures.

In areas where the consensus was not unanimous, some participants chose to have their dissents recorded. Where requested, these dissents have been recorded in the chronological records of the meetings but are not recorded in this summary document.

Asterisks *in the text that follows* indicate the areas where the consensus is to proceed with a political accord.

I: UNITY AND DIVERSITY

A. PEOPLE AND COMMUNITIES

1. *Canada Clause*

A new clause should be included as section 2 of the *Constitution Act, 1867* that would express fundamental Canadian values. The Canada Clause would guide the courts in their future interpretation of the entire Constitution, including the Canadian Charter of Rights and Freedoms.

The *Constitution Act, 1867* is amended by adding thereto, immediately after section 1 thereof, the following section:

"2. (1) The Constitution of Canada, including the *Canadian Charter of Rights and Freedoms*, shall be interpreted in a manner consistent with the following fundamental characteristics:

(a) Canada is a democracy committed to a parliamentary and federal system of government and to the rule of law;

(b) the Aboriginal peoples of Canada, being the first peoples to govern this land, have the right to promote their languages, cultures and traditions and to ensure the integrity of their societies, and their governments constitute one of three orders of government in Canada;

(c) Quebec constitutes within Canada a distinct society, which includes a French-speaking majority, a unique culture and a civil law tradition;

(d) Canadians and their governments are committed to the vitality and development of official language minority communities throughout Canada;

(e) Canadians are committed to racial and ethnic equality in a society that includes citizens from many lands who have contributed, and continue to contribute, to the building of a strong Canada that reflects its cultural and racial diversity;

(f) Canadians are committed to a respect for individual and collective human rights and freedoms of all people;

(g) Canadians are committed to the equality of female and male persons; and

(h) Canadians confirm the principle of the equality of the provinces at the same time as recognizing their diverse characteristics.

(2) The role of the legislature and Government of Quebec to preserve and promote the distinct society of Quebec is affirmed.

(3) Nothing in this section derogates from the powers, rights or privileges of the Parliament or the Government of Canada, or of the legislatures or governments of the provinces, or of the legislative bodies or governments of the Aboriginal peoples of Canada, including any powers, rights or privileges relating to language and, for greater certainty, nothing in this section derogates from the aboriginal and treaty rights of the Aboriginal peoples of Canada."

2. *Aboriginal Peoples and the Canadian Charter of Rights and Freedoms*

The Charter provision dealing with Aboriginal peoples (section 25, the non-derogation clause) should be strengthened to ensure that nothing in the Charter abrogates or derogates from Aboriginal, treaty or other rights of Aboriginal peoples, and in particular any rights or freedoms relating to the exercise or protection of their languages, cultures or traditions.

3. *Linguistic Communities in New Brunswick*

A separate constitutional amendment requiring only the consent of Parliament and the legislature of New Brunswick should be added to the *Canadian Charter of Rights and Freedoms*. The amendment would entrench the equality of status of the English and French linguistic communities in New Brunswick, including the right to distinct educational institutions and such distinct cultural institutions as are necessary for the preservation and promotion of these communities. The amendment would also affirm the role of the legislature and government of New Brunswick to preserve and promote this equality of status.

B. CANADA'S SOCIAL AND ECONOMIC UNION

4. *The Social and Economic Union*

A new provision should be added to the Constitution describing the commitment of the governments, Parliament and the legislatures within the federation to the principle of the preservation and development of Canada's social and economic union. The new provision, entitled *The Social and Economic Union*, should be drafted to set out a series of policy objectives underlying the social and the economic union, respectively. The provision should not be justiciable.

The policy objectives set out in the provision on the social union should include, but not be limited to:

- providing throughout Canada a health care system that is comprehensive, universal, portable, publicly administered and accessible;
- providing adequate social services and benefits to ensure that all individuals resident in Canada have reasonable access to housing, food and other basic necessities;
- providing high quality primary and secondary education to all individuals resident in Canada and ensuring reasonable access to post-secondary education;
- protecting the rights of workers to organize and bargain collectively; and
- protecting, preserving and sustaining the integrity of the environment for present and future generations.

The policy objectives set out in the provision on the economic union should include, but not be limited to:

- working together to strengthen the Canadian economic union;
- the free movement of persons, goods, services and capital;
- the goal of full employment;
- ensuring that all Canadians have a reasonable standard of living; and
- ensuring sustainable and equitable development.

A mechanism for monitoring the Social and Economic Union should be determined by a First Ministers' Conference.

A clause should be added to the Constitution stating that the Social and Economic Union does not abrogate or derogate from the *Canadian Charter of Rights and Freedoms*.

5. *Economic Disparities, Equalization and Regional Development*

Section 36 of the *Constitution Act, 1982* currently commits Parliament and the Government of Canada and the governments and legislatures of the provinces to promote equal opportunities and economic development throughout the country and to provide reasonably comparable levels of public services to all Canadians. Subsection 36(2) currently commits the federal government to the principle of equalization payments. This section should be amended to read as follows:

"Parliament and the Government of Canada are committed to making equalization payments so that provincial governments have sufficient revenues to provide reasonably comparable levels of public services at reasonably comparable levels of taxation."

Subsection 36(1) should be expanded to include the territories.

Subsection 36(1) should be amended to add a commitment to ensure the provision of reasonably comparable economic infrastructures of a national nature in each province and territory.

The Constitution should commit the federal government to meaningful consultation with the provinces before introducing legislation relating to equalization payments.

A new Subsection 36(3) should be added to entrench the commitment of governments to the promotion of regional economic development to reduce economic disparities.

Regional development is also discussed in item 36 of this document.

6. *The Common Market*

Section 121 of the *Constitution Act, 1867* would remain unchanged.

Detailed principles and commitments related to the Canadian Common Market are included in the political accord of August 28, 1992. First Ministers will decide on the best approach to implement these principles and commitments at a future First Ministers' Conference on the economy. First Ministers would have the authority to create an independent dispute resolution agency and decide on its role, mandate and composition. (*)

II: INSTITUTIONS

A. THE SENATE

7. *An Elected Senate*

The Constitution should be amended to provide that Senators are elected, either by the population of the provinces and territories of Canada or by the members of their provincial or territorial legislative assemblies.

Federal legislation should govern Senate elections, subject to the constitutional provision above and constitutional provisions requiring that elections take place at the same time as elections to the House of Commons and provisions respecting eligibility and mandate of Senators. Federal legislation would be sufficiently flexible to allow provinces and territories to provide for gender equality in the composition of the Senate.

Matters should be expedited in order that Senate elections be held as soon as possible, and, if feasible, at the same time as the next federal general election for the House of Commons.

8. *An Equal Senate*

The Senate should initially total 62 Senators and should be composed of six Senators from each province and one Senator from each territory.

9. *Aboriginal Peoples' Representation in the Senate*

Aboriginal representation in the Senate should be guaranteed in the Constitution. Aboriginal Senate seats should be additional to provincial and territorial seats, rather than drawn from any province or territory's allocation of Senate seats.

Aboriginal Senators should have the same role and powers as other Senators, plus a possible double majority power in relation to certain matters materially affecting Aboriginal people. These issues and other details relating to Aboriginal representation in the Senate (numbers, distribution, method of selection) will be discussed further by governments and the representatives of the Aboriginal peoples in the early autumn of 1992. (*)

10. *Relationship to the House of Commons*

The Senate should not be a confidence chamber. In other words, the defeat of government-sponsored legislation by the Senate would not require the government's resignation.

11. *Categories of Legislation*

There should be four categories of legislation:

1) Revenue and expenditure bills ("Supply bills");
2) Legislation materially affecting French language or French culture;
3) Bills involving fundamental tax policy changes directly related to natural resources;
4) Ordinary legislation (any bill not falling into one of the first three categories).

Initial classification of bills should be by the originator of the bill. With the exception of legislation affecting French language or French culture (see item 14), appeals should be determined by the Speaker of the House of Commons, following consultation with the Speaker of the Senate.

12. *Approval of Legislation*

The Constitution should oblige the Senate to dispose of any bills approved by the House of Commons, within thirty sitting days of the House of Commons, with the exception of revenue and expenditure bills.

Revenue and expenditure bills would be subject to a 30 calendar-day suspensive veto. If a bill is defeated or amended by the Senate within this period, it could be repassed by a majority vote in the House of Commons on a resolution.

Bills that materially affect French language or French culture would require approval by a majority of Senators voting and by a majority of the Francophone Senators voting. The House of Commons would not be able to override the defeat of a Bill in this category by the Senate.

Bills that involve fundamental tax policy changes directly related to natural resources would be defeated if a majority of Senators voting cast their votes against the bill. The House of Commons would not be able to override the Senate's veto. The precise definition of this category of legislation remains to be determined.

Defeat or amendment of ordinary legislation by the Senate would trigger a joint sitting process with the House of Commons. A simple majority vote at the joint sitting would determine the outcome of the bill.

The Senate should have the powers set out in this Consensus Report. There would be no change to the Senate's current role in approving constitutional amendments. Subject to the Consensus Report, Senate powers and procedures should mirror those in the House of Commons.

The Senate should continue to have the capacity to initial bills, except for money bills.

If any bill initiated and passed by the Senate is amended or rejected by the House of Commons, a joint sitting process should be triggered automatically.

The House of Commons should be obliged to dispose of legislation approved by the Senate within a reasonable time limit.

13. *Revenue and Expenditure Bills*

In order to preserve Canada's parliamentary traditions, the Senate should not be able to block the routine flow of legislation relating to taxation, borrowing and appropriation.

Revenue and expenditure bills ("supply bills") should be defined as only those matters involving borrowing, the raising of revenue and appropriation as well as matters subordinate to these issues. This definition should exclude fundamental policy changes to the tax system (such as the Goods and Services Tax and the National Energy Program).

14. *Double Majority*

The originator of a bill should be responsible for designating whether it materially affects French language or French culture. Each designation should be subject to appeal to the Speaker of the Senate under rules to be established by the Senate. These rules should be designed to provide adequate protection to Francophones.

On entering the Senate, Senators should be required to declare whether they are Francophones for the purpose of the double majority voting rule. Any process for challenging these declarations should be left to the rules of the Senate.

15. *Ratification of Appointments*

The Constitution should specify that the Senate ratify the appointment of the Governor of the Bank of Canada.

The Constitution should also be amended to provide the Senate with a new power to ratify other key appointments made by the federal government.

The Senate should be obliged to deal with any proposed appointments within thirty sitting-days of the House of Commons.

The appointments that would be subject to Senate ratification, including the heads of the national cultural institutions and the heads of federal regulatory boards and agencies, should be set out in specific federal legislation rather than the Constitution. The federal government's commitment to table such legislation should be recorded in a political accord. (*)

An appointment submitted for ratification would be rejected if a majority of Senators voting cast their votes against it.

16. *Eligibility for Cabinet*

Senators should not be eligible for Cabinet posts.

B. THE SUPREME COURT

17. *Entrenchment in the Constitution*

The Supreme Court should be entrenched in the Constitution as the general court of appeal for Canada.

18. *Composition*

The Constitution should entrench the current provision of the *Supreme Court Act*, which specifies that the Supreme Court is to be composed of nine members, of whom three must have been admitted to the bar of Quebec (civil law bar).

19. *Nominations and Appointments*

The Constitution should require the federal government to name judges from lists submitted by the governments of the provinces and territories. A provision should be made in the Constitution for the appointment of interim judges if a list is not submitted on a timely basis or no candidate is acceptable.

20. *Aboriginal Peoples' Role*

The structure of the Supreme Court should not be modified in this round of constitutional discussions. The role of Aboriginal peoples in relation to the Supreme Court should be recorded in a political accord and should be on the agenda of a future First Ministers' Conference on Aboriginal issues. (*)

Provincial and territorial governments should develop a reasonable process for consulting representatives of the Aboriginal peoples of Canada in the preparation of lists of candidates to fill vacancies on the Supreme Court. (*)

Aboriginal groups should retain the right to make representations to the federal government respecting candidates to fill vacancies on the Supreme Court. (*)

The federal government should examine, in consultation with Aboriginal groups, the proposal that an Aboriginal Council of Elders be entitled to make submissions to the Supreme Court when the court considers Aboriginal issues. (*)

C. HOUSE OF COMMONS

21. *Composition of the House of Commons*

The composition of the House of Commons should be adjusted to better reflect the principle of representation by population. The adjustment should include an initial increase in the size of the House of Commons to 337 seats, to be made at the time Senate reform comes into effect. Ontario and Quebec would each be assigned eighteen additional seats. British Columbia four additional seats, and Alberta two additional seats, with boundaries to be developed using the 1991 census.

An additional special Canada-wide redistribution of seats should be conducted following the 1996 census, aimed at ensuring that, in the first subsequent general election, no province will have fewer than 95% of the House of Commons seats it would receive under strict representation-by-population. Consequently, British Columbia and Ontario would each be assigned three additional seats and Alberta two additional seats. As a result of this special adjustment, no province or territory will lose seats, nor will a province or territory which has achieved full representation-by-population have a smaller share of House of Commons seats than its share of the total population in the 1996 census.

The redistribution based on the 1996 census and all future redistributions should be governed by the following constitutional provisions:

(a) A guarantee that Quebec would be assigned no fewer than 25 percent of the seats in the House of Commons;

(b) The current Section 41(b) of the *Constitution Act, 1982*, the "fixed floor," would be retained;

(c) Section 51A of the *Constitution Act, 1867*, the "rising floor," would be repealed;

(d) A new provision that would ensure that no province could have fewer Commons seats than another province with a smaller population, subject to the provision in item (a) above;

(e) The current provision that allocates two seats to the Northwest Territories and one seat to Yukon would be retained.

A permanent formula should be developed and Section 51 of the *Constitution Act, 1867*, should be adjusted to accommodate demographic change, taking into consideration the principles suggested by the Royal Commission on Electoral Reform and Party Financing.

22. *Aboriginal Peoples' Representation*

The issue of Aboriginal representation in the House of Commons should be pursued by Parliament, in consultation with representatives of the Aboriginal peoples of Canada, after it has received the final report of the House of Commons Committee studying the recommendations of the Royal Commission on Electoral Reform and Party Financing. (*)

D. FIRST MINISTERS' CONFERENCES

23. *Entrenchment*

A provision should be added to the Constitution requiring the Prime Minister to convene a First Ministers' Conference at least once a year. The agendas for these conferences should not be specified in the Constitution.

The leaders of the territorial governments should be invited to participate in any First Ministers' Conference convened pursuant to this constitutional provision. Representatives of the Aboriginal peoples of Canada should be invited to participate in discussions on any item on the agenda of a First Ministers' Conference that directly affects the Aboriginal peoples. This should be embodied in a political accord. (*)

The role and responsibilities of First Ministers with respect to the federal spending power are outlined at item 25 of this document.

E. THE BANK OF CANADA

24. *Bank of Canada*

The Bank of Canada was discussed and the consensus was that this issue should not be pursued in this round, except for the consensus that the Senate should have a role in ratifying the appointment of its Governor.

III: ROLES AND RESPONSIBILITIES

25. *Federal Spending Power*

A provision should be added to the Constitution stipulating that the Government of Canada must provide reasonable compensation to the government of a province that chooses not to participate in a new Canada-wide shared-cost program that is established by the federal government in an area of exclusive provincial jurisdiction, if that province carries on a program or initiative that is compatible with the national objectives.

A framework should be developed to guide the use of the federal spending power in all areas of exclusive provincial jurisdiction. Once developed, the framework could become a multilateral agreement that would receive constitutional protection using the mechanism described in Item 26 of this report. The framework should ensure that when the federal spending power is used in areas of exclusive provincial jurisdiction, it should:

(a) contribute to the pursuit of national objectives;
(b) reduce overlap and duplication;
(c) not distort and should respect provincial priorities; and
(d) ensure equality of treatment of the provinces, while recognizing their different needs and circumstances.

The Constitution should commit First Ministers to establishing such a framework at a future conference of First Ministers. Once it is established, First Ministers would assume a role in annually reviewing progress in meeting the objectives set out in the framework.

A provision should be added (as Section 106A(3)) that would ensure that nothing in the section that limits the federal spending power affects the commitments of Parliament and the Government of Canada that are set out in Section 36 of the *Constitution Act, 1982.*

26. *Protection of Intergovernmental Agreements*

The Constitution should be amended to provide a mechanism to ensure that designated agreements between governments are protected from unilateral change. This would occur when Parliament and the legislature(s) enact laws approving the agreement.

Each application of the mechanism should cease to have effect after a maximum of five years but could be renewed by a vote of Parliament and the legislature(s) readopting similar legislation. Governments of Aboriginal peoples should have access to this mechanism. The provision should be available to protect both bilateral and multilateral agreements among federal, provincial and territorial governments, and the governments of Aboriginal Peoples. A government negotiating an agreement should be accorded equality of treatment in relation to any government which has already concluded an agreement, taking into account different needs and circumstances.

It is the intention of governments to apply this mechanism to future agreements related to the Canada Assistance Plan. (*)

27. *Immigration*

A new provision should be added to the Constitution committing the Government of Canada to negotiate agreements with the provinces relating to immigration.

The Constitution should oblige the federal government to negotiate and conclude within a reasonable time an immigration agreement at the request of any province. A government negotiating an agreement should be accorded equality of treatment in relation to any government which has already concluded an agreement, taking into account different needs and circumstances.

28. *Labour Market Development and Training*

Exclusive federal jurisdiction for unemployment insurance, as set out in Section 91(2A) of the *Constitution Act, 1867*, should not be altered. The federal government should retain exclusive jurisdiction for income support and its related services delivered through the Unemployment Insurance system. Federal spending on job creation programs should be protected through a constitutional provision or a political accord. (*)

Labour market development and training should be identified in section 92 of the Constitution as a matter of exclusive provincial jurisdiction. Provincial legislatures should have the authority to constrain federal spending that is directly related to labour market development and training. This should be accomplished through justiciable intergovernmental agreements designed to meet the circumstances of each province.

At the request of a province, the federal government would be obligated to withdraw from any or all training activities and from any or all labour market development activities, except Unemployment Insurance. The federal government should be required to negotiate and conclude agreements to provide reasonable compensation to provinces requesting that the federal government withdraw.

The Government of Canada and the government of the province that requested the federal government to withdraw should conclude agreements within a reasonable time.

Provinces negotiating agreements should be accorded equality of treatment with respect to terms and conditions of agreements in relation to any other province that has already concluded an agreement, taking into account the different needs and circumstances of the provinces.

The federal, provincial and territorial governments should commit themselves in a political accord to enter into administrative arrangements to improve efficiency and client service and ensure effective coordination of federal Unemployment Insurance and provincial employment functions. (*)

As a safeguard, the federal government should be required to negotiate and conclude an agreement within a reasonable time, at the request of any province not requesting the federal government to withdraw, to maintain its labour market development and training programs and activities in that province. A similar safeguard should be available to the territories.

There should be a constitutional provision for an ongoing federal role in the establishment of national policy objectives for the national aspects of labour market development. National labour market policy objectives would be established through a process which could be set out in the Constitution including the obligation for presentation to Parliament for debate. Factors to be considered in the establishment of national policy objectives could include items such as national economic conditions, national labour market requirements, international labour market trends and changes in international economic conditions. In establishing national policy objectives, the federal government would take into account the different needs and circumstances of the provinces; and there would be a provision, in the Constitution or in a political accord, committing the federal, provincial, and territorial governments to support the development of common occupational standards, in consultation with employer and employee groups. (*)

Provinces that negotiated agreements to constrain the federal spending power should be obliged to ensure that their labour market development programs are compatible with the national policy objectives, in the context of different needs and circumstances.

Considerations of service to the public in both official languages should be included in a political accord and be discussed as part of the negotiation of bilateral agreements. (*)

The concerns of Aboriginal peoples in this field will be dealt with through the mechanisms set out in item 40 below.

29. *Culture*

Provinces should have exclusive jurisdiction over cultural matters within the provinces. This should be recognized through an explicit constitutional amendment that also recognizes the continuing responsibility of the federal government in Canadian cultural matters. The federal government should retain responsibility for national cultural institutions, including grants and contributions delivered by these institutions. The Government of Canada commits to negotiate cultural agreements with provinces in recognition of their lead responsibility for cultural matters within the province and to ensure that the federal government and the province work in harmony. These changes should not alter the federal fiduciary responsibility for Aboriginal people. The non-derogation provisions for Aboriginal peoples set out in item 40 of this document will apply to culture.

30. *Forestry*

Exclusive provincial jurisdiction over forestry should be recognized and clarified through an explicit constitutional amendment.

Provincial legislatures should have the authority to constrain federal spending that is directly related to forestry.

This should be accomplished through justiciable intergovernmental agreements, designed to meet the specific circumstances of each province. The mechanism used would be the one set out in item 26 of this document, including a provision for equality of treatment with respect to terms and conditions. Considerations of service to the public in both official languages should be considered a possible part of such agreements. (*)

Such an agreement should set the terms for federal withdrawal, including the level and form of financial resources to be transferred. In addition, a political accord could specify the form the compensation would take (i.e., cash transfers, tax points, or others) (*). Alternatively, such an agreement could require the federal government to maintain its spending in that province. A similar safeguard should be available to the territories. The federal government should be obliged to negotiate and conclude such an agreement within a reasonable time.

These changes and the ones set out in items 31, 32, 33, 34 and 35 should not alter the federal fiduciary responsibility for Aboriginal people. The provisions set out in item 40 would apply.

31. *Mining*

Exclusive provincial jurisdiction over mining should be recognized and clarified through an explicit constitutional amendment and the negotiation of federal-provincial agreements. This should be done in the same manner as set out above with respect to forestry. (*)

32. *Tourism*

Exclusive provincial jurisdiction over tourism should be recognized and clarified through an explicit constitutional amendment and the negotiation of federal-provincial agreements. This should be done in the same manner as set out above with respect to forestry. (*)

33. *Housing*

Exclusive provincial jurisdiction over housing should be recognized and clarified through an explicit constitutional amendment and the negotiation of federal-provincial agreements. This should be done in the same manner as set out above with respect to forestry. (*)

34. *Recreation*

Exclusive provincial jurisdiction over recreation should be recognized and clarified through an explicit constitutional amendment and the negotiation of federal-provincial agreements. This should be done in the same manner as set out above with respect to forestry. (*)

35. *Municipal and Urban Affairs*

Exclusive provincial jurisdiction over municipal and urban affairs should be recognized and clarified through an explicit constitutional amendment and the negotiation of federal-provincial agreements. This should be done in the same manner as set out above with respect to forestry. (*)

36. *Regional Development*

In addition to the commitment to regional development to be added to Section 36 of the *Constitution Act, 1982* (described in item 5 of this document), a provision should be added to the Constitution that would oblige the federal government to negotiate an agreement at the request of any province with respect to regional development. Such agreements could be protected under the provision set out in item 26 ("Protection of Intergovernmental Agreements"). Regional development should not become a separate head of power in the Constitution.

37. *Telecommunications*

The federal government should be committed to negotiate agreements with the provincial governments to coordinate and harmonize the procedures of their respective regulatory agencies in this field. Such agreements could be protected under the provision set out in item 26 ("Protection of Intergovernmental Agreements").

38. Federal Power of Disallowance and Reservation

This provision of the Constitution should be repealed. Repeal requires unanimity.

39. Federal Declaratory Power

Section 92(10)(c) of the *Constitution Act, 1867*, permits the federal government to declare a "work" to be for the general advantage of Canada and bring it under the legislative jurisdiction of Parliament. This provision should be amended to ensure that the declaratory power can only be applied to new works or rescinded with respect to past declarations with the explicit consent of the province(s) in which the work is situated. Existing declarations should be left undisturbed unless all of the legislatures affected wish to take action.

40. Aboriginal Peoples' Protection Mechanism

There should be a general non-derogation clause to ensure that division of powers amendments will not affect the rights of the Aboriginal peoples and the jurisdictions and powers of governments of Aboriginal peoples.

IV: FIRST PEOPLES

Note: References to the territories will be added to the legal text with respect to this section, except where clearly inappropriate. Nothing in the amendments would extend the powers of the territorial legislations.

A. THE INHERENT RIGHT OF SELF-GOVERNMENT

41. The Inherent Right of Self-Government

The Constitution should be amended to recognize that the Aboriginal peoples of Canada have the inherent right of self-government within Canada. This right should be placed in a new section of the *Constitution Act, 1982*, section 35.1(1).

The recognition of the inherent right of self-government should be interpreted in light of the recognition of Aboriginal governments as one of three orders of government in Canada.

A contextual statement should be inserted in the Constitution, as follows:

"The exercise of the right of self-government includes the authority of the duly constituted legislative bodies of Aboriginal peoples, each within its own jurisdiction:

(a) to safeguard and develop their languages, cultures, economies, identities, institutions and traditions; and,
(b) to develop, maintain and strengthen their relationship with their lands, waters and environment

so as to determine and control their development as peoples according to their own values and priorities and ensure the integrity of their societies."

Before making any final determination of an issue arising from the inherent right of self-government, a court or tribunal should take into account the contextual statement referred to above, should enquire into the efforts that have been made to resolve the issue through negotiations and should be empowered to order the parties to take such steps as are appropriate in the circumstances to effect a negotiated resolution.

42. Delayed Justiciability

The inherent right of self-government should be entrenched in the Constitution. However, its justiciability should be delayed for a five-year period through constitutional language and a political accord. (*)

Delaying the justiciability of the right should be coupled with a constitutional provision which would shield Aboriginal rights.

Delaying the justiciability of the right will not make the right contingent and will not affect existing Aboriginal and treaty rights.

The issue of special courts or tribunals should be on the agenda of the first Ministers' Conference on Aboriginal Constitutional matters referred to in item 53. (*)

43. Charter Issues

The *Canadian Charter of Rights and Freedoms* should apply immediately to governments of Aboriginal peoples.

A technical change should be made to the English text of Sections 3, 4, and 5 of the *Canadian Charter of Rights and Freedoms* to ensure that it corresponds to the French text.

The legislative bodies of Aboriginal peoples should have access to section 33 of the *Constitution Act, 1982* (the notwithstanding clause) under conditions that are similar to those applying to Parliament and the provincial legislatures but which are appropriate to the circumstances of Aboriginal peoples and their legislative bodies.

44. Land

The specific constitutional provision on the inherent right and the specific constitutional provision on the commitment to negotiate land should not create new Aboriginal rights to land or derogate from existing aboriginal or treaty rights to land, except as provided for in self-government agreements.

B. METHOD OF EXERCISE OF THE RIGHT

45. Commitment to Negotiate

There should be a constitutional commitment by the federal and provincial governments and the Indian, Inuit and Métis peoples in the various regions and communities of Canada to negotiate in good faith with the objective of concluding agreements elaborating the relationship between Aboriginal governments and the other orders of government. The negotiations would focus on the implementation of the right of self-government including issues of jurisdiction, lands and resources, and economic and fiscal arrangements.

46. *The Process of Negotiation*

Political Accord on Negotiation and Implementation
— A political accord should be developed to guide the process of self-government negotiations. (*)

Equity of Access
— All Aboriginal peoples of Canada should have equitable access to the process of negotiation.

Trigger for Negotiations
— Self-government negotiations should be initiated by the representatives of Aboriginal peoples when they are prepared to do so.

Provision for Non-Ethnic Governments
— Self-government agreements may provide for self-government institutions which are open to the participation of all residents in a region covered by the agreement.

Provision for Different Circumstances
— Self-government negotiations should take into consideration the different circumstances of the various Aboriginal peoples.

Provision for Agreements
— Self-government agreements should be set out in future treaties, including land claims agreements or amendments to existing treaties, including land claims agreements. In addition, self-government agreements could be set out in other agreements which may contain a declaration that the rights of the Aboriginal peoples are treaty rights, within the meaning of Section 35(1) of the *Constitution Act, 1982*.

Ratification of Agreements
— There should be an approval process for governments and Aboriginal peoples for self-government agreements, including Parliament, the legislative assemblies of the relevant provinces and/or territories and the legislative bodies of the Aboriginal peoples. This principle should be expressed in the ratification procedures set out in the specific self-government agreements.

Non-Derogation Clause
— There should be an explicit statement in the Constitution that the commitment to negotiate does not make the right of self-government contingent on negotiations or in any way affect the justiciability of the right of self-government.

Dispute Resolution Mechanism
– To assist the negotiation process, a dispute resolution mechanism involving mediation and arbitration should be established. Details of this mechanism should be set out in a political accord. (*)

47. *Legal Transition and Consistency of Laws*

A constitutional provision should ensure that federal and provincial laws will continue to apply until they are displaced by laws passed by governments of Aboriginal peoples pursuant to their authority.

A constitutional provision should ensure that a law passed by a government of Aboriginal peoples, or an assertion of its authority based on the inherent right provision may not be inconsistent with those laws which are essential to the preservation of peace, order and good government in Canada. However, this provision would not extend the legislative authority of Parliament or of the legislatures of the provinces.

48. *Treaties*

With respect to treaties with Aboriginal peoples, the Constitution should be amended as follows:

– treaty rights should be interpreted in a just, broad and liberal manner taking into account the spirit and intent of the treaties and the context in which the specific treaties were negotiated;
– the Government of Canada should be committed to establishing and participating in good faith in a joint process to clarify or implement treaty rights, or to rectify terms of treaties when agreed to by the parties. The governments of the provinces should also be committed, to the extent that they have jurisdiction, to participation in the above treaty process when invited by the government of Canada and the Aboriginal peoples concerned or where specified in a treaty;
– participants in this process should have regard, among other things and where appropriate, to the spirit and intent of the treaties as understood by Aboriginal peoples. It should be confirmed that all Aboriginal peoples that possess treaty rights shall have equitable access to this treaty process;
– it should be provided that these treaty amendments shall not extend the authority of any government or legislature, or affect the rights of Aboriginal peoples not party to the treaty concerned.

C. ISSUES RELATED TO THE EXERCISE OF THE RIGHT

49. *Equity of Access to Section 35 Rights*

The Constitution should provide that all of the Aboriginal peoples of Canada have access to those Aboriginal and treaty rights recognized and affirmed in Section 35 of the *Constitution Act, 1982* that pertain to them.

50. *Financing*

Matters relating to the financing of governments of Aboriginal peoples should be dealt with in a political accord. The accord would commit the governments of Aboriginal peoples to:

- promoting equal opportunities for the well-being of all Aboriginal peoples;
- furthering economic, social and cultural development and employment opportunities to reduce disparities in opportunities among Aboriginal peoples and between Aboriginal peoples and other Canadians; and
- providing essential public services at levels reasonably comparable to those available to other Canadians in the vicinity.

It would also commit federal and provincial governments to the principle of providing the governments of Aboriginal peoples with fiscal or other resources, such as land, to assist those governments to govern their own affairs and to meet the commitments listed above, taking into account the levels of services provided to other Canadians in the vicinity and the fiscal capacity of governments of Aboriginal peoples to raise revenues from their own sources.

The issues of financing and its possible inclusion in the Constitution should be on the agenda of the first Ministers' Conference on Aboriginal Constitutional matters referred to in item 53. (*)

51. *Affirmative Action Programs*

The Constitution should include a provision which authorizes governments of Aboriginal Peoples to undertake affirmative action programs for socially and economically disadvantaged individuals or groups and programs for the advancement of Aboriginal languages and cultures.

52. *Gender Equality*

Section 35(4) of the *Constitution Act, 1982*, which guarantees existing Aboriginal and treaty rights equally to male and female persons should be retained. The issue of gender equality should be on the agenda of the first Ministers' Conference on Aboriginal Constitutional matters referred to under item 53. (*)

53. *Future Aboriginal Constitutional Process*

The Constitution should be amended to provide for four future First Ministers' Conferences on Aboriginal constitutional matters beginning no later than 1996, and following every two years thereafter. These conferences would be in addition to any other First Ministers' Conferences required by the Constitution. The agendas of these conferences would include items identified in this report and items requested by Aboriginal peoples.

54. *Section 91(24)*

For greater certainty, a new provision should be added to the *Constitution Act, 1867* to ensure that Section 91(24) applies to all Aboriginal peoples.

The new provision would not result in a reduction of existing expenditures by governments on Indians and Inuit or alter the fiduciary and treaty obligations of the federal government for Aboriginal peoples. This would be reflected in a political accord (*)

55. *Métis in Alberta/Section 91(24)*

The Constitution should be amended to safeguard the legislative authority of the Government of Alberta for Métis and Métis Settlements lands. There was agreement to a proposed amendment to the *Alberta Act* that would constitutionally protect the status of the land held in fee simple by the Métis Settlements General Council under letters patent from Alberta.

56. *Métis Nation Accord* (*)

The federal government, the provinces of Ontario, Manitoba, Saskatchewan, Alberta, British Columbia and the Métis National Council have agreed to enter into a legally binding, justiciable and enforceable accord on Métis Nation issues. Technical drafting of the Accord is being completed. The Accord sets out the obligations of the federal and provincial governments and the Métis Nation.

The Accord commits governments to negotiate: self-government agreements; lands and resources; the transfer of the portion of Aboriginal programs and services available to Métis; and cost sharing arrangements relating to Métis institutions, programs and services.

Provinces and the federal government agree not to reduce existing expenditures on Métis and other Aboriginal people as a result of the Accord or as a result of an amendment to section 91(24). The Accord defines the Métis for the purposes of the Métis Nation Accord and commits governments to enumerate and register the Métis Nation.

V: THE AMENDING FORMULA

Note: All of the following changes to the amending formula require the unanimous agreement of Parliament and the provincial legislatures.

57. *Changes to National Institutions*

Amendments to provisions of the Constitution related to the Senate should require unanimous agreement of Parliament and the provincial legislatures, once the current set of amendments related to Senate reform has come into effect. Future amendments affecting the House of Commons, including Quebec's guarantee of a least 25 percent of the seats in the House of Commons, and amendments which can now be made under Section 42 should also require unanimity.

Sections 41 and 42 of the *Constitution Act, 1982* should be amended so that the nomination and appointment process of Supreme Court judges would remain subject to the general (7/50) amending procedure. All other matters related to the Supreme Court, including its entrenchment, its role as the general court of appeal and its composition, would be matters requiring unanimity.

58. *Establishment of New Provinces*

The current provisions of the amending formula governing the creation of new provinces should be rescinded. They should be replaced by the pre-1982 provisions allowing the creation of new provinces through an Act of Parliament, following consultation with all of the existing provinces at a First Ministers' Conference. New provinces should not have a role in the amending formula without the unanimous consent of all of the provinces and the federal government, with the exception of purely bilateral or unilateral matters described in Sections 38(3), 40, 43, 45, and 46 as it relates to 43, of the *Constitution Act, 1982*. Any increase in the representation for new provinces in the Senate should also require the unanimous consent of all provinces and the federal government. Territories that become provinces could not lose Senators or members of the House of Commons.

The provision now contained in Section 42(1)(e) of the *Constitution Act, 1982*, with respect with the extension of provincial boundaries into the Territories should be repealed and replaced by the *Constitution Act, 1871*, modified in order to require the consent of the Territories.

59. *Compensation for Amendments that Transfer Jurisdiction*

Where an amendment is made under the general amending formula that transfers legislative powers from provincial legislatures to Parliament, Canada should provide reasonable compensation to any province that opts out of the amendment.

60. *Aboriginal Consent*

There should be Aboriginal consent to future constitutional amendments that directly refer to the Aboriginal peoples. Discussions are continuing on the mechanism by which this consent would be expressed with a view to agreeing on a mechanism prior to the introduction in Parliament of formal resolutions amending the Constitution.

VI: OTHER ISSUES

Other constitutional issues were discussed during the multilateral meetings. The consensus was not to pursue the following issues:

- personal bankruptcy and insolvency;
- intellectual property;
- interjurisdictional immunity;
- inland fisheries;
- marriage and divorce;
- residual power;
- legislative interdelegation;

- changes to the "notwithstanding clause";
- Section 96 (appointment of judges);
- Section 125 (taxation of federal and provincial governments);
- Section 92A (export of natural resources));
- requiring notice for changes to federal legislation respecting equalization payments;
- property rights;
- implementation of international treaties.

Other issues were discussed by were not finally resolved, among which were:

- requiring notice for changes to federal legislation respecting Established Programs Financing;
- establishing in a political accord a formal federal-provincial consultation process with regard to the negotiation of international treaties and agreements;
- Aboriginal participation in intergovernmental agreements respecting the division of powers;
- establishing a framework for compensation issues with respect to labour market development and training;
- consequential amendments related to Senate reform, including by-elections;
- any other consequential amendments required by changes recommended in this report.

Notes

INTRODUCTION

COOK: CANADA'S PREDICAMENT

1 American readers will find a concentrated and readable review of
Canadian constitutional politics in the following articles in *PS* 26, no. 1
(March 1993): 32–48: Kent Weaver, "Introduction"; Peter H. Russell,
"The End of Mega Constitutional Politics in Canada?"; Stéphane Dion,
"The Quebec Challenge to Canadian Unity"; Richard Johnson, "An
Inverted Logroll: The Charlottetown Accord and the Referendum."
Current History 90, no. 560 (December 1991) is also helpful, especially
Kenneth McRoberts, "Canada's Constitutional Crisis," 411–16.
2 Kenneth McNaught, *The Penguin History of Canada* (Markham: Penguin
Books of Canada, 1988), ch. 4.
3 Samuel P. Huntington, *American Politics: The Promise of Disharmony*
(Cambridge: Belknap Press of Harvard University Press, 1981), ch. 2.
4 Leon Wieseltier, "Spoilers at the Party," *National Interest*, Fall 1989, 12–16.
5 Allan R. Gregg, Mitch Patten, and Joan Fischer, "Canadian Politics in
1993," *Public Perspective*, March/April 1993, 25–8.
6 James Madison, "Federalist Paper 37," in *The Federalist*, ed. Edward
Mead Earle (New York: Modern Library, n.d.), 227.

CHAPTER ONE

CAIRNS: THE CHARLOTTETOWN ACCORD

1 See Philip Resnick, "Canada: Three Sociological Nations," *Canadian
Forum*, October 1992, for a brief discussion of Canada as a three-nation

multinational federation. Ten academics from the University of Toronto and York University and the writer Christina McCall recently supported a three-nations view of the desired direction of constitutional change. See "Three Nations in a Delicate State," *Toronto Star*, 4 February 1992. See also "Speaking Notes by Ron George, President, NCC, to the Policy Conference on 'Identity, Rights and Values,'" 6–9 February 1992, Toronto, for advocacy of a three-nations view of Canada and for a "National Covenant" negotiated and signed by their representatives.

2 For a powerful expression of this view, see Ovide Mercredi, Assemblée nationale, *Journal des débats*, Commission parlementaire spéciale, Commission d'étude des questions afférentes à l'accession du Québec à la souveraineté, no. 27 (11 February 1992): CEAS 826.

3 See, for example, many of the essays in Duncan Cameron and Miriam Smith, eds., *Constitutional Politics: The Canadian Forum Book on the Federal Constitutional Proposals 1991–92* (Toronto: James Lorimer, 1992), which view Canada through a two- or three-nation lens. See also Arthur Keppel-Jones and Hugh G. Thorburn, "Why Not a Two-Nations Canada?" *Policy Options*, May 1992, 21–2. As far as Quebec/ROC constitutional aspirations are concerned, this approach frequently leads to support for asymmetrical federalism. See Duncan Cameron, "The Asymmetrical Alternative"; A.W. Johnson, "A National Government in a Federal State," 89–91; and Philip Resnick, "The West Wants In," 198–9; all in Cameron and Smith, *Constitutional Politics*. Two- or three-nation perspectives are central themes in the post-referendum analyses of Kari Levitt, "Requiem for a Referendum"; Mel Watkins, "A Flawed Process"; Philip Resnick, "Beyond October 26"; and Frank Cunningham, "Democracy and Three-Nation Asymmetry"; all in *Canadian Forum*, December 1992.

4 See the report of the Constitutional Committee of the Quebec Liberal Party, *A Québec Free to Choose* (28 January 1991) (the Allaire Report) for a good example.

5 *Report of the Commission on the Political and Constitutional Future of Québec* (Québec, 1991), 1 (the Bélanger-Campeau Report).

6 Kari Levitt, "Requiem for a Referendum," 13. See also Casey Vander Ploeg, *The Referendum on the Charlottetown Accord: An Assessment* (Calgary: Canada West Foundation, January 1993), 16–20.

7 Guy Laforest, "The Referendum and Its Aftermath in Quebec," *Canada Watch*, November/December 1992, 57.

8 For this genre of analysis, see John McCallum, "What If the Vote Is NO?" *Network* 2, no. 8 (October 1992): 7–8.

9 Resnick, "Canada: Three Sociological Nations," 27.

10 J.L. Granatstein and Kenneth McNaught, "Introduction," 12; Reg Whitaker, "With or without Quebec?" 18; and Tom Kent, "An Emergency

Operation for the Constitution," 324; all in *"English Canada" Speaks Out*, ed. J.L. Granatstein and Kenneth McNaught (Toronto: Doubleday Canada, 1991).

11 Whitaker, "With or without Quebec?" 18. Tom Kent agrees with Mulroney: "No federal government elected to run the federal affairs of the country as a whole, has any right, legal or moral, to represent one part of the country in constitutional negotiations with another part ... no entitlement to respond to Quebec on behalf of Canada outside Quebec"; Kent, "An Emergency Operation for the Constitution," 323.

12 Whitaker, "With or without Quebec?" 19.

13 Reg Whitaker, "Bearing It without a Grin," *Canadian Forum*, October 1992, 29.

14 See, for example, the various essays in *"English Canada" Speaks Out*, ed. Granatstein and McNaught, especially comments by the editors, 12; see also the various essays in *Negotiating with a Sovereign Quebec*, ed. Daniel Drache and Roberto Perin (Toronto: James Lorimer, 1992). The emergence of a distinct ROC or English-Canadian constitutional self-consciousness was frequently noted in the Spicer Report – *Citizens' Forum on Canada's Future: Report to the People and Government of Canada* (Ottawa: Supply and Services, 1991).

15 Barbara Cameron, "A Constitution for English Canada," in *Negotiating with a Sovereign Quebec*, ed. Drache and Perin, 230–1. Mel Watkins detects "recurring evidence over the years that English-speaking Canadians outside Quebec, their regionalism notwithstanding, think and act like a distinct people": Watkins, "A Flawed Process," *Canadian Forum*, December 1992, 14.

16 For the latter, see David J. Bercuson and Barry Cooper, *Deconfederation: Canada without Quebec* (Toronto: Key Porter Books, 1991), and various essays in *"English Canada" Speaks Out*, ed. Granatstein and McNaught.

17 This discussion of the Quebec components of the Charlottetown Accord is based on *Consensus Report on the Constitution, Charlottetown, August 28, 1992, Final Text*, and *Draft Legal Text, October 9, 1992*.

18 Report of the Constitutional Committee, *A Québec Free to Choose*.

19 *Reformer*, special edition, Fall 1992.

20 Both this discussion of the Aboriginal components of the Charlottetown Accord and the discussion in the following sections are based on the *Consensus Report* and *Draft Legal Text*.

21 Radha Jhappan, "Aboriginal Self-Government," *Canadian Forum*, October 1992, 15–16.

22 Tony Hall, "Aboriginal People and the Third Option in the Referendum" (6 October 1992, mimeo), 1.

23 Douglas Sanders, "Lesbians and Gays and the Charlottetown Accord" (10 October 1992, mimeo), 8.

24 Bradford Morse, "Indigenous Peoples in Quebec and Canada," *Literary Review of Canada*, October 1992, 12.

25 Ron George, "Saying NO to a Generation of Hope," *Network* 2, no. 8 (October 1992): 3. Elsewhere he described the Aboriginal components of the accord as marking "an historic shift in our relationship with the government ... the dawn of a new era. The future is ours"; George, "Equity of Access for Aboriginal Peoples," in *Referendum Round-Table: Perspectives on the Charlottetown Accord*, Points of View, no. 3, ed. Kate Sutherland (Edmonton: Centre for Constitutional Studies, University of Alberta, 1992), 34.

26 An undated "best efforts draft" for final review by first ministers and Aboriginal leaders described the "Métis Nation ... as a unique nation with its own language, culture and forms of self-government." For the purposes of the accord: (a) "'Métis' means an Aboriginal person who self-identifies as Métis, who is distinct from Indian and Inuit and is a descendant of those Métis who received or were entitled to receive land grants and/or scrip under the provisions of the *Manitoba Act*, 1870, or the *Dominion Lands Acts*, as enacted from time to time. [And] (b) 'Métis Nation' means the community of Métis persons in subsection (a) and persons of Aboriginal descent who are accepted by that community." Métis Nation Accord, mimeo, Best Efforts Draft.

27 Jhappan, "Aboriginal Self-Government," 16.

28 *Native Women's Association of Canada, Gail Stacey-Moore and Sharon McIvor v. Her Majesty the Queen*, Federal Court of Appeal, August 20, 1992.

29 The Report of the Special Joint Committee of the Senate and the House of Commons, *The Process for Amending the Constitution of Canada* (Ottawa: Supply and Services, 1991), 16.

30 Conference Report of Co-Chairs Joseph A. Ghiz and Mary Simon, *First Peoples and the Constitution* (Ottawa: Privy Council Office, 1992).

31 Commissioner's Report, Assembly of First Nations, *To the Source* (Ottawa, 1992).

32 *Report of the Royal Commission of Inquiry on Constitutional Problems* (Quebec, 1956) (the Tremblay Report).

33 Mary Ellen Turpel, "Does the Road to Quebec Sovereignty Run through Aboriginal Territory?" in *Negotiating with a Sovereign Quebec*, ed. Drache and Perin, 105–6.

34 Tony Hall, "Aboriginal People and the Third Option," 5.

35 Tony Hall, "The Assembly of First Nations and the Demise of the Charlottetown Accord," (30 November 1992, mimeo), 1.

36 The *Consensus Report*, 22, indicated that "the issue of Aboriginal representation in the House of Commons should be pursued by Parliament, in consultation with representatives of the Aboriginal peoples of Canada, after it has received the final report of the House of Com-

mons Committee studying the recommendations of the Royal Commission on Electoral Reform and Party Financing."

37 *Shaping Canada's Future Together: Proposals* (Ottawa: Supply and Services, 1991), 4–9.

38 Shawn Henry, *Public Opinion and the Charlottetown Accord* (Calgary: Canada West Foundation, January 1993), 4.

39 Jean-François Lisée, "Les dossiers secrets de Bourassa," *L'Actualité*, 1 November 1992, 67–9.

40 Guy Laforest, "L'Accord d'Ottawa-Charlottetown et la réconciliation des aspirations nationales au Canada," in Claude Bariteau, et al., *Référendum, 26 octobre 1992: les objections de 20 spécialistes aux offres fédérales* (Montréal: Éditions Saint-Martin, 1992). In the same work, Daniel Latouche makes a similar comparison, focusing on the division of powers, in "le partage des pouvoirs: ceux des Autochtones, ceux du Québec et ceux qu'on peut-être oubliés."

41 Trudeau's views are cogently, indeed polemically, presented in his *Trudeau: "A Mess that Deserves a Big NO"* (Toronto: Robert Davies Publishing, 1992).

42 Assistance in tracing this policy evolution is provided by Douglas Sanders, "The Renewal of Indian Special Status," in *Equality Rights and the Canadian Charter of Rights and Freedoms*, ed. Anne F. Bayefsky and Mary Eberts (Toronto: Carswell, 1985); and Sally M. Weaver, 'A New Paradigm in Canadian Indian Policy for the 1990s,' *Canadian Ethnic Studies* 22, no. 3 (1990).

43 *Transition* 6, no. 1 (January 1993): 10.

44 Richard Gwyn, "A Second Sovereignty," in *"English Canada" Speaks Out*, ed. Granatstein and McNaught, 387.

45 Douglas Sanders, "An Uncertain Path: The Aboriginal Constitutional Conferences," in *Litigating the Values of a Nation: The Canadian Charter of Rights and Freedoms*, ed. Joseph M. Weiler and Robin M. Elliot (Toronto, 1986), 72–3; and Bryan Schwartz, *First Principles, Second Thoughts: Aboriginal Peoples, Constitutional Reform and Canadian Statecraft* (Montreal, 1986), 324.

46 For another example, see Ed Finn, "A Vote to Reject," *Canadian Forum*, October 1992, 31.

47 Thomas J. Courchene and Lisa M. Powell, "A First Nations Province," School of Policy Studies, Queen's University (April 1992, mimeo), 49.

48 "Referendum File: What Happens Next," *Maclean's*, 2 November 1992, 17. The question was: "Which of the following reasons for voting No comes closest to your main reason?" See also Henry, *Public Opinion and the Charlottetown Accord*, 4, for the far greater antipathy to the "Quebec concessions" than to the Aboriginal constitutional package. (The gap is much greater if Quebec is excluded from the comparison, but Henry

does not provide this data.) Even where dislike of Aboriginal self-government was greatest (12 per cent of respondents in British Columbia and Saskatchewan), opposition to the Quebec concessions was still four times greater, at 47 per cent.

49 P.A. Monture-Okanee and M.E. Turpel, "Aboriginal Peoples and Canadian Criminal Law: Rethinking Justice," *University of British Columbia Law Review*, special edition (1992): 256, 258, 264. Andrew Bear Robe concurs, asserting that Indian First Nations had no voice in the constitutional settlements of 1867 or 1982. "We have," he continued, "no sense of ownership regarding the federal and provincial laws that apply to us simply because those laws were forced upon us without our consent, consultation or input, especially the much despised federal *Indian Act*"; see "Treaty Federalism," *Constitutional Forum* 4, no. 1 (Fall 1992): 6.

50 Bercuson and Cooper, *Deconfederation*, 169.

51 Tony Hall, "Aboriginal Issues and the New Political Map of Canada," 136–9; and Bruce W. Hodgins, "The Northern Boundary of Quebec: The James Bay Crees as Self-Governing Canadians"; both in *"English Canada" Speaks Out*, ed. Granatstein and McNaught.

52 See also Mary Ellen Turpel, "Does the Road to Quebec Sovereignty Run through Aboriginal Territory?"; and Kent McNeill, "Aboriginal Nations and Quebec's Boundaries: Canada Couldn't Give What It Didn't Have"; both in *Negotiating with a Sovereign Quebec*, ed. Drache and Perin. Turpel refers to "embittered relationships between aboriginal peoples and the [Quebec] provincial government" (95). McNeil asserts: "The Québécois cannot assert a right of self-determination for themselves and at the same time deny that right to the aboriginal nations ... The aboriginal nations may decide to align themselves with Canada, or go with Québec, or set off on their own. If the country disintegrates, the choice must be up to them."

Ovide Mercredi's blunt presentation to the Quebec National Assembly committee studying sovereignty, and the hostile reactions of nationalist committee members, graphically revealed the tensions and conflicts between rival views of "Who is a people?," "Who has the right to self-determination?," and "Can a seceding Quebec depart with all its territory, taking all of its peoples with it?" See Assemblé nationale, *Journal des débats*, no. 27.

Criticism of Quebec's relation to Aboriginal peoples needs to be tempered by the recognition that in many policy areas Quebec's response has been very positive and enlightened compared with that of other provinces in Canada. For a discussion, see Bradford Morse, "Indigenous Peoples in Quebec and Canada," *Literary Review of Canada*, October 1992.

53 Roger Tassé, "Finding the Balance: Comments on the Proposals to Amend the Division of Powers," *Network Analysis*, Analysis no. 6, October 1992, 10–11. De facto asymmetries would, of course, emerge as different provincial governments struck different arrangements with the federal government.

54 Courchene and Powell, "A First Nations Province," 3, 55. Their proposal would apply to on-reserve Indians, about 60 per cent of the status population. See also David J. Elkins, *Where Should the Majority Rule? Reflections on Non-Territorial Provinces and Other Constitutional Proposals*, Points of View, no. 1 (Edmonton: Centre for Constitutional Studies, University of Alberta, 1992).

55 If the proposals were implemented, presumably it would mean that Aboriginal Canadians would not be considered citizens of the traditional ten provinces, but only of the new territorially fragmented Aboriginal province, and hence that they would have no vote or voice in, for example, British Columbia elections.

56 See Native Women's Association of Canada, "Native Women and the Charter: A Discussion Paper" (Ottawa, n.d.), and "Native Women and Self-Government: A Discussion Paper" (Ottawa, n.d.). The first round of public hearings of the Royal Commission on Aboriginal Peoples elicited recurrent expressions of fear that Aboriginal self-government would be an instrument for the domination of Aboriginal women by Aboriginal men and that the application of the Charter of Rights and Freedoms was an essential safeguard: see "Royal Commission on Aboriginal Peoples, Public Hearings: Overview of the First Round" (prepared by Michael Cassidy Ginger Group Consultants, October 1992), 4, 27, 36, 40–1, 46.

57 Commissioners' Report, Assembly of First Nations, *To the Source.*

58 Mary Ellen Turpel, "Aboriginal Peoples and the Canadian *Charter*: Interpretive Monopolies, Cultural Differences," *Canadian Human Rights Yearbook* (1989–90).

59 According to law professor L.E. Weinrib, basing her interpretation primarily on the strengthening of the existing section 25 Charter exemption of Aboriginal, treaty, or other rights or freedoms of the Aboriginal people from the Charter's application, its application to Aboriginal government would be minimal. She also noted that the section 33 override made available to Aboriginal governments might not be subject to the same safeguards and political costs that attend to the open political process of federal and provincial legislatures, a weakness that might be especially pronounced when self-government, including Aboriginal leadership selection, followed traditional norms; see "Charlottetown Accord Constitutional Proposals: Legal Analysis of Draft Legal Text of October 12, 1992" (prepared by Professor L.E. Weinrib, Faculty

of Law, University of Toronto, 21 October 1992, mimeo), 23, 26–7.
Weinrib argued that the overall impact of the accord, not just its Aboriginal sections, was Charter weakening. Thirteen legal colleagues
agreed with the Weinrib analysis.

   Professor Anne Bayefsky concurs with the Weinrib analysis, stating
that "the insulation of aboriginal self-government from Charter rights
and freedoms has been greatly expanded." Although she was referring
to an earlier draft legal text, the final wording appears to confirm the
validity of her statement; see Anne F. Bayefsky, "The Effect of Aboriginal Self-Government on the Rights and Freedoms of Women," *Network
Analysis: Reactions; Comments on Analysis no. 4*, October 1992, 2.

60 An Aboriginal third order was, of course, much more threatening to
   the Québécois' sense of themselves as a national people in possession
   of Quebec territory, and doubly so to the advocates of independence.

CHAPTER TWO
NOËL: DELIBERATING A CONSTITUTION

1 The results for Canada outside Quebec and for Indian reserves are
  unofficial results obtained from Elections Canada and the Assembly of
  First Nations; for the Indian reserves, the error may be as much as
  17 per cent. For Quebec, the results are official and are reported in
  Rapport des résultats officiels du scrutin: référendum du 26 octobre 1992
  (Quebec: Directeur général des élections, 1992).

2 See Susan Delacourt, "Loss of Faith," *Globe and Mail*, 24 October 1992,
  D1; Graham Fraser, "What Does It Mean for Government? How to
  Decide What to Do Next?" *Globe and Mail*, 27 October 1992, A1; and
  Gilles Lesage, "Une gifle magistrale," *Le Devoir*, 27 October 1992, A1.

3 Graham Fraser, "Referendum Had to Be Held, Politicians Say," *Globe
  and Mail*, 24 October 1992, A1; François Brousseau, "Un référendum
  sert souvent à exprimer la mauvaise humeur de l'électorat," *Le Devoir*,
  26 October 1992, A1.

4 Craig McInnes, "The Invisible Angels of Yes," *Globe and Mail*,
  24 October 1992, D2; Anthony Wilson-Smith, "As Time Runs Out,"
  Maclean's, 19 October 1992, 16.

5 Respectively, Peter C. Newman, "How the Yes Side Lost its Marbles,"
  Maclean's, 2 November 1992, 22; Edward Broadbent, "Think We, Not
  Me on Referendum Day," *Globe and Mail*, 20 October 1992, A23; and
  Jeffrey Simpson, "Les alliances singulières," *Le Devoir*, 28 September
  1992, 16.

6 Ross Laver and Bruce Wallace, "The Meaning of No," *Maclean's*,
  2 November 1992, 16–17.

7 Canadian Press, "Quebec Voters Led Turnout in Referendum," *Globe and Mail*, 29 October 1992, A6; Fraser, "What Does It Mean for Government?"

8 Thomas J. Courchene, "What Does It Mean for the Nation? Death of a Political Era," *Globe and Mail*, 27 October 1992, A1.

9 Harold D. Clarke, Jane Jenson, Lawrence LeDuc, and Jon H. Pammett, *Absent Mandate: The Politics of Discontent in Canada* (Toronto: Gage, 1984), 10–16, 181–3.

10 Richard Simeon, "We Are All Smiley's People: Some Observations on Donald Smiley and the Study of Federalism," in *Federalism and Political Community: Essays in Honour of Donald Smiley*, ed. David P. Shugarman and Reg Whitaker (Peterborough: Broadview, 1989), 412–13.

11 Alan C. Cairns, "Political Science, Ethnicity and the Canadian Constitution," in *Federalism and Political Community*, ed. Shugarman and Whitaker, 113–18.

12 Garth Stevenson, "The Decline of Consociational Democracy in Canada" (Paper presented at the annual meeting of the American Political Science Association, Washington, D.C., 29 August – 1 September 1991), 9–10. See also R. Kent Weaver, who states explicitly the difference between Lijphart's model and the narrower notion of consociationalism used in Canada, in his "Political Institutions and Canada's Constitutional Crisis," in *The Collapse of Canada?* ed. Weaver, (Washington: Brookings, 1992), 12.

13 See Kenneth McRae, "The Meech Lake Impasse in Theoretical Perspective," in *Democracy with Justice: Essays in Honour of Khayyam Zev Paltiel*, ed. Alain-G. Gagnon and A. Brian Tanguay (Ottawa: Carleton University Press, 1992).

14 Leif Lewin, *Self-Interest and Public Interest in Western Politics* (Oxford: Oxford University Press, 1991), 19.

15 See Reg Whitaker, *A Sovereign Idea: Essays on Canada as a Democratic Community* (Montreal: McGill-Queen's University Press, 1992), 207.

16 See, respectively, H. D. Forbes, "Absent Mandate '88? Parties and Voters in Canada," in *Party Politics in Canada*, 6th edition, ed. Hugh G. Thorburn (Scarborough: Prentice-Hall, 1991); Cairns, "Political Science, Ethnicity and the Canadian Constitution"; and McRae, "The Meech Lake Impasse in Theoretical Perspective."

17 Jane J. Mansbridge, "The Rise and Fall of Self-Interest in the Explanation of Political Life," in *Beyond Self-Interest*, ed. Mansbridge (Chicago: University of Chicago Press, 1990).

18 See, for instance, Samuel L. Popkin, *The Reasoning Voter: Communication and Persuasion in Presidential Campaigns* (Chicago: University of Chicago Press, 1991), 20–1.

19 Charles Taylor, "Alternative Futures: Legitimacy, Identity and Alienation in Late Twentieth Century Canada," in *Constitutionalism, Citizenship
and Society in Canada*, ed. Alan Cairns and Cynthia Williams, vol. 33 of
the research studies of the Royal Commission on the Economic Union
and Development Prospects for Canada (Toronto: University of
Toronto Press, 1985).

20 Alan C. Cairns, *Charter versus Federalism: The Dilemmas of Constitutional
Reform* (Montreal: McGill-Queen's University Press, 1992), 10.

21 Richard Johnston, André Blais, Henry E. Brady, and Jean Crête, *Letting the People Decide: Dynamics of a Canadian Election* (Montreal: McGill-
Queen's University Press, 1992), 15; underlined in the original. One
can contrast this account with the more conventional interpretation of
the same election proposed by Harold D. Clarke and Allan Kornberg
in "Risky Business: Partisan Volatility and Electoral Choice in Canada,
1988," *Electoral Studies* 11, no. 2 (June 1992): 138–56.

22 Cairns, *Charter versus Federalism*, 98; Peter H. Russell, *Constitutional
Odyssey: Can Canadians Be a Sovereign People?* (Toronto: University of
Toronto Press, 1992), 190.

23 Cairns, *Charter versus Federalism*, 98.

24 Jon Elster, "The Market and the Forum: Three Varieties of Political
Theory," in *Foundations of Social Choice Theory*, ed. Elster and Aanund
Hylland (Cambridge: Cambridge University Press, 1986).

25 Bernard Manin, "Volonté générale ou délibération? Esquisse d'une
théorie de la délibération politique," *Le Débat* 33 (January 1985): 85–7.

26 Robert A. Dahl, "Myth of the Presidential Mandate," *Political Science
Quarterly* 105, no. 3 (Fall 1990): 371.

27 Jon Elster, "The Possibility of Rational Politics," *Archives européennes de
sociologie* 28, no. 1 (1987): 89, 98.

28 Manin, "Volonté générale ou délibération?" 88.

29 Michael Harrington, *The Next Left: The History of a Future* (New York:
Henry Holt, 1986), 15.

30 This contrast between two viewpoints obviously masks important differences between the various behavioural and rational choice interpretations; in fact, many studies stand somewhere between these two polar
views. The purpose of the dichotomy is simply to contrast clearly the
interpretation proposed here with conventional understandings of politics. A similar contrast between economic explanations and accounts
stressing deliberation is suggested in James A. Caporaso and David P.
Levine, *Theories of Political Economy* (Cambridge: Cambridge University
Press, 1992), 155; see also Benjamin I. Page and Robert Y. Shapiro,
The Rational Public: Fifty Years of Trends in Americans' Policy Preferences
(Chicago: Chicago University Press, 1992).

31 Quoted in Graham Fraser, "Referendum Had to Be Held, Politicians Say." See also Pierre O'Neill, "Tout dépend encore du vote des indécis," *Le Devoir*, 7 October 1992, A1.

32 Quoted in Hugh Windsor, "Learning the Lessons from the Ballot Box," *Globe and Mail*, 7 November 1992, A5.

33 R. Darcy and Michael Laver, "Referendum Dynamics and the Irish Divorce Amendment," *Public Opinion Quarterly* 54, no. 1 (Spring 1990): 1–20.

34 Scott Feschuk, "Yes and No Sides Make Their Pitch with Series Ads," *Globe and Mail*, 20 October 1992, A1.

35 See Thomas E. Cronin, *Direct Democracy: The Politics of Initiative, Referendum, and Recall* (Cambridge: Harvard University Press, 1989), 84–7.

36 Ibid., 86.

37 Miriam Smith, "Institutional Reform," *Canadian Forum*, October 1992, 17.

38 Ross Howard, "Yes Campaign Needs Focus, Political Strategists Agree," *Globe and Mail*, 21 October 1992, A5.

39 Alan C. Cairns, "Constitutional Change and the Three Equalities," in *Options for a New Canada*, ed. Ronald L. Watts and Douglas M. Brown (Toronto: University of Toronto Press, 1991), 77.

40 See Pierre Elliott Trudeau, *Ce gâchis mérite un gros non!* (Montréal: L'Étincelle, 1992).

41 "Special Edition: Know More!" *Reformer*, Fall 1992.

42 Philippe Cantin, "Elijah Harper invite les autochtones à boycotter le scrutin," *La Presse*, 22 October 1992, A1; Agnès Gruda, "Le Non autochtone," *La Presse*, 30 October 1992, B2.

43 Comité du Non, "A ce prix là, c'est non," in *Québec: référendum 92* (Quebec: Directeur général des élections,1992), 2–3.

44 Elster, "The Possibility of Rational Politics," 97.

45 McInnes, "The Invisible Angels of Yes"; Newman, "How the Yes Side Lost Its Marbles."

46 "Special Edition: Know More!"

47 Cairns, "Constitutional Change and the Three Equalities"; Peter H. Russell, *Constitutional Odyssey.*

48 Peter H. Russell, "Can the Canadians Be a Sovereign People?," *Canadian Journal of Political Science* 24, no. 4 (December 1991): 708.

49 Johnston, Blais, Brady, and Crête, *Letting the People Decide*, 106.

50 Julian Beltrame, "Majority Want Canada to Stay United," *Gazette*, 7 November 1992, A1.

51 Courchene, "What Does It Mean for the Nation?"; Stéphane Dion, "Le Canada malade de la politique symbolique," *La Presse*, 26 February 1992, B3.

52 Edouard Cloutier, Jean H. Guay, and Daniel Latouche, *Le virage: l'évo-lution de l'opinion publique au Québec depuis 1960* (Montreal: Québec/ Amérique, 1992); Maurice Pinard, "The Dramatic Reemergence of the Quebec Independence Movement," *Journal of International Affairs* 45, no. 2 (Winter 1992): 471–97; André Blais and Richard Nadeau, "To Be or Not to Be Sovereignist: Quebeckers' Perennial Dilemma," *Canadian Public Policy* 18, no. 1 (March 1992): 89–103.

53 Courchene, "What Does It Mean for the Nation?"

54 Duncan Cameron, "Rallying around the Referendum," *Canadian Forum*, October 1992, 12.

55 See Jane Jenson, "Beyond Brokerage Politics: Towards the Democracy Round," in *Constitutional Politics*, ed. Duncan Cameron and Miriam Smith (Toronto: Lorimer, 1992).

56 Manin, "Volonté générale ou délibération?" 84; the quotation is pre-sented as translated in Manin, "On Legitimacy and Political Delibera-tion," *Political Theory* 15, no. 3 (August 1987): 352–3.

57 Russell, *Constitutional Odyssey*, 177.

58 James S. Fishkin, *Democracy and Deliberation: New Directions for Demo-cratic Reform* (New Haven: Yale University Press, 1991), 81–4.

59 The representativeness of the participants was often questioned. *La Presse* columnist Lysiane Gagnon noted that half of the Quebec popula-tion – the sovereigntists and those on the left – remained conspicuously absent, and that on the side of English Canada, social and political activ-ists of all stripes appeared overrepresented; see "Où est l'autre moitié du Québec?" *La Presse*, 3 February 1992, A1, and "Le triomphe des non-élus," *La Presse*, 25 February 1992, B3. An earlier experiment conducted by *Maclean's* suggests, however, that a more representative sample of "ordinary" citizens might yield not so different results; see Robert Mar-shall, "The People's Verdict: How Canadians Can Surmount Differences to Agree on Their Future," *Maclean's*, 1 July 1991, 10–11.

60 Russell, *Constitutional Odyssey*, 177.

61 Reg Whitaker, "Bearing It Without a Grin," *Canadian Forum*, October 1992, 28–9; Kenneth McRoberts, "Blame It on a Fundamentally Flawed Accord," *Globe and Mail*, 29 October 1992, A19.

62 Adam Przeworski, *Democracy and the Market: Political and Economic Reforms in Eastern Europe and Latin America* (Cambridge: Cambridge University Press, 1991), 15.

63 Ibid., 18.

64 Laura Stoker, "Interests and Ethics in Politics," *American Political Science Review* 86, no. 2 (June 1992): 369–80.

65 Kenneth McRoberts, *English Canada and Quebec: Avoiding the Issue* (Toronto: Robarts Centre for Canadian Studies, 1991); Guy Laforest, *Trudeau et la fin d'un rêve canadien* (Sillery: Septentrion, 1992).

66 Przeworski, *Democracy and the Market*, 83–7.
67 David Butler and Austin Ranney, "Summing Up," in *Referendums: A Comparative Study of Practice and Theory*, ed. Butler and Ranney (Washington: American Enterprise Institute for Public Policy Research, 1978), 223.
68 Michel Vastel, "Cinq jours en août," *L'Actualité*, 1 November 1992, 71.
69 Denis Lessard, "'Touche pas à mon Boubou...'" *La Presse*, 24 October 1992, B1.
70 John Zaller and Stanley Feldman argue that such ambivalence is not a failure of rationality but a normal feature of personality; see "A Simple Theory of the Survey Response: Answering Questions versus Revealing Preferences," *American-Journal of Political Science* 36, no. 3 (August 1992): 579–616.
71 Christian Dufour, *La rupture tranquille* (Montreal: Boréal, 1992), 144–5; Jean-François Lisée, "Le Canada dans la peau," *L'Actualité*, July 1992, 21–8.
72 Manin, "Volonté générale ou délibération?" 93.
73 Gilles Normand, "Parizeau invite les Québécois à s'unir pour relancer l'économie," *La Presse*, 27 October 1992, A3.
74 Michel Crête, "Une journée dans la vie d'un référendum," *Nouvelles CSN*, 30 October 1992, 11–12.
75 See Charles Taylor, "Shared and Divergent Values," in *Options for a New Canada*, ed. Watts and Brown, 75–6.

CHAPTER THREE

COOPER: LOOKING EASTWARD, LOOKING
BACKWARD

1 For purposes of this argument, *Canadians* refers to the multiethnic English-speaking citizens of Canada; *Québécois* refers to the French-speaking citizens of the Province of Quebec who identify with the ethnic descendants of the colonists of New France, whether or not they are *pure laine*, or "old stock," in any genealogical sense. This commonsensical distinction was central to the argument by David Bercuson and myself in *Deconfederation: Canada without Quebec* (Toronto: Key Porter, 1991).
2 For the classical statement, see Robert Presthus, *Elite Accommodation in Canadian Politics* (Toronto: Macmillan, 1973).
3 Harvey Mansfield, Jr., *America's Constitutional Soul* (Baltimore: Johns Hopkins University Press, 1991), 102. Hannah Arendt makes an equivalent argument from a considerably different starting point than Mansfield in *The Human Condition* (Chicago: University of Chicago Press, 1958), part 2, and *On Revolution* (New York: Viking, 1963), ch. 2.

4 See Barry Cooper, *The End of History: An Essay on Modern Hegelianism* (Toronto: University of Toronto Press, 1984); and Eric Voegelin, "On Hegel: A Study in Sorcery," in *Published Essays, 1966–1985,* vol. 12 of *The Collected Works of Eric Voegelin* (Baton Rouge: Louisiana State University Press, 1990), 213–55.

5 For details, see Harvey Mansfield, Jr., *The Taming of the Prince: The Ambivalence of Modern Executive Power* (New York: Free Press, 1989), esp. chs. 5–7; and Mansfield, *America's Constitutional Soul,* ch. 8.

6 The best account of this problem is Hubert Guindon, *Quebec Society: Tradition, Modernity and Nationhood* (Toronto: University of Toronto Press, 1988). We followed his analysis in Bercuson and Cooper, *Deconfederation: Canada without Quebec.*

7 See Ralph Heintzman, "The Political Culture of Quebec, 1840–1960," *Canadian Journal of Political Science* 16 (1983): 3–59.

8 The results have on occasion been bizarre. For a witty discussion of Quebec's language laws, see Mordecai Richler, *Oh Canada! Oh Quebec! Requiem for a Divided Country* (Toronto: McClelland & Stewart, 1992).

9 Northrup Frye, *The Bush Garden* (Toronto: Anansi, 1971), i–iii; 225–6; Margaret Atwood, *Survival: A Thematic Guide to Canadian Literature* (Toronto: Anansi, 1972), 32.

10 Frye, *Bush Garden,* 163. Sylvia B. Bashevkin made essentially the same mistake as Frye in her *True Patriot Love: The Politics of Canadian Nationalism* (Toronto: Oxford University Press, 1991). This is rather more surprising, because Bashevkin is fully aware of the limited, not to say provincial, outlook of the generally left-wing Toronto intellectuals whom she identified as the *fons et origo* of "pan-Canadian" nationalism.

11 Dennis Duffy, *Gardens, Covenants, Exiles: Loyalism in the Literature of Upper Canada/Ontario* (Toronto: University of Toronto Press, 1982), 131–2.

12 Jean-Jacques Rousseau, *Du contrat social,* vol. 2, ch. 1.

13 I have argued this point at greater length in my "Western Political Consciousness," in *Political Thought in Canada: Contemporary Perspectives,* ed. Stephen Brooks (Toronto: Irwin, 1984), 213–38; "The West: A Political Minority," in *Minorities and the Canadian State,* ed. Neil Nevitte and Allan Kornberg (Toronto: Mosaic, 1985), 203–20; and "Did George Grant's Canada Ever Exist?" in *George Grant and the Future of Canada,* ed. Yusuf K. Umar (Calgary: University of Calgary Press, 1992), 151–64.

14 One may add, parenthetically, that the garrison mentality of Ontario is far more compatible with the myth of *la survivance* of Quebec than it is with the myths of western Canada. This compatibility is what makes the composite myth – the founding of Canada by *deux nations*/two

nations – easily acceptable in central Canada and widely resisted in the West.

15 See, however, Leo Strauss, *What Is Political Philosophy? And Other Studies* (Glencoe: Free Press, 1959), 9–55; and Eric Voegelin, *The Nature of the Law*, vol. 27 of *Collected Works* (Baton Rouge: Louisiana State University Press, 1991), 1–69.

16 My understanding of this question has been guided chiefly by Eugene Forsey. See, in particular, Forsey, *Freedom and Order: Collected Essays* (Toronto: McClelland & Stewart, 1974). Andrew Heard, *Canadian Constitutional Conventions: The Marriage of Law and Politics* (Toronto: Oxford University Press, 1991) is also useful, as well as any number of "*X* on Con" books by law professors. Hogg on Con – that is, Peter Hogg, *Constitutional Law in Canada*, 2d ed. (Toronto: Carswell, 1985) – is probably the standard work.

17 See Alan Cairns, *Charter versus Federalsim: The Dilemmas of Constitutional Reform* (Montreal: McGill-Queen's University Press, 1992), 72. The distinctions amid their interrelationships were explored in Cairns's earlier collection, *Disruptions: Constitutional Struggles from the Charter to Meech Lake* (Toronto: McClelland & Stewart, 1991).

18 See Janet Ajzenstat, "Modern Mixed Government: A Liberal Defence of Inequality," *Canadian Journal of Political Science* 18 (1985): 119–34; Philip Resnick, "Montesquieu Revisited: Or the Mixed Constitution and the Separation of Powers in Canada," ibid., 20 (1987): 97–116; and Ajzenstat, "Comment: The Separation of Powers in 1867," ibid., 20 (1987): 117–20.

19 See Thomas L. Pangle, *The Ennobling of Democracy: The Challenge of the Postmodern Age* (Baltimore: Johns Hopkins University Press, 1992).

20 Mansfield, *America's Constitutional Soul*, 16.

21 Charles Murray, *Losing Ground: American Social Policy, 1950–1980* (New York: Basic Books, 1984); Christopher Sarlo, *Poverty in Canada* (Vancouver: Fraser Institute, 1992).

22 See Rainer Knopff, *Human Rights and Social Technology: The New War on Discrimination* (Ottawa: Carleton University Press, 1989).

23 Mansfield, *America's Constitutional Soul*, 82.

24 Cairns, *Charter versus Federalism*, 98.

25 Peter H. Russell, *Constitutional Odyssey: Can Canadians Be a Sovereign People?* (Toronto: University of Toronto Press, 1992).

26 Cairns, *Charter versus Federalism*, 94.

27 See, for example, Scott Reid, *The Breakup of Quebec: Democracy and the Dangers of Partition* (Peterborough: Broadview, 1992).

28 Cairns, *Charter versus Federalism*, 101; see also his *Disruptions*, ch. 9.

29 Cairns, *Charter versus Federalism*, 124.

30 David J. Elkins, "Facing Our Destiny: Rights and Canadian Distinctiveness," *Canadian Journal of Political Science* 22 (1989): 699–716; F.L.
Morton, "Group Rights versus Individual Rights in the Charter: The
Special Case of Natives and the Québécois," in *Minorities and the Canadian State*, ed. Nevitte and Kornberg, 71–85.

31 R. Kent Weaver, "Political Institutions and Canada's Constitutional
Crisis," in *The Collapse of Canada?* ed. Weaver (Washington: Brookings,
1992), 7–75.

32 See, for example, Guy Laforest, *Trudeau et la fin d'un rêve canadien*
(Montreal: Septentrion, 1992), chs. 6–8. See also Bercuson and Cooper,
Deconfederation.

33 Pierre Foglia, "Look at Erie Street," *La Presse*, 17 October 1992, A5.

34 Allen Buchanan, *Secession: The Morality of Political Divorce from Fort
Sumter to Lithuania and Quebec* (Boulder: Westview, 1991), 74–7.

35 Ibid., 77.

36 See Kenneth McRae, "The Meech Lake Impasse in Theoretical Per-
spective," in *Democracy with Justice: Essays in Honour of Khayyam Zev Pal-
tiel*, ed. Alain-G. Gagnon and A. Brian Tanguay (Ottawa: Carleton
University Press, 1992); and Charles Taylor, "Shared and Divergent
Values," in *Options for a New Canada*, ed. Ronald L. Watts and Douglas
M. Brown (Toronto: University of Toronto Press, 1991).

37 These percentages are based on 1982–83 data for all levels of government; see Å. G. Blomqvist, "Political Economy of the Canadian Welfare
State," in *Approaches to Economic Well-Being*, ed. David Laidler, vol. 4 of
the research studies of the Royal Commission on the Economic Union
and Development Prospects for Canada (Toronto: University of
Toronto Press, 1985), 90.

38 The 25 per cent figure is for 1982–86; see Economic Council of
Canada, *The New Face of Poverty: Income Security Needs of Canadian Fami-
lies* (Ottawa: Economic Council of Canada, 1992). On the turnover
among beneficiairies, see Keith G. Banting, *The Welfare State and Canadian Federalism*, 2d ed. (Montreal: McGill-Queen's University Press,
1987), 29.

39 David J. Bercuson and Barry Cooper, *Goodbye … et bonne chance: les
adieux du Canada anglais au Québec* (Montreal: Le Jour, 1991), 155–82,
193.

CHAPTER FOUR
AJZENSTAT: CONSTITUTION MAKING

1 For an argument about the destructive consequences of political debate
on constitutional issues, see Michael Foley, *The Silence of Constitutions:*

Gaps, "Abeyances" and Political Temperament in the Maintenance of Government (London: Routledge, 1989).

2 Keith Spicer argued that a "new constitution" was necessary; see *Citizens' Forum on Canada's Future: Report to the People and Government of Canada* (the Spicer Report) (Ottawa: Supply and Services, 1991), 5. *Maclean's* argued for reinventing Canada; see "The People's Verdict," *Maclean's*, 1 July 1991. Recent articles speak of "fixing Canada," "reconfederation," "steps to a new Canada"; see contributions by G.T. Rayner and Robert Patterson in *Policy Options* 13 (1992).

3 Mark O. Dickerson and Thomas Flanagan, *An Introduction to Government and Politics: A Conceptual Approach*, 3d ed. (Scarborough: Nelson, 1990), 61.

4 See the minority report of the Beaudoin-Edwards committee. *The Process for Amending the Constitution of Canada, The Report of the Special Joint Committee of the Senate and the House of Commons* (Beaudoin-Edwards Report), 20 June 1991, 74.

5 "One of the strongest messages the Forum received from participants was that they have lost their faith in the political process and their political leaders"; see *Citizens' Forum on Canada's Future*, 96. See also the testimony of the participants in the forum sponsored by *Maclean's*: "The People's Verdict." Much of this dissatisfaction took the form of hostility to the prime minister. A public opinion poll on Mr Mulroney's performance as prime minister, released by the *Globe and Mail* and CBC in the fall of 1990, showed that 85 per cent in Ontario, 83 per cent in British Columbia, and 87 per cent on the prairies felt that he was doing a poor or very poor job; see Roger Gibbins, "Constitutional Politics in the West and the Rest," in *Confederation in Crisis*, ed. Robert Young (Toronto: Lorimer, 1991), 21. Provincial leaders who had participated in the debate also suffered loss of public confidence, as Gibbins notes.

6 Vaughan Lyon, "Stalemated Democracy? The Canadian Case," *Journal of Canadian Studies* 26 (1991). See also Ken Hanly, "Constitutional Initiatives and Referenda: Only in Switzerland, You Say? Pity!" *Policy Options* 13 (1992): 19, where he states: "Given that people are becoming more frustrated in politics and feel a sense of powerlessness in the face of the existing parliamentary system, surely what we need is more real power for the people, even if it comes at the expense of those politicians the people have elected."

7 The Citizens' Forum found "striking unity" among forum participants in their "demand to be more involved in the process that will define Canada's future"; see "The Forum: A Report to the People from the Citizens' Forum on Canada's Future," *Globe and Mail*, 29 June 1991, A7.

The Canadians polled by *Maclean's* agreed. A typical academic opinion is expressed in Edouard Cloutier, "We the People: Public Opinion, Sovereignty and the Constitution," in *Confederation in Crisis*, ed. Young. Cloutier states, "The introduction of the people as a constitutional actor will bring about a saner way of looking at everything, at least in Quebec," 9. The Spicer Report concluded by arguing that Canadians were in danger of forgetting substantive issues in the "great preoccupation with process and personalities"; *Citizens' Forum*, 143.

8 Statement to the Special Joint Committee on the 1987 Constitutional Accord, cited in *Meech Lake and Canada: Perspectives from the West*, ed. Roger Gibbins et al. (Edmonton: Academic, 1988), 100. Beverley Baines spoke of "the almost pathological secrecy of the patriarchal process that ultimately gave us the final version of the accord"; Baines, "After Meech Lake: The Ms/Representation of Gender in Scholarly Spaces," in *After Meech Lake, Lessons for the Future*, ed. David E. Smith, Peter MacKinnon, and John C. Courtney (Saskatoon: Fifth House, 1991), 206. Witnesses before the Beaudoin-Edwards committee complained in similar terms about the secrecy of the Meech process; see Beaudoin-Edwards Report, 20 June 1991.

9 Among the foremost advocates of a constituent assembly was Keith Spicer, chairman of the Citizens' Forum. In his foreword to the final report, he urged the government to adopt a constituent assembly or some "similar process allowing citizens to feel directly involved in constitution-making"; see *Citizens' Forum on Canada's Future*, 5. The majority of witnesses (158 out of 181) testifying to the Beaudoin-Edwards committee recommended a constituent assembly. Among the organizations that supported the idea of a constituent assembly were the Reform Party of Canada, the New Democratic Party of Ontario, the federal NDP, the Ontario wing of the federal Liberals, the National Action Committee on the Status of Women, and the Canada West Foundation. Clyde Wells, premier of Newfoundland, outspokenly supported a constituent assembly. A number of academics endorsed more or less moderate variations on the assembly, among them Kenneth McRoberts and David Elton. As John Dafoe noted, "Almost everyone likes the idea of a constituent assembly but the Mulroney government"; see "Assembly Idea Has Seized the Political Imagination," *Globe and Mail*, 6 July 1991, D2.

10 Difficulties posed by the proposal for a country-wide referendum are outlined in Peter H. Russell's moderate proposal for a constituent assembly, "Towards a New Constitutional Process," in *Options for New Canada*, ed. Ronald L. Watts and Douglas M. Brown (Toronto: University of Toronto Press, 1991).

11 Willard Z. Estey and Peter J. Nicholson, "Giving Power to the People," *Globe and Mail*, 22 April 1991, A13.

12 Deborah Wilson, Miro Cernetig, and Susan Delacourt, "Filmon to Press for People's Assembly," *Globe and Mail*, 26 August 1991, A7.

13 The argument that Parliament has more legitimacy than a constituent assembly was made by the Beaudoin-Edwards committee. Mr Mulroney's Speech from the Throne in the spring of 1991 argued that public involvement in the constitutional process was essential, that all-party parliamentary committees would facilitate it, and that recommendations made by such committees were not narrow, partisan pronouncements; see House of Commons, *Debates*, vol. 132, 13 May 1991, 1–6. See also Graham Fraser and Susan Delacourt, "Ottawa Must Reach Out, Clark Says," *Globe and Mail*, 8 May 1991, A4. The government's constitutional proposals were widely advertised in the fall of 1991 and winter of 1992, and were available on request without cost; see *Shaping Canada's Future Together* (Ottawa: Supply and Services, 1991). Views on the government's package were solicited by the Special Joint Committee of the Senate and the House of Commons (chaired first by Claude Castonguay and Dorothy Dobbie, and after Senator Castonguay's resignation, by Dobbie and Gérald Beaudoin) which toured the country in the fall of 1991. Debate continued in the national conferences of early 1992. In addition to these federally sponsored opportunities, there were the various provincial commissions.

14 Anne Bayefsky, *Globe and Mail*, 10 January 1992, A13. See also Alex N. McLeod, "If We Want to Fix the Constitution, First We Have to Fix the Process," *Policy Options* 31 (1992): 11.

15 Ken Hanly, "Constitutional Initiatives and Referenda: Only in Switzerland?" 19. Hanly's comments prefaced a recommendation for the introduction of the initiative at the constitutional level.

16 Alan C. Cairns, "The Politics of Constitutional Conservatism," in *And No One Cheered: Federalism, Democracy and the Constitution Act*, ed. Keith Banting and Richard Simeon (Toronto: Methuen, 1983), 28. Roger Gibbins notes that "prior to the 1981 Accord, the Canadian public had been involved, and often intensely involved, in the constitutional process. Canadians had gone through at least five years of protracted constitutional debate that reached well beyond the First Ministers to embrace seemingly endless task forces, televised confrontations, townhall meetings, editorial commentary, articles in *Saturday Night*, and the groves of academe"; see "A Sense of Unease: The Meech Lake Accord and Constitution-Making in Canada," in *Meech Lake and Canada*, ed. Gibbins et al., 123.

17 David Milne, *The Canadian Constitution, from Patriation to Meech Lake* (Toronto: Lorimer, 1989), 89, 159–60. The groups' appearances before

joint parliamentary committees in the fall of 1980 were especially note-worthy.

18 See, for example, Reg Whitaker, "Democracy and the Canadian Consti-tution," in *And No One Cheered*, ed. Banting and Simeon. In their con-cluding essay in this volume, Banting and Simeon welcome the idea that the 1982 Act will open avenues for group activity in constitution making: "Groups can bring pressure to bear on individual govern-ments to initiate 'their' amendment"; "Federalism, Democracy and the Future," in *And No One Cheered*, 357.

19 See Milne, *The Canadian Constitution*, 158–9; and Chaviva Hosek, "Women and the Constitutional Process," in *And No One Cheered*, ed. Banting and Simeon.

20 Douglas E. Sanders, "The Indian Lobby," in *And No One Cheered*, ed. Banting and Simeon.

21 See Anthony Parel, "The Meech Lake Accord and Multiculturalism," in *Meech Lake and Canada*, ed. Gibbins et al., 171; and H.G. Thorburn, "Ethnic Minorities and the Canadian State," in *Canadian Constitution-alism 1791–1991*, ed. Janet Ajzenstat (Ottawa: Canadian Study of Par-liament Group, 1992).

22 The organizations that succeeded in enshrining their conceptions of rights are commonly referred to as "Charter groups." Alan Cairns's analysis of the Charter groups is the political scientist's guide. See, for example Cairns, "Ottawa, the Provinces and Meech Lake," in *Meech Lake and Canada*, ed. Gibbins et al., 116–7. Among the Charter Cana-dians, according to Cairns, are "women, aboriginals, linguistic minori-ties, multicultural groups, the disabled, and a more diffuse category of rights bearers who regard the Charter as a progressive advance." The Beaudoin-Edwards Report refers to the Charter Canadians as the "new constitutional players," noting that they have "a kind of special proprie-torial interest" in the document; see Beaudoin-Edwards, 36n.

23 That rights are universal and inalienable appears to be the premise of the Charter. Section 15 begins with a declaration of the universality: "Every individual is equal before and under the law." But the fact that the lobbies fought to see categories describing their clients and mem-bers specifically mentioned in section 15 and elsewhere in the docu-ment argues that they did not regard the declaration of universality as a sufficient guarantee for those members, or that they wanted privi-leges that would go beyond equal treatment.

24 Mahoney, "Women's Rights," in *Meech Lake and Canada*, ed. Gibbins et al. Not all feminists are of the opinion that the Charter has been such a blessing; see Gwen Brodsky and Shelagh Day, *Canadian Charter Equality Rights for Women: One Step Forward or Two Steps Backward?* (Ottawa: Canadian Advisory Council on the Status of Women, 1989).

25 See, for example, Rainer Knopff and F.L. Morton, *Charter Politics* (Scarborough: Nelson, 1992), especially chs. 2 and 4.

26 Nor do I want to suggest that losers have no recourse outside of constitutional amendment. Recent court decisions have recognized gay rights under the Canadian Human Rights Code. Sean Fine analyses the development in "Gays Finally Board Train of Rights Advances: Legal Triumphs Sure Signal for MPS," *Globe and Mail*, 24 November 1992, A1.

27 See "Eleven Men and the Constitution," in Robert M. Campbell and Leslie A. Pal, *The Real Worlds of Canadian Politics, Cases in Process and Policy* (Peterborough: Broadview Press, 1989). See also "Introduction: Human Rights," in *Meech Lake and Canada*, ed. Gibbins et al, 156, which reads: "Relatively new actors on the political stage – organized, and articulate groups – will not be as easily ignored as they were in the past. The framers of the Meech Lake Accord largely ignored women, natives, and other groups. They did so at the Accord's peril." Kathleen Mahoney agrees: "In 1987, five years after the ultimate had apparently been won by the inclusion of equality guarantees for women in sections 15 and 28 of the Charter, ten provincial premiers and the prime minister of Canada re-negotiated women's rights without their notice, consent or participation"; Mahoney, "Women's Rights," in *Meech Lake and Canada*. Multicultural groups feared that Meech would "emasculate" section 27 of the Charter; see Parel, "The Meech Lake Accord and Multiculturalism," in *Meech Lake and Canada*, 174.

28 Gibbins suggests that the Charter has exacerbated some aspects of regionalism. He notes, for example, that the Charter has legitimized a subterranean anti-Quebec, anti-French sentiment that was always part of regional politics: "People who in the past simply disliked Quebec can now wrap themselves in the flag of the Charter and come charging forward in the defence of universal rights"; Gibbins, "Constitutional Politics in the West and the Rest," 23. Knopff and Morton explore the idea that the Charter has a divisive effect in "A Note on the Charter and National Integration," *Charter Politics*, 374–84. Alan Cairns describes the competing notions of citizenship that are emerging, in Cairns, "Constitutional Theory in the Post-Meech Era: Citizenship as an Emergent Constitutional Category," in *Canadian Constitutionalism 1791–1991*, ed. Ajzenstat. Peter Russell notes that if Meech Lake had been ratified, another round of divisive constitutional politicking would have followed immediately; see Russell, "Can Canadians Be a Sovereign People?", *Canadian Journal of Political Science* 24 (1991).

29 Graham Fraser, "Difficult Task Tests Minister's Constitution," *Globe and Mail*, 17 June 1991, A4.

30 See J. David Hulchanski's argument in "Property Rights No, Housing Rights Yes," *Policy Options* 13 (1992).

31 The National Action Committee argues that a social charter is essential for women. Property rights, on the other hand are a "disaster for women"; see Susan Jackel, "Women and Constitutional Reform," *Network*, November/December 1991, 9. For a broader discussion, see Tom Pocklington, "Against Inflating Human Rights," *Windsor Yearbook of Access to Justice* 2 (1982): 77, and Sam Ajzenstat's response in the same number, 320.

32 Donald Smiley, *The Federal Condition in Canada* (Toronto: McGraw-Hill Ryerson, 1987), 68.

33 Milne, *The Canadian Constitution*, 19.

34 The complete story would suggest how often governments encouraged group participation. Trudeau's description of the Charter as a "people's package" was an invitation to Canadians to become involved.

35 Even socially disadvantaged groups accepted the idea of constitutional neutrality. The Regina Manifesto assumed that constitutional means would bear the socialist Co-operative Commonwealth Federation to power.

36 That the constitutional principles honouring political dissent and guaranteeing freedom of political speech have a long history in this country is argued in Janet Ajzenstat, "Canada's First Constitution: Pierre Bédard on Tolerance and Dissent," *Canadian Journal of Political Science* 23 (1990).

37 Alan C. Cairns, *Constitution, Government and Society in Canada: Selected Essays by Alan C. Cairns*, ed. Douglas E. Williams (Toronto: McClelland & Stewart, 1988), 230.

38 See the essays by Allan Hutchinson and Patrick Monahan, Philippe Nonet, and Duncan Kennedy in *The Rule of Law, Ideal or Ideology?* ed. Hutchinson and Monahan (Toronto: Carswell, 1987). The rule of law in this collection is understood as the defining principle of the liberal constitution. The question, then, is exactly whether the liberal constitution is the expression of class interest and ideology. The editors, and contributors Nonet and Kennedy, agree that the rule of law is mere ideology.

39 See, for example, essays in *Feminist Perspectives, Philosophical Essays on Method and Morals*, ed. Lorraine Code, Sheila Mullett, and Christine Overall (Toronto: University of Toronto Press, 1988). The editors argue that feminist philosophy regards "ideals" such as objectivity and autonomy as products of a way of thinking that has facilitated the repression of women; see "Editors' Introduction," 3.

40 Cited in John Dafoe, "Assembly Idea Has Seized the Political Imagination."

41 "Chairman's Foreword," *Citizens' Forum on Canada's Future*, 5.

42 Beaudoin-Edwards, 75.

43 "Chairman's Foreword," *Citizens' Forum on Canada's Future*, 5. Proponents of a constituent assembly sometimes appeal to the U.S. example. But the Philadelphia Convention of 1787 was notably elitist.

44 *Globe and Mail*, 22 April 1991, A13.

45 See Douglas Verney on democracy: *The Analysis of Political Systems* (Glencoe: Free Press, 1959).

46 Donna Greschner, "Commentary," in *After Meech Lake*, ed. David E. Smith, 224.

47 Michael Valpy, "Changes Sought, Forum Finds: Canadians feel they are not being governed in accordance with their values," *Globe and Mail*, 19 June 1991, A7.

48 Estey and Nicholson, "Giving Power to the People," *Globe and Mail*. Estey did not propose to leave elected politicians out of the picture altogether. Delegates to the constituent assembly would be chosen by lot from a pool of names put forward by the elected representatives in Canada's eleven legislatures. Henry Wiseman, describing the symposium on the constitution held at the University of Guelph, October 1991, noted that the planning committee was careful not to invite politicians "whose presence would have hindered more than helped"; *Network*, November/December 1991, 12–13. In the same issue, John Trent makes a similar point about the Towards 2000 conference held in Ottawa at the end of October.

49 Beaudoin-Edwards, 74–5.

50 "The People's Verdict," *Maclean's*, 1 July 1991, 10–76.

51 Ibid., 32. *Maclean's* argued that Canadians are profoundly disillusioned with the institutions of Parliament; 27, 30–1, 39. One participant summed up the group's feeling: "Let's get the politicians out of it."

52 Bernard Crick, *In Defense of Politics* (Chicago: University of Chicago Press, 1972).

53 One must feel some alarm at the suggestion embodied in the Spicer Report that Canadians want stronger political leaders, leaders with "vision and courage," who will not "govern by the polls or play sterile partisan games"; *Citizens' Forum on Canada's Future*, 8. This is the language of fascism. Mr Spicer allows himself in these passages to speak of Canada'a "spiritual crisis."

54 For the importance of new politics in Canada, see Neil Nevitte and Roger Gibbins, *New Elites in Old Societies: Ideologies in the Anglo-American Democracies* (Toronto: Oxford University Press, 1990).

55 Nevitte, "New Politics," in *Introductory Readings in Government and Politics*, 3d edition, ed. Mark Dickerson, Thomas Flanagan, and Neil Nevitte (Scarborough: Nelson, 1991), 161. (Nevitte is drawing on the observations of Ronald Inglehart.)

56 Idem.

57 Gibbins voices dissent from the enthusiasm for popular participation in constitution making, arguing that it may overload the constitutional process. He speaks of "constitutional meltdown," in his "Constitutional Politics in the West and the Rest." Many witnesses before the Dobbie-Beaudoin committee argued that the constitutional agenda should be limited; see Susan Delacourt, "Caution, Prudence Deflates Debate," *Globe and Mail*, 27 December 1991, A13. The Canadian Bar Association was one of these; see André Picard, "Lawyers Weigh into Debate," *Globe and Mail*, 12 December 1991, A10.

58 *Citizens' Forum on Canada's Future*, 161 and appendix B.

59 See Peter H. Russell, "Commentary," in *After Meech Lake*, ed. David E. Smith, 67. A *Globe and Mail*/CBC News poll of October, 1990 reported that 56 per cent of English Canadians believed that political leaders should get on with matters other than constitutional reform. Only 39 per cent were prepared to envisage the start of new negotiations with Quebec. See also Russell, "Can Canadians Be a Sovereign People?" where he states: "No other country in the world today has been engaged ... for so long in searching for the constitutional conditions of its continuing unity ... It is time to bring it to an end."

60 Robert J. Jackson and Doreen Jackson, *Politics in Canada* (Toronto: Prentice-Hall, 1990), 489.

61 Robert J. Jackson and Doreen Jackson, *Stand Up for Canada: Leadership and the Canadian Crisis* (Toronto: Prentice-Hall, 1992).

CHAPTER FIVE
MORTON: JUDICIAL POLITICS

1 *Final Report of the Special Joint Committee of the Senate and the House of Commons on the Constitution* (Ottawa: Information Canada, 1972), 11–12.

2 *The Constitutional Amendment Bill: Text and Explanatory Notes*, June 1978 (Ottawa: Government of Canada, 1978), 1.

3 *Towards a New Canada* (Montreal: Committee on the Constitution, Canadian Bar Association, 1978), 9.

4 "Priorities for a New Canadian Constitution," proposed by the Government of Canada, 9 June 1980, tabled in the House of Commons, 10 June 1980. In Anne F. Bayefsky, *Canada's Constitution Act: A Documentary History* (McGraw-Hill Ryerson, 1989), 598.

5 *Final Report on the Constitution*, 11.

6 However, the explanatory notes also declare that the preamble "would serve as a guide to the courts where the courts are interpreting a substantive section of the Bill [whose meaning] is not clear"; see *Constitutional Amendment Bill: Text and Explanatory Notes*, 1.

7 *Towards a New Canada*, 10.

8 The only exception was Trudeau's objection to Quebec's counterpro-
posal to add a recognition of "le peuple québécois" to the June 1980
"statement of principles." This phrase was inaccurate, said Trudeau,
because it implied a linguistic and cultural homogeneity (such as that
of the Inuit) which pluralistic Quebec lacked. Trudeau subsequently
proposed an alternative, the recognition of a "société québécoise"; see
"Déclarations des principes: Trudeau accepte de reconnaitre la société
québécoise," Le Devoir, 12 Sep 1980, 1. The Gazette (Montreal's English-
language daily) also reported this difference, quoting Trudeau as
declaring that the federal negotiators "carefully avoided using the
words 'nation' or 'people' so as not to get caught up in this debate"; see
"Leaders Can't Agree on Poetic Preamble," Gazette, 12 Sep 1980, 9.
Also see fn. 11.

9 A good example of the perception of courts as secondary actors in
Canadian constitutional development may be found in Alan Cairns's
influential article, "The Living Canadian Constitution," Queen's Quarterly 77, no. 4 (Winter 1970): 1–16.

10 Peter Hogg, Constitution Act, 1982 Annotated (Toronto:.Carswell, 1982),
72.

11 Gil Rémillard, Le fédéralisme canadien: le repatriation de la constitution
(Montreal: Québec/Amerique, 1985), 118. Quebec negotiators vigorously objected to the federal government's failure to recognize the
distinct nature of the Québécois people as one of the two founding
nations and its right to self-determination in its June 1980 "statement
of principles." In July, Trudeau responded by declaring that the
wording of the proposed preamble was open to improvements. He
rejected the use of the French terms "peuple" or "nation," because their
meaning had been "badly distorted by centuries of hypernationalist
commentary"; see Claude Morin, Lendemains piégés: du référendum à la
nuit des longues couteaux (Montreal: Boréal, 1988), 91. However, Trudeau was willing to accept a clause recognizing "the existence of the
two principal linguistic communities of Canada." A subsequent draft of
the federal proposal included recognition of "la société québécoise." At
the September 1980 First Ministers' Conference, René Levesque proposed to strike out "société québécoise" and to substitute the phrase
"peuple québécois." (He also wanted a second clause declaring that
Canada was founded on the free will of each province to belong.) Neither of these proposals was acceptable to Trudeau (see fn. 8), contributing to the failure of the conference; Morin, 123.

12 Morin, Lendemains piégés, 123. Morin makes it clear that this was not
what he and Lévesque were looking for.

13 The cause of the court's change in behaviour is disputed. The court
itself and most lawyers point to the new constitutionally entrenched
status of rights since 1982. Recent American experience reveals the

inadequacy of this legalistic explanation: the debate over judicial activism versus judicial self-restraint is just as active in a legal system with constitutionally entrenched rights. For a postmaterialist, sociological explanation, see F.L. Morton and Rainer Knopff, "The Supreme Court as the Vanguard of the Intelligentsia: Charter Politics as the Politics of Postmaterialism," in *Canadian Constitutionalism 1791–1991*, ed. Janet Ajzenstat (Ottawa: Canadian Study of Parliament Group, 1992).

14 *The Queen v. Drybones*, [1970] SCR 282.

15 *Brownridge v. The Queen*, [1972] SCR 926.

16 *Hogan v. The Queen*, [1975] 2 SCR 574.

17 *Morgentaler v. The Queen*, [1976] 1 SCR 616.

18 *Attorney-General of Canada v. Lavell and Bedard*, [1974] SCR 1349.

19 Wayne MacKay, "Fairness after the Charter: A Rose by Any Other Name," *Queen's Law Journal* 263 (1985): 10.

20 J.R. Mallory, *The Timlin Lecture* (Saskatoon: University of Saskatchewan, 1984), 8.

21 F.L. Morton, Peter H. Russell, and Michael J. Withey, "The Supreme Court's First One Hundred Charter of Rights Decisions: A Statistical Analysis," *Osgoode Hall Law Journal* 30, no. 1 (1992): 1–56.

22 Ibid.

23 *R. v. Collins*, [1987] 1 SCR 265.

24 *R. v. Manninen*, [1987] 1 SCR 1233.

25 *R. v. Hebert*, [1990] 2 SCR 151.

26 R. Harvie and H. Foster, "Different Drummers, Different Drums: The Supreme Court, American Jurisprudence and the Revision of Canadian Criminal Law under the Charter," *Ottawa Law Review* 39 (1990): 24.

27 See F.L. Morton, *Morgentaler v. Borowski: Abortion, the Charter and the Courts* (Toronto: McClelland & Stewart, 1992).

28 *Andrews v. Law Society of British Columbia*, [1989] 1 SCR 143.

29 *Haig (and Birch) v. Canada* (1992), 5 OR (3D) 245; and *Leshner v. Ministry of the Attorney-General* (Sept. 1992), unreported.

30 *Schachter v. Canada* (9 July 1993) (SCC), unreported.

31 This is my revision of a prediction made in 1982 by Eugene Forsey, the late elder statesman of Canadian constitutional scholars: "The Charter will be a field-day for crackpots; a headache for judges; and a goldmine for lawyers"; Martland Lecture, University of Calgary, 1983.

32 See Sherene Razack, *The Women's Legal Education and Action Fund* (Toronto: Second Story Press, 1992).

33 *Andrews v. Law Society of British Columbia*.

34 *Haig (and Birch) v. Canada*; and *Leshner v. Ministry of the Attorney-General*.

35 *Mahé v. Alberta*, [1990] 1 SCR 342.

36 *Sparrow v. British Columbia*, [1990] 1 SCR 1075.

37 Feminists and civil libertarians have found themselves on opposite sides of such issues as the rape shield law and the public disclosure of the names of victims in rape cases. Feminists and Aboriginal groups have fiercely disputed the application of the Charter to Aboriginal forms of self-government.

38 Alan Cairns, "Citizens (Outsiders) and Governments (Insiders) in Constitution Making: The Case of Meech Lake," *Canadian Public Policy* 14, supplement (1988): s125.

39 Rainer Knopff and F.L. Morton, *Charter Politics* (Toronto: Nelson Canada, 1992), 88.

40 F.L. Morton, "The Charter Revolution and the Court Party," forthcoming in *Osgoode Hall Law Journal.*

41 See Alan C. Cairns, *Charter versus Federalism: The Dimensions of Constitutional Reform* (Montreal: McGill-Queens University Press, 1992), 115–16.

42 Monahan, "The Charter Then and Now," 12.

43 *Re Resolution to Amend the Constitution,* [1981] 1 SCR 753.

44 Michael Mandel, *The Charter of Rights and the Legalization of Politics in Canada* (Toronto: Wall and Thompson, 1989), 29–32.

45 Quebec's interest in obtaining the nominating power for "its" Supreme Court judges dates back to the 1950s, following the abolition of appeals from the Supreme Court of Canada to the JCPC, a reform that Quebec opposed.

46 *Attorney-General of Quebec v. Quebec Association of Protestant School Boards,* [1984] 2 SCR 66.

47 "Projet d'accord constitutionnel: propositions du Gouvernement du Québec," (Gouvernement du Québec, Dépot légal, Bibliothèque nationale du Québec, May 1985). This recognition was a precondition for further demands that the Charter of Rights and Freedoms (except sections 3–5) not apply in Quebec and that Quebec be given exclusive jurisdiction to legislate on all aspects of language policy falling within its normal section 92 jurisdictions. These proposals could never have been accepted by the Mulroney government. Lévesque must have known this but was probably using them as part of his "beau risque" strategy: to appear to be giving federalism another chance by making an offer to Ottawa, but then to be able to blame Ottawa for not accepting them. If this was his strategy, it surely misfired. It alienated the hard-core nationalist wing of the party, contributing to the PQ's electoral defeat later that year.

48 "Maîtriser l'avenir" (Document de travail, Parti libéral du Québec, February 1985). The Liberals' "distinct society" proposal was clearly more politically feasible than the PQ's, and reflected the Liberals' more receptive attitude towards the Charter of Rights and Freedoms. After its

election victory in December 1985, the new Bourassa government announced that it would no longer follow the PQ practice of inserting the *non obstante* clause in every new statute. In 1987, it refused to renew Bill 78, the retroactive "blanket override" passed by the PQ in 1982.

49 Patrick J. Monahan, *Meech Lake: The Inside Story* (Toronto: University of Toronto Press, 1991), 44. The Parti Québécois document phrased it somewhat differently: "that the Constitution explicitly recognize the existence of a people of Quebec." Cf. Draft Agreement on the Constitution: Proposals by the Government of Quebec (Government of Quebec, May 1985), 11.

50 Monahan, *Meech Lake*, 56.

51 Ibid., 66.

52 Ibid., 67.

53 Ibid., 94.

54 Ibid., 105, 125.

55 Ibid., 106.

56 For a fuller analysis of the "two-step," see Knopff and Morton, *Charter Politics*, ch. 3.

57 *R. v. Oakes*, [1986] 1 SCR 104 is the leading case on section 1 jurisprudence.

58 Monahan, *Meech Lake*, 110,111.

59 *Quebec v. Ford et al.*, [1988] 2 SCR 712.

60 Peter H. Russell, *Constitutional Odyssey: Can Canadians Be a Sovereign People?* (Toronto: University of Toronto Press, 1992), 146–7.

61 See Russell, *Constitutional Odyssey*, 146.

62 Monahan, *Meech Lake*, 164.

63 See Russell, *Constitutional Odyssey*, 149–50.

64 Ibid.

65 "The Referendum: Just Saying No," *Globe and Mail*, 17 October 1992.

66 L.E. Weinrib, "Legal Analysis of Draft Legal Text of October 12, 1992" (Toronto: Faculty of Law, University of Toronto), 2. This study was widely disseminated and relied upon by most feminist critics of the accord.

67 William Shabas, "La société distincte et l'interprétation de la Charte canadienne des droits et libertés," in *Référendum 26 octobre 1992: Les objections de 20 spécialistes aux offres fédérales* (Montréal: Éditions Saint-Martin, 1992), 57–62. Shabas argues (correctly) that the addition of the clause calling for the expansion and development of minority language communities "neutralizes" any potential effect of the distinct society clause.

68 Henri Brun et al., "La clause relative à la société distincte du Rapport du consensus sur la Constitution: un recul pour le Québec," *Les objections de 20 spécialistes*, 56.

69 Claude Bariteau, "La société distincte: un cheval de Troie devenu une épée de Damoclès," in *Les objections de 20 spécialistes*, 45–51.

70 Judy Rebick, "Why Not Women?" *Canadian Forum*, October 1992, 14.

71 Shelagh Day, "What's Wrong with the Canada Clause," *Canadian Forum*, October 1992, 22.

72 Consider the post-referendum comments of the president of the Fisheries Council of British Columbia, Michael Hunter, criticizing the federal government's plan to grant special commercial salmon fishing privileges to Anoriginals: "The people of this province said no to inequality on the 26th of October. But this government is still proceeding in dealing with people on the basis of race"; "Salmon Loss a Serious Setback," *Globe and Mail*, 8 Dec 1992, A2.

73 Russell, *Constitutional Odyssey*, 2d ed., ch. 11, forthcoming.

74 The useful concepts of "micro-" and "macro-level" constitutional politics are adopted from Christopher Manfredi's insightful paper, "Litigation and Institutional Design: The Charter of Rights and Freedoms and Micro-Constitutional Politics" (Paper presented at the annual meeting of the Canadian Political Science Association, Ottawa, 6–8 June 1993).

75 The very presence of nongovernmental actors as formal participants in the process of constitutional negotiations suggests a regime whose legitimacy is being contested. The clear implication of such a practice is that existing governmental structures have somehow failed to represent relevant societal interests adequately. To the extent that the "outsiders" succeed in their challenge to the "insiders," this may mark the end of one regime and the beginning of a new one.

76 H.L.A. Hart, *The Concept of Law* (Oxford: Oxford University Press, 1961), 124.

77 Manfredi, "Micro-Constitutional Politics."

78 Russell, *Constitutional Odyssey*.

79 Patrick J. Monahan also makes a connection between the collectivist bent of the court's Charter jurisprudence and the appearance of group claims in the Charlottetown Accord; see "The Charter Then and Now" (Paper presented at the Conference on the Tenth Anniversary of the Charter, sponsored by the British Columbia Civil Liberties Association, May 1992), 16.

CHAPTER SIX

TULLY: DIVERSITY'S GAMBIT DECLINED

1 Alain Dubuc, "Anatomie d'un échec," *La Presse*, 27 October 1992.

2 Peter Russell, *Constitutional Odyssey: Can Canadians Become a Sovereign People?* (Toronto: University of Toronto Press, 1992).

3 Jean-Francois Lisée, "Le Canada dans la peau," *L'Actualité*, July 1992, 21–8.

4 See Russell, *Constitutional Odyssey*, 154–90; and Alain-G. Gagnon and Daniel Latouche, *Allaire, Bélanger, Campeau et les autres: les Québécois s'interrogent sur leur avenir* (Montréal: Éditions Québec/Amérique, 1991), 21–90, for summaries.

5 See, for example, Reform Party of Canada, *Reformer*, special edition, Fall 1992; Philip Resnick, "Saying a Pro-Canada No," *Globe and Mail*, 9 October 1992; Pierre Elliott Trudeau, *A Mess that Deserves a Big No* (Toronto: Robert Davies Publishing, 1992); and Comité du Non, "A ce prix-là, c'est non," in *Québec: référendum 92* (Québec: Directeur général des élections, 1992).

6 Richard Simeon, in *Competing Constitutional Visions – The Meech Lake Accord*, ed. K.E. Swinton and C.J. Rogerson (Toronto: Carswell, 1988), 295–6.

7 Timothy F. Fuller, ed., *The Voice of Liberal Learning: Michael Oakeshott on Education* (New Haven: Yale University Press, 1989), 15.

8 The concept of a middle ground has been developed by the anthropologist James Clifford in *The Predicament of Culture* (Cambridge, Mass.: Harvard University Press, 1988). It has been brilliantly applied to early modern Aboriginal-French-English relations by Richard White, *The Middle Ground: Indians, Empires and Republics in the Great Lakes Region, 1650–1815* (New York: Cambridge University Press, 1991).

9 See Alan C. Cairns, *Charter versus Federalism: The Dilemmas of Constitutional Reform* (Montreal: McGill-Queen's University Press, 1992); Cairns, *Disruptions: Constitutional Struggles, from the Charter to Meech Lake*, ed. Douglas E. Williams (Toronto: McClelland & Stewart, 1991); and Donald G. Lenihan, "Is There a Vision? Looking for the Philosophy behind the Reforms," *Network Analysis*, Analysis no. 7, September 1992.

10 Angus Reid, "Public Opinion: A New Variable in the Constitutional Equation," *Network*, special edition, 2 (6–7 June–July 1992): 3–5.

11 For the origins of this view, see Jennifer Smith, "Canadian Confederation and the Influence of American Federalism," *Canadian Journal of Political Science* 21, no. 3 (September 1989): 444–63.

12 See Brian Slattery, "A Theory of the Charter," *Osgoode Hall Law Journal* 25 (1987): 701–47, and Peter Russell, "Standing Up for Notwithstanding," *Alberta Law Review* 29 (1991): 293–309.

13 I am indebted to my colleagues Alain-G. Gagnon and Charles Taylor for this point and others with regard to Quebec. For the main objections to the accord in Québec, see Claude Bariteau, ed., *Référendum 26 octobre 1992: les objections de 20 spécialistes aux offres fédérales* (Montréal: Éditions Saint-Martin, 1992).

14 For the background to the next three sections, see James Tully, "Multirow Federalism and the Charter," in *The Charter-Ten Years After*, ed. Phil Bryden, Stephen Davis, and John Russell (Toronto: University of Toronto Press, 1993).

15 *Attorney General of Manitoba et al. v. Attorney General of Canada et al.* in *Federalism and the Charter*, ed. Peter Russell, Rainer Knopff, and F.L. Morton (Ottawa: Carleton University Press, 1990), 706–59.

16 See Lord Mansfield, *Campbell v. Hall*, I Cowp. 204–11 (1774), in William Knox, *The Justice and Policy of the Late Act of Parliament for Making More Effectual Provision for the Government of the Province of Quebec*, London: 1774; and James Tully, "Placing the *Two Treatises*," in *Political Discourse in Early Modern Britain*, ed. Quentin Skinner and Nicholas Phillipson (Cambridge: Cambridge University Press, 1993), 253–83.

17 *Re: Objection to a Resolution to Amend the Constitution* (Québec veto reference), 1982, in *Federalism*, ed. Russell, Knopff, and Morton, 760–71.

18 See Hilda Neatby, *The Quebec Act: Protest and Policy* (Scarborough: Prentice-Hall, 1972).

19 Lord Watson, *Liquidators of the Maritime Bank v. Receiver General of New Brunswick* (1892), cited in the patriation reference (1981), in *Federalism*, ed. Russell, Knopff, and Morton, 749. For an introduction to this vast literature, see Paul Romney, "The Nature and Scope of Provincial Autonomy: Oliver Mowat, the Quebec Resolutions and the Construction of the *British North America Act*," *Canadian Journal of Political Science* 25, no. 1 (March 1992): 3–28.

20 William Molyneux, *The Case of Ireland Being Bound by Acts of the Parliament of England* (Dublin: 1698).

21 For the background, see James Tully, *An Approach to Political Philosophy: Locke in Contexts* (Cambridge: Cambridge University Press, 1993), 9–70. John Rawls has reformulated his liberal theory in a way conformable to these conventions in "Justice as Fairness: Political Not Metaphysical," *Philosophy and Public Affairs* 14 (1985): 223–52, and "Justice as Fairness: A Briefer Restatement" (Cambridge: Harvard University, 1990, unpublished ms). The remaining differences between liberals and communitarians occur within these shared conventions; see Tully, *An Approach to Political Philosophy*, 315–23.

22 Guy Laforest, *Trudeau et la fin d'un rêve canadien* (Sillery: Éditions du Septentrion, 1992), 55–80.

23 Cf. Russell, *Constitutional Odyssey*, 142–5.

24 A.C. Parker, ed., *The Constitution of the Five Nations or the Iroquois Book of the Great Law* (Ohsweken: Iroquois Reprints, 1984). See Paul Wallace, *The White Roots of Peace* (Philadelphia: University of Pennsylvania Press, 1986).

25 Mary Ellen Turpel, "Aboriginal Peoples and the Canadian Charter: Interpretive Monopolies, Cultural Differences," and Patricia Monture, "Reflections on Flint Women," in *First Nations Issues*, ed. Richard E. Devlin (Toronto: Emond Montgomery Publications, 1991), respectively 40–73 and 13–26.

26 Parker, *The Constitution*, 53.

27 See Tully, *An Approach to Political Philosophy*, 137–78, and Joe Sanders, "First Nations Sovereignty and Self-Determination," in *Aboriginal Self-Determination*, ed. Frank Cassidy (Lantzville, B.C.: Oolichan Books, 1991), 186–97.

28 Cited in Michael Mitchell, "Akwesasne: An Unbroken Assertion of Sovereignty," in *Drumbeat: Anger and Renewal in Indian Country*, ed. Boyce Richardson (Toronto: Summerhill Press, 1989), 109–10.

29 See Francis Jennings et al., eds., *The History and Culture of Iroquois Diplomacy* (Syracuse: Syracuse University Press, 1985); Brian Slattery, *The Land Rights of Indigenous Canadian People as Affected by the Crown's Acquisition of their Territory* (Saskatoon: University of Saskatchewan, 1979); and J.R. Miller, *Skyscrapers Hide the Heavens: A History of Indian-White Relations in Canada* (Toronto: University of Toronto Press, 1989). For a sample of the treaties, see Alexander Morris, *The Treaties of Canada with the Indians of Manitoba and the North-West Territories* (Saskatoon: Fifth House, 1990) (reprint).

30 The Six Nations, *The Redman's Appeal for Justice: The Position of the Six Nations that They Constitute an Independent State* (Brantford: Six Nations, 1924). See Geoffrey York and Loreen Pindera, *People of the Pines: The Warriors and the Legacy of Oka* (Toronto: Little, Brown, 1991).

31 See Brian Slattery, "Aboriginal Sovereignty and Imperial Claims: Reconstructing North American History," in Cassidy, *Aboriginal Self-Determination*, 197–218 and references. For the continued recognition of Aboriginal sovereignty during treaty making, see Darlene Johnston, *The Taking of Indian Lands in Canada* (Saskatoon: University of Saskatchewan Native Law Centre, 1989), esp. 52–68.

32 Elijah Harper, "Keynote Speech," *Lessons from Oka: Forging a Better Relationship* (Montreal: Aboriginal Law Society of McGill University, 1991), 78–83.

33 Compare Brian Slattery, "First Nations and the Constitution: A Question of Trust," *Canadian Bar Review* 71 (1992). I am indebted to this fine article although we differ to some extent on Aboriginal and Canadian sovereignty. By the criteria of recognition and continuity, international law and Two-Row, it is Canada's sovereignty that rests on recognition by the First Nations, not vice versa (see notes 14 and 27).

34 Canada, House of Commons, *Debates*, 1916, IV, 3618, cited in Ramsay Cook, *Provincial Autonomy, Minority Rights and the Compact Theory 1867–*

1921 (Ottawa: Information Canada, 1969), 61. For the official language minorities, see Roderick A. MacDonald, "Meech Lake to the Contrary Notwithstanding," *Osgoode Hall Law Journal* 29, no. 2 (1991): 253–328; and 29, no. 3 (1991).

35 Lord Durham, *Report*, in *Search for a Nation: Canada's Crises in French-English Relations 1759–1980*, ed. Janet Morchain and Mason Wade (Toronto: Fitzhenry & Whiteside, 1984), 118–19.

36 See Richardson, ed., *Drumbeat*; J.R. Miller, ed., *Sweet Promises: A Reader on Indian-White Relations in Canada* (Toronto: University of Toronto Press, 1991); Geoffrey York, *The Dispossessed: Life and Death in Native Canada* (London: Vintage, 1990); Darlene Johnston, *The Taking of Indian Lands in Canada*; and Ken Coates, ed., *Aboriginal Land Claims in Canada: A Regional Perspective* (Mississauga: Copp Clark Pitman, 1992).

37 See, for example, National Action Committee on the Status of Women, "NAC Response to Federal Constitutional Proposals," 25 October 1991.

38 For the background conventions of the U.S. constitution see Philip Bobbitt, *Constitutional Interpretation* (Oxford: Basil Blackwell, 1991), and the review by Dennis Patterson, "Conscience and the Constitution," *Columbia Law Review* 93, no. 1 (1993): 270–307.

39 For an introduction, see Jennings, *History of Iroquois Diplomacy*; White, *The Middle Ground*; and Morris, *Treaties of Canada with the Indians*.

40 See, for these two points, Jamake Highwater, *The Primal Mind: Vision and Reality in Indian America* (New York: New American Library, 1981); Gisday Wa and Delgam Uukw, *The Spirit in the Land* (Gabriola, B.C.: Reflections, 1992); and Marcel Mauss, *The Gift: Forms and Functions of Exchange in Archaic Societies*, tr. Ian Cunnison (New York: Norton, 1977).

41 *Quebec v. Ford et al.*, in Russell, Knopff, and Morton, *Federalism*, 557–82.

42 There is a fine analysis of this form of reasoning by Avigail Eisenberg, "The Politics of Individual and Group Difference in Canadian Jurisprudence," unpublished ms, 1993. More generally, see Iris Marion Young, *Justice and the Politics of Difference* (Princeton: Princeton University Press, 1990), 96–121; and Albert R. Jonsen and Stephen Toulmin, *The Abuse of Casuistry: A History of Moral Reasoning* (Berkeley: University of California Press, 1988).

43 See Ian Gilp, *The Distinct Society Clause and the Charter of Rights and Freedoms*, York University Constitutional Reform Project, study 5 (North York: York University, 1992).

44 Sarah Scott, "Premiers' Lunch 'Political Suicide': Parizeau," *Gazette*, 31 July 1992.

45 See Simon Langlois, "Le choc de deux sociétés globales," in *Le Québec et la restructuration du Canada 1980–1992*, ed. Louis Balthazar, Guy Laforest, and Vincent Lemieux (Sillery: Éditions du Septentrion, 1992),

95–108; and Alain-G. Gagnon and Francois Rocher, eds., *Répliques aux détracteurs de la souveraineté du Québec* (Montréal: VLB éditeur, 1992). See also the important and expansive reinterpetation of the "community of communities" view by Jeremy Webber, *Imagining Canada: Language, Culture, Community and the Canadian Constitution* (Montreal: McGill-Queen's University Press, 1993).

46 See Frank Cassidy, ed., *Aboriginal Title in British Columbia: Delgamuukw v. The Queen* (Lantzville, B.C.: Oolichan Books, 1992); and for the background to the stereotypes, see Tully, "Placing the *Two Treatises*."

47 Rudy Platiel, "Native Council to Back Yes Side: Accord Endorsed by 3 of 4 Aboriginal Groups Who Signed It," *Globe and Mail*, 20 October 1992. I am indebted to Anoush Terjanian for this and the following two references.

48 Robert Matas, "Aboriginals Divided on Accord Too," *Globe and Mail*, 19 October 1992. I would like to thank Gerald R. Alfred of the Kanienkehaka nation at Kahnawake for clarification of these and other points concerning Aboriginal sovereignty.

49 Jeffrey Simpson, "Accord a Big Break for Natives? Not According to Many Chiefs," *Globe and Mail*, 19 October 1992. See Murray Angus, *"And the Last Shall Be First": Native Policy in an Era of Cutbacks* (Toronto: NC Press, 1991).

50 For the historical background of these practices of diplomacy, see William N. Fenton, "Structure, Continuity and Change in the Process of Iroquois Treaty Making," in Jennings, *The History of Iroquois Diplomacy*, 3–37. For the indispensability of trust, see John Dunn, "Trust and Political Agency," in *Interpreting Political Responsibility* (Princeton: Princeton University Press, 1990), 26–45.

51 Gail Stacey-Moore, "Aboriginal Women, Self-Government, the Canadian Charter of Rights and Freedoms, and the 1991 Canada Package on the Constitution," Native Women's Association of Canada, 3 December 1991.

52 For the background to these arguments, see Mary Ellen Turpel, "Aboriginal Peoples and the Canadian Charter"; Patricia Monture, "Reflecting on Flint Women"; Rupert Ross, *Dancing with a Ghost: Exploring Indian Reality* (Markham, Ont.: Octopus Publishing Group, 1992); Frank Cassidy and Robert Bish, *Indian Government: Its Meaning in Practice* (Lantzville, B.C.: Oolichan Books, 1989); J. Anthony Long, "Political Revitalization in Canadian Native Indian Societies," *Canadian Journal of Political Science* 23, no. 4 (1990): 751–74; Diane Engelstad and John Bird, eds., *Nation to Nation: Aboriginal Sovereignty and the Future of Canada* (Concord, Ont.: House of Anansi, 1992); Helen Buckley, *From Wooden Ploughs to Welfare: Why Indian Policy Failed in the Prairie Provinces* (Montreal: McGill-Queen's University Press, 1992);

Young, *Justice and Difference*, 39–65. For a concrete example, see The Innu Nation and the Mushuau Innu Band Council, *Gathering Voices: Finding Strength to Help our Children* (Utshimasists, Ntesinan, Labrador, June 1992). I am indebted to the discussions of these issues at McGill University by Ardith Walkem of the Nlaka'pamux Nation and Ellen Gabriel of Kanesatake.

53 Mary Ellen Turpel, "Aboriginal Peoples and the Canadian Charter," and Wendy Moss, "Indigenous Self-Government in Canada and Sexual Equality under the Indian Act: Resolving Conflicts between Collective and Individual Rights," *Queen's Law Journal* 15, nos. 1–2 (1990): 279–305.

54 See Brian Slattery, "The Legal Basis of Aboriginal Title," in Cassidy, *Aboriginal Title*, 113–32.

55 Cf. Ludwig Wittgenstein, *Philosophical Investigations*, tr. Elizabeth Anscombe (Oxford: Basil Blackwell, 1958), ss. 65–75.

56 Cairns, *Disruptions*, passim; Russell, *Constitutional Odyssey*, 190–3; and Charles Taylor, "Shared and Divergent Values," in *Options for a New Canada*, ed. Ronald L. Watts and Douglas M. Brown (Toronto: University of Toronto Press, 1991), 53–77. These three non-Aboriginal male elders should be read in exchange with the words and deeds of three Aboriginal male elders, such as Bill Reid, Georges Erasmus, and Oren Lyons, and, applying sections 28 and 15(2) of the Charter, with at least ten Aboriginal and non-Aboriginal female elders.

57 See Ulli Steltzer and Robert Bringhurst, eds., *The Black Canoe: Bill Reid and the Spirit of Haida Gwaii* (Vancouver: Douglas & McIntyre, 1991).

58 For the Royal Commission on Aboriginal Peoples, to whom the spirit of diversity has been entrusted.

CHAPTER SEVEN
EMBERLEY: GLOBALISM AND LOCALISM

1 See David B. Allison, ed., *The New Nietzsche: Contemporary Styles of Interpretations* (Cambridge, Mass.: MIT Press, 1985).

2 I have used the word "pastiche" following Frederic Jameson's essay "Postmodernism of the Cultural Logic of Late Capitalism," *New Left Review*, July/August 1984, 146.

3 Of course, as the *Protagoras* and *Laws* make clear, Plato's humanism is one that identifies the distinctively human as the impulse of transcendence towards the divine or eternal. However, these are apprehended through the human measure of the Good.

4 Simply stated, I am suggesting that the events and realignments occurring in our decade overreach the explanatory power of modern philosophies of history. My argument is not restricted to counterclaims

supported by empirical fact. Rather, I am suggesting that the metaphysic of the modern analyses is increasingly irrelevant to the contemporary situation. (Nor would I deny that that metaphysic may have underwritten a safer and more decent era of human association than that upon which we are about to embark. We simply cannot know.) The viability of a metaphysic to comprehend the forms of human intercourse, I believe, is vouchsafed by the distinctive institutions, practices, ways of life, skills, forms of education, and self-interpretations of a specific society at a unique juncture of its history. I am not making a statement regarding the truth of a specific metaphysic. What I am saying is that however "true" the metaphysic may be abstractly, or even when assented to in private experience, it is an instrument for illuminating the cardinal components of a political regime only when it is concretely actuated. Modern philosophies of history (Hegelian, Marxist, liberal) – with their metaphysical assumptions of pure origins, sequential time, spatial order, teleological processes, and intelligible totalities – were vouchsafed by the power structures and ideology of the nation-state. With the disintegration of the nation-state, these philosophies of history have become obsolete.

5 Historically, and especially in Europe, Arendt argues, the nation-state's fragility meant that its principle was almost immediately corrupted. The disintegration occurred internally when society emancipated itself from public concerns. The nation-state broke down when the state was overwhelmed by the dominance of one social interest defined by a single class, the bourgeoisie. The dynamic of this class's interest unleashed a process of never-ending accumulation of power to make possible its never-ending accumulation of capital. Imperialist expansion arose from an economic crisis of an overproduction of capital which could not be productively invested within national boundaries. Coming up against national limitations to its economic expansion, the bourgeoisie would not give up the capitalist system of constant economic growth, and the nation-state proved unfit for the further growth of the capitalist economy.

6 The new Canadian drug bill, c-91, which will be locked in to the North American Free Trade Agreement, is an example of the erosion of national sovereignty in the face of the imperatives pursued by multinational pharmaceutical companies.

7 Examining the "epistemology" which underscores and legitimates our contemporary self-interpretation is, however, only a first step. It is the step taken by such thinkers as Marshall McLuhan and Walter Ong. Critics of their "neo-Kantian" analyses, such as Michel Foucault and Jacques Donzelot, have directed their attention to the modality of power in contemporary society which undergirds the categories of

consciousness informing contemporary self-interpretation. I would argue that even a more far-reaching perspective that examines the "psyche" in its totality would be necessary to grasp its essence fully. However, one must begin somewhere.

8 To be clear, many of the new nations, ethnic associations, and social movements (especially those asserting themselves after the experience of oppression at the hands of imperial power or illiberal regimes) are interpreting and legitimating their actions by appeal to the modern discourse. Many have no other tools at their disposal as they recapitulate the historical development of the modern nation-state. But this is simply a catch-up phase prior to being caught up by the dynamic that is overtaking the modern period.

9 See Hannah Arendt, *The Human Condition* (Chicago: University of Chicago Press, 1958); George Grant, "Knowing and Making," *Transactions of the Royal Society of Canada*, 4th series, vol. 12, 1967; Martin Heidegger, "The Question Concerning Technology," in *Basic Writings*, ed. David F. Krell (New York: Harper and Row, 1977), 287–317; and Carl Mitcham and Robert Mackey, eds., *Philosophy and Technology: Readings in the Philosophical Problems of Technology* (New York: Free Press, 1971).

10 Jacques Ellul, *The Technological Society* (New York: Vintage, 1964), xxv.

11 Marshall McLuhan, *The Gutenberg Galaxy* (Toronto: University of Toronto Press, 1962) and *Understanding Media* (New York: Mentor, 1964).

12 Jean Baudrillard, "Implosion of Meaning in the Media," in *In the Shadow of the Silent Majorities – or The End of the Social, and Other Essays*, (New York: Semiotexte, 1983), 102.

Contributors

JUAN D. LINDAU   The Colorado College

CURTIS COOK   The Colorado College

ALAN C. CAIRNS   The University of British Columbia

ALAIN NOËL   Université de Montréal

BARRY COOPER   The University of Calgary

JANET AJZENSTAT   McMaster University

ROBERT JACKSON   Carleton University

F.L. MORTON   The University of Calgary

JAMES TULLY   McGill University

PETER EMBERLEY   Carleton University

DAVID HENDRICKSON   The Colorado College

Index

Inuit Tapirisat 191
Iroquois 161, 175

Lévesque, René 31, 135
Liberal party 30, 119,
128–9
of Manitoba 51
of Ontario 119
of Quebec 140–1
Locke, John 92, 173–4,
201, 204
Lower Canada 170

Macdonald, Sir John A.
131, 191
Machiavelli, Niccolò 91,
98, 107–8, 112
McLuhan, Marshall 212–
13
Manitoba 28, 30, 51, 57,
74, 141, 160, 174, 177,
180
Manitoba Act, 1870
178
Liberal party 51
Manning, Preston 74–5,
83, 110, 144
Marx, Karl 221
Meech Lake Accord 4, 28,
90, 113–16 passim,
140–3, 152, 185
Aboriginal peoples and
8, 18, 50, 174–9
Quebec and 8, 31, 90–
1, 106, 139, 166, 171,
174, 188
Mercredi, Ovide 45, 49,
65, 192–3
Métis 27, 39, 41, 46, 52,
59–62, 96–7, 154, 162,
180, 196
Métis National Council
42, 191
Mic'mac 179
Mohawk 160, 163
Montesquieu, Charles
Louis de 102
Mulroney, Brian 65, 72–5,
82, 87, 101, 114, 118,
129–31, 140

multiculturalism 30, 133,
158–66, 178–80, 184,
188, 197
See also Constitution
Act, 1982, s. 27

Naskapi 162
National Action Com-
mittee on the Status of
Women 51, 74, 145,
180, 182
nationalism, multination-
alism 4–5, 7–8, 26–9,
181–3, 207–8, 213
Aboriginal 4, 8, 26–8
Canadian, pan-Cana-
dian 4, 26–7, 188
Quebec 4, 26, 29–38,
82, 93, 150, 188
ROC 4, 8, 26–7, 33, 35
Native Council of Canada
40, 191
Native Women's Associa-
tion of Canada 43, 58,
152, 181, 193–4
New Brunswick 72
New Democratic Party
119, 129
Newfoundland 60, 72, 92,
162, 172, 174
Nietzsche, Friedrich 201
Nova Scotia 30, 154, 180
Nunavut 46, 54, 56–7,
162

Oakes test 185
Official Languages Act 52
Oka 38, 51, 165, 177,
180, 183
Ontario 42, 72, 96–8,
105–8, 119, 136, 141,
166, 178–9, 216

Parizeau, Jacques 32, 81,
156, 187
Parti Québécois 30–2, 80–
3, 88, 135, 139–41,
156, 174
patriation 4, 15, 31, 152,
154, 181

Aboriginals and 174,
177
Supreme Court and
138–9, 169–71
Pepin-Roberts task force
31
Plato 201, 207
Prince Edward Island 72
Progressive Conservative
party 72, 82, 87, 114,
131
public opinion
Charlottetown Accord
52, 72, 84
polls 23, 65–6, 77, 86,
113, 124, 129

Quebec 4, 8, 10, 104–11,
166, 179–82
as Charter loser 138–9
distinct society 10, 90–
4, 104, 111, 133–44
passim, 155–8
passim, 170, 182–8
Liberal party 140–1
and Meech Lake Ac-
cord 31, 140–3, 174
as multiethnic society
111, 188
nationalism 4, 29–34,
82, 84, 139, 146, 188
objections to Charlotte-
town Accord 49, 146,
182
and patriation 138–9,
169–71, 174
Quiet Revolution 10,
93–4, 119
referendum of 1980
30–1, 133
relationship with ROC
26–38, 93–4, 104–11
separatism 94, 151, 174
treatment by Supreme
Court 133, 139–43,
169–71, 185, 195
use of notwithstanding
clause 59, 140, 143
vote on Charlottetown
Accord 153, 166